A Guide for the Hospitality Industry

Professional
Sales and Selling

for Meetings · Expositions · Events · Conventions · Groups

Kendall Hunt
publishing company

Jeffrey Beck · George Fenich

Cover images © Shutterstock, Inc.

Kendall Hunt
publishing company

www.kendallhunt.com
Send all inquiries to:
4050 Westmark Drive
Dubuque, IA 52004-1840

Published in the United States of America

BRIEF CONTENTS

Chapter 1   Introduction to Meetings, Events, Exhibitions and Conventions, and Allied Hospitality Industries   1

Chapter 2   The Road-map to Sales: Marketing   13

Chapter 3   Introduction to Sales for MEEC and Hospitality   33

Chapter 4   Professional Development in Hospitality Sales   59

Chapter 5   Communication Skills for Sales   79

Chapter 6   Market Segment Behaviors   99

Chapter 7   Developing a Strategy for Selling the Product   121

Chapter 8   Gaining Access to the Prospect   139

Chapter 9   Establishing the Sales Dialogue   153

Chapter 10   Presenting the Hospitality Product   171

Chapter 11   Getting the Customer to Say Yes   187

Chapter 12   Asking for the Sale   201

Chapter 13   Service after the Sale   215

Chapter 14   Management of the Sales Force and Practical Applications (Part 1)   229

Chapter 15   Management of the Sales Force and Practical Applications (Part 2)   247

Glossary   269
Index   279

CONTENTS

Prologue by Robert Gilbert   xi
About the Authors   xii
About the Contributing Authors   xiv

Chapter 1   **Introduction to Meetings, Events, Exhibitions and Conventions, and Allied Hospitality Industries**   1

Introduction   2
The Process of MEEC Planning   5
What YOU will learn from this Book   8
The Outline of this Book   9

Chapter 2   **The Road-map to Sales: Marketing**   13

Introduction   14
Marketing Principles   14
Learning About Marketing Through Analogy   16
Marketing Research   18
Marketing Function   19
Marketing Tactics   23

Chapter 3   **Introduction to Sales for MEEC and Hospitality**   33

Introduction   34
The Nature of MEEC and Hospitality Sales: Different Responsibilities   34
Various Roles of the MEEC Salesperson   37
Different Job Opportunities   38
Job Descriptions and Career Overviews   40
The Relationship of Sales to Marketing   48
The Sales Organization in MEEC   49
The Sales Organization   50
Sales Meetings   53
Individual Sales Manager Organizational Activities   56

Chapter 4   **Professional Development in Hospitality Sales**   **59**

Introduction   60

What Makes a GREAT Hospitality Sales
    Professional?   62

Management of Self   63

Business Etiquette   63

Introducing a Client or Guest   64

Shaking Hands During Introductions   64

Communication Etiquette   65

Sales Letter Writing   66

Professional Appearance   68

Time Management   69

Networking   71

The Thirty-Second Commercial   72

Ethics   74

Chapter 5   **Communication Skills for Sales**   **79**

Introduction   80

The Sales Relationship: Communication Styles   80

Types of Communication   89

Selling to the Hospitality Customer:
    The Customer's Buying Process   90

The Hospitality Customer's Buying Objectives   91

Customer Buying Theories Applied
    to Sales   93

Chapter 6   **Market Segment Behaviors**   **99**

Introduction   100

Who Are We Selling To?   100

Major Market Segments in Hospitality   101

The Association Market Segment   101

Selling to Associations   105

The Corporate Market Segment   106

Selling to the Corporate Meetings Market   108

Other Markets   112
Still Other Markets   114
The Hospitality Sales Process   117

Chapter 7   **Developing a Strategy for Selling the Product   121**
Four Levels of Product   124
Solution Selling   126
Positioning   133

Chapter 8   **Gaining Access to the Prospect   139**
Prospecting   140
Sources of Prospects   144
Collecting Information during Prospecting
    for Access   147
Meeting the Prospect Face to Face   149

Chapter 9   **Establishing the Sales Dialogue   153**
Introduction   154
Types of Sales Communication   155
The Sales Contact Plan   156
Objectives of the Sales Dialogue   156
Techniques for Beginning the Sales Dialogue   157
Determining Customer Needs   160
Hospitality Sales Questioning Process   161
The Beck-Farrar Hospitality Question Model   163
Being a Trusted Consultant: Listening   165
Establishing Buying Objectives from the
    Sales Dialogue   166

Chapter 10   **Presenting the Hospitality Product   171**
Introduction – The Importance of the
    Hospitality Sales Presentation   172
Describing Features   173
Offering Benefits   173

Linking Features and Benefits   174
Prevent Feature Overload   175
ACTIVITY: Identifying Benefits Based
    on a Feature   175
The Presentation Process   175
Presentation Formats   177
Presentation Techniques   178
Making Effective Presentations   180
Planning the Effective Presentation   181
Strategic Selling Materials   181
Types of SSMs   182
Making the Presentation   183
Practice before Presentation   184

Chapter 11 **Getting the Customer to Say Yes**   **187**
Introduction   188
Reasons for Concern   189
Forms of Objections   190
Sales Stop Signs   190
The Plan for Addressing Concerns   192
Techniques for Overcoming
    Objections   193
Revenue Management and Sales   195
Negotiation Techniques   197

Chapter 12 **Asking for the Sale**   **201**
Introduction   202
The Plan to Close the Sale   203
Techniques for Closing the Sale   204
Hospitality Contracts   208
The Start of the Relationship   212

Chapter 13   **Service after the Sale**   **215**
              Introduction   216
              Providing Service that Strengthens the
                  Relationship   216
              On-Property Service   219
              Catering/Convention/Event Services   220
              The On-Site Service Process   222
              Resolving Issues   224
              Post-Event Follow Up   225

Chapter 14   **Management of the Sales Force and Practical**
              Applications (Part 1)   **229**
              Introduction   230
              On-Property Sales   231
              Above Property Sales   233
              Global Sales Manager   235
              Experience   236
              Education   236
              A Day in the Life of a Global Sales Director   236
              About Me   237
              About the Center   238
              About Our Team   239
              Marketing/Communications   239
              Type of Events   240
              How We Book Events   240
              Determining Rental   242
              Generating a Proposal   243
              Site Visits   244
              New Orleans is Selected to Host
                  the Meeting, What's Next   245
              In Conclusion   246

Chapter 15 **Management of the Sales Force and Practical
Applications (Part 2)**   **247**
How Do Prospects Buy Professional Services?   248
Types of Office Configuration   257
Lead Generation   258
Lead Management   260
The Lukewarm Call vs. the Cold Call   260
Do Your Research: Drilling Down into the Lead 261
Affiliated Suppliers Can be a Great Option
   and Fit   265
Average Tenure in the Industry Is 21.5 years. 265
Reasons for Affiliated Industry Desirability   265

Glossary   *269*
Index   *279*

There is an old adage in hospitality that is still true today: Nothing happens until you sell something. Whether readers of this book have career aspirations in sales or as a general manager or owner or asset manager, this fundamental truth will always be relevant. The role of sales in any successful business is vital.

Indeed, as the landscape of hospitality sales continues to evolve, the sales discipline at hotels, conference centers, and other venues is more important than ever. This book outlines the core competencies of hotel sales as it relates to one of the biggest segments in the hotel industry: meetings, conventions, and events.

Authors Jeffrey Beck and George Fenich are two academics who have invested time over their careers to engage with industry, giving them a unique advantage when it comes to writing a textbook on this subject. They understand first-hand the nature of hospitality sales, the attributes of a successful salesperson, and the composition of a complex industry landscape.

And more than anything, they understand that, even as sales adapts to the shifting sands of customer needs, technology, and business processes, we can't lose focus on what is most important: the customer.

My thanks to Professor Beck and Professor Fenich for creating a text that provides a valuable learning tool for the fundamental discipline of sales.

Robert A. Gilbert

Robert A. Gilbert, CHME, CHBA
President & CEO
Hospitality Sales and Marketing Association International
www.hsmai.org

ABOUT THE AUTHORS

Jeff Beck and George Fenich have been involved in hospitality and specifically meetings and events for many years. When this opportunity to write a hands-on textbook about selling in this industry came about, we wanted to pool our resources and take the challenge. As such, we wanted you to know more about us, the authors. After all, as we know that in the sales industry, it all begins with trust. You must trust the salesperson before you can buy into what they are selling.

Photo by Sarah Morreim Photography. Reprinted by permission.

Jeff Beck, Ph.D. Dr. Beck is an Associate Professor in The School of Hospitality Business within the Eli Broad College of Business at Michigan State University. He teaches courses in hospitality sales and revenue management. Jeff Beck has over 20 years of experience in the lodging industry. His industry experience includes 10 years with Marriott Hotels, Resorts, and Suites in various management positions. In 1989, Beck was on the opening management team of the San Francisco Marriott, a 1500-room convention hotel. He was honored with the Director of Services of the Year award, Northwest Region, for his outstanding performance and achievements. He later moved to the Marriott regional office in San Ramon, California as a Total Quality Management (TQM) Facilitator where he worked with the 17 hotel executive committees in the Northwest Region to develop strategic initiatives for each hotel.

Dr. Beck received his doctorate from Purdue University where he also taught Meeting and Convention Management, Guest Service Management, and Lodging Management. At Oklahoma State University he was the Charles Lanphere Professor of Hotel Administration, recognized twice as Outstanding Undergraduate Advisor. He has written several research articles and is currently president elect of the International Council of Hotel, Restaurant, and Institutional Educators for 2019-2020. He earned his bachelor's degree in Marketing from the Kelley School of Business at Indiana University, and his master's degree from Purdue University.

George G. Fenich, Ph.D. Dr. Fenich holds the rank of Full Professor in the School of Hospitality Leadership at East Carolina University. He earned his Ph.D. from Rutgers University, his master's from Rensselaer Polytechnic Institute, and his bachelor's degree from SUNY Cortland. His teaching and research focus is on meetings/events/conventions. George worked in the hospitality industry prior to joining the academy with positions in management and in group sales. He had titles such as Division Vice President and General Manager. Dr. Fenich has provided extensive service to hospitality education, especially ICHRIE. He has served as a Board Member, Chapter President, chapter officer positions, and meetings/events/convention SIG Chair, and was a founder and one of the first officers of the Accreditation Commission for Programs in Hospitality Administration (ACPHA). He has served on boards, commissions, and task forces for industry associations such as the Professional Convention Management Association (PCMA), Meeting Professionals International (MPI), the Destination Marketing Association International (DMAI), the International Association of Events and Exhibitions (IAEE), and the Society for Incentive Travel Excellence (SITE). He is currently the Editor-in-Chief of the *Journal of Convention and Event Tourism* and serves on the editorial boards of six additional journals. He has authored over a dozen textbooks on the hospitality industry and published over 60 articles in academic journals. He has delivered educational programs around the world, from China and Japan to Turkey, France, Mauritius, and South Africa. He has been named the PCMA Educator of the Year, is an inductee into the DMAI Hall of Fame and received the Fletcher Career Achievement Award from ICHRIE.

Photo by Chuck Fazio. Reprinted by permission.

George is a principal in the firm Fenich & Associates LLC. The firm provides consulting services to the hospitality industry with a focus on DMOs and casinos. Their analysis aids DMOs in achieving their sales goals. The firm has developed a database of over 60 metrics or attractor variable?s for almost 150 cities in the United States. These are the attractors that are important to travelers when selecting a destination. They are used in an "Destination Attractiveness Analysis" that has been completed for over 50 DMOs in the United States. These same attractor metrics are also used to mathematically determine a DMO's fair share of the convention market. Fenich also developed the algorithms for what is now the TAP Report and is the owner of the intellectual property for this report.

ABOUT THE CONTRIBUTING AUTHORS

Gus Vonderheide, Vice President of Global Sales—Americas Hyatt Hotels & Resorts

In his role as Vice President of Global Sales—Americas, Gus Vonderheide has the responsibility over Hyatt's transient and business travel segments. He provides leadership over a global strategic team who manages relationships with Hyatt's largest corporate, consortia and travel management companies. These customers, all based in the Americas and doing business globally, generate over $1B annually for the brand. Part of a larger team, Hyatt's Global Sales Force can be found in 20 additional locations around the world. Gus is Hyatt's Executive Sponsor for disABILITIES, a diversity resource group within the company.

A 25 year Hyatt employee, Gus has led the sales teams at the Hyatt Regency Louisville, KY, Hyatt Regency Dearborn, MI and the Grand Hyatt Washington, DC. He also spent time in the Worldwide Reservation Center in Omaha, NE where he managed the Western Worldwide Sales Office and group call desk. Prior to his Hyatt career, hotel management experience includes Sales, Front Office, Purchasing and Convention Services.

Gus continues to fill leadership roles in a number of industry organizations—A past member of the GBTA Board of Directors, past chair of the MPI Foundation and a member of BTN Group Advisory Board.

Elaine Williams, CMP

Elaine Williams is the Director of Sales at the New Orleans Ernest N. Morial Convention Center. Williams joined the sales team in 2007 as a national sales manager. As Director, Williams is responsible for targeting new business as well as selling and servicing the Center's national association and corporate accounts.

Williams brings solid and extensive operational knowledge and sales skills to the position from a career that has spanned over twenty years in the convention and hospitality industries. Her career with ARAMARK at the New Orleans Ernest N. Morial Convention Center began in 1996 when she was named sales manager. Over the years, Williams rose through the ranks to achieve the position of director of sales and later director of operations. She most recently held the title of interim general manager of ARAMARK at the Center.

Williams has also served as a national account executive for AVW Audio Visual Services, a Freeman Company, and as vice president of sales for Joel's Grand Cuisine, a premier local catering and destination management company.

In 2005, she successfully completed the CMP exam and became a Certified Meeting Professional (CMP) designated by the Convention Industry Council. In 2016, Williams received her certification in Exhibition Management (CEM), a globally recognized designation that demonstrates the highest professional standard throughout the exhibition and event management arena. A graduate of the University of New Orleans, Williams has completed several Hospitality Management Training programs consisting of both internal ARAMARK programs as well as those offered by Affiliate Hospitality Associations.

Terri Woodin, CMP

Terri Woodin, CMP, is Vice President of Marketing and Global Meeting Services at Meeting Sites Resource (MSR). She has been with MSR since 2012 and is responsible for strategically partnering with MSR customers on all facets of global site research, custom hotel contract negotiations, meeting support services, and Strategic Meetings Management (SMM) solutions.

Terri is an industry veteran with 35 years in the hospitality industry with extensive experience in hotel operations, hotel sales, and as a meeting planner. Committed and passionate about the industry, she is engaged and contributes by presenting workshops and writing articles for many industry publications.

Terri leads by example and continues to give back through her many volunteer positions. She currently serves globally on The Meeting Professional Advisory Board for MPI and with her alma mater, The School of Hospitality Business at Michigan State University Board of Directors.

Terri continues to make a difference by engaging in the community with Project Angel Heart, Ronald McDonald House, and Children's Hospital. Most recently, Terri was awarded one of the Top 25 Women Industry Leaders by SMART Meetings Magazine and awarded the (MIC) Meetings Industry Council Leadership Award.

She obtained the Certified Meeting Professional (CMP) designation in 1997.

Professional memberships include Meeting Professionals International (MPI) since 1996.

Jim LaBadie, National Account Executive with Houston First/Visit Houston

Jim graduated from Michigan State University in 1974. His hospitality career has spanned 45 years including 25 years in hotels and resorts. The last 20 years Jim has spent in destination marketing managing both domestic and international convention and trade show sales for North American cities, the state of Hawaii and islands in the Caribbean.

After early beginnings in operations at a resort in northern Michigan and a hotel in suburban Cincinnati, Jim found his way into sales. Throughout his hotel/resort portion of his career, he held positions as a sales manager and Director of Sales at a variety of properties including downtown, suburban and airport hotels. He eventually elevated to a regional position with as many at 20 hotels and their sales departments under his direction. Mr. LaBadie was responsible for sales training, business and market plans and the overall development of sales in every market, individualized for each hotel.

Jim moved to Chicago where he was Vice President of The Hyland Group, managing Midwest operations for the sales representation company. The Hyland Group had contracts with a dozen cities and over 25 independent hotels and resorts to staff their regional sales business development in Chicago and Washington DC. And it was here that he was first exposed to destination marketing.

Mr. LaBadie left the Hyland Group to become Vice President of Sales for Visit Grand Rapids in western Michigan. He earned his Certified Association Sales Executive (CASE) certification from the Professional Convention Management Association (PCMA). Subsequently, Jim ran Midwest sales operations for several destinations including Fort Worth, Los Angeles and the state of Hawaii. In 2011, he re-opened the office for Houston where he now works.

Jim is an active member of PCMA, the American Society of Association Executives, the Association Forum and the International Association for Exhibitions and Events. He has served on the Board of Directors for both the Association Forum and the International Association of Association Management Companies.

David Rome

David Rome is from New Orleans, Louisiana and joined BBC Destination Management, A Global DMC Partner, in 2003 as an Account Executive and in 2005 became the Director of Sales. He is committed to sharing the value of DMCs to both internal and external stakeholders of the DMC and hospitality community. He has served as the 2011-12 President of the Gulf States Chapter of Meeting Professionals International and earned his DMCP and CMP certifications in 2010. Most recently, he was the President of the Association of Destination Management Executives International (ADMEI) in 2016 and was an adjunct professor of hospitality management at Delgado Community College from 2010 to 2017.

John Flood

John is the Founder and Managing Partner of **elevate.** John graduated from Michigan State University in 1980. He has been engaged in the hospitality business for 39 years working on the affiliated, supply side of the industry. After a successful career, John retired in 2017 and now spends his time sharing his expertise consulting with the industry and as an annual guest lecturer at MSU.

CHAPTER 1

Introduction to Meetings, Events, Exhibitions and Conventions, and Allied Hospitality Industries

Weddings are one type of special event
© Erman Erikoglu/Shutterstock.com

LEARNING OBJECTIVES

- Define the term MEEC
- Outline the steps of the MEEC planning process
- Name the various companies and organizations that support MEEC events
- Describe the three industry segments that support the hospitality and tourism industries.

Introduction

Tourism is defined as the activities of individuals traveling to and staying in places outside their usual environment for no less than 24 hours for business and other purposes. As it pertains to leisure, individual activities in tourism do not exceed one year. The **hospitality industry** benefits from tourism activities; many segments of hospitality gain from tourism. These categories include lodging, food and beverage establishments, theme parks, transportation, cruise lines, **MEEC**, and additional fields within the tourism industry. These additional fields are the allied industries that support hospitality and tourism; the suppliers of products and services that support the delivery of service to the customer/end user. All of these segments of hospitality and tourism employ some form of sales and marketing to create awareness and interest in the corresponding products and services.

The term **MEEC** is an acronym that describes an important sector of the hospitality industry that describes business events and activities. **Meetings** are a coming together of a group of people to discuss or exchange information. Meetings can include conferences, lectures, workshops, board meetings, training meetings, and corporate retreats. Meetings can be organized and held by corporations, associations, and government entities. **Events**, according to the Event Industry Council, are organized occasions such as special celebrations, gala dinners, marketing events, incentive group events, and product launches. Events can be held by corporations, associations, government agencies, and individuals. **Exhibitions** have different meanings in different parts of the world. Exhibitions can be trade shows, expositions, fairs, and expos. Exhibitions are designed to display, and potentially sell, goods

© pcruciatti/Shutterstock.com

and services to customers in a particular market segment. While some exhibitions may be open to the public, others are closed to the public and open only to members of the particular industry and members of the press. Exhibitions can be organized by trade associations, private organizations seeking to use the exhibition as a business activity for profit, or individuals with personal art or other collections to share.

Conventions are a type of event where the primary purpose is for attendees to experience educational sessions, participate in meetings and discussions, network, and attend recognition events. These recognition events can be gala dinners, awards luncheons, and sponsorship events. Typically, conventions have an exhibit component; exhibits can be an income stream for the sponsor organization. Sponsoring organizations of conventions tend to be associations, which rely heavily on attendance and exhibitors to make up the majority of the annual budget revenues for the association. The European word for a convention is a **congress**; attendees are referred to as delegates.

The MEEC segment of the hospitality and tourism industry is of great value to countries, cities, and local businesses. Individuals traveling for the purpose of a business meeting or event are likely to spend more than the traditional leisure traveler. Those traveling for association conventions sometimes combine business and leisure travel, particularly if the destination is attractive. The new term for this "combination" is **bleisure travel**. Because destinations have different travel seasons based on geography, MEEC activities can be scheduled at different times of the year, allowing for flexibility and satisfying price-sensitive attendees. Forward looking sales efforts are important in lodging and convention sales, as MEEC events can be planned anywhere from one month in advance for small corporate events to many years in advance for large association conventions. A MEEC event and its attendees will have similar requirements for goods and services, making it straightforward for the hospitality and tourism entity to provide outstanding and consistent service. There are many ancillary businesses and suppliers that support MEEC events. These suppliers include set-up companies, decoration companies, florists, carpenters, shipping firms, and technology providers. All of these ancillary companies have sales and service representatives that practice the sales function. The destination where the MEEC event is held can provide for a positive image for the organization holding the event. Ease of access by travel method, such as airport convenience, train routes, and highway access, are all elements MEEC planners use to consider a destination. Hospitality salespeople representing these destinations use access as a key selling point when speaking with MEEC planners. Finally, MEEC events are not necessarily in fixed locations; in fact, many national and international organizations rotate among various countries and cities to provide variety to attendees or delegates. A corporation based in the United States may choose to hold an event in Europe, where many of its customers may reside. MEEC events can be held in both traditional and non-traditional sites, requiring sales and marketing efforts by museums, parks, athletic facilities, and other unique venues.

According to the Event Industry Council (EIC), business events generated $612.4 billion (US) of gross domestic product (GDP) in 2017. Globally, business events contributed $1.5 trillion to the global gross domestic product. Further, the global business events industry would rank larger than the GDP's of countries such as Australia, Mexico, Spain, and Indonesia. The $1.5 trillion dollars in expenditures represents the planning, producing, attending, and/or hosting of a business event. The EIC defines a **business event** for the economic report as "a gathering of 10 or more participants for a minimum of four hours in a contracted venue." These business events include conventions, conferences, exhibitions, and incentive travel (EIC Website, accessed June 2019).

These business events involved more than 1.5 billion participants from more than 180 countries. On average, over $700 U.S. was spent on each business event participant; business events supported 10.3 million direct jobs globally. According to the EIC, the meetings sector supported more direct jobs than the machinery, auto manufacturing, and telecommunications industries in the US in 2016. In 2016, 1.9 million meetings were held in the US. It is clear from these statistics that the MEEC industry impacts the national economy.

The integral role that MEEC events have on the livelihood of destinations, convention centers and other venues, lodging facilities, food and beverage establishments, and allied hospitality and tourism suppliers cannot be ignored. The commerce that occurs thanks to MEEC events is stimulated by the interaction between MEEC planners and the sales and service professionals that represent the hospitality and tourism organizations described.

The Process of MEEC Planning

Planning a MEEC event requires skills in project management; a schedule of activities to be performed sequentially and concurrently is developed by the MEEC planner. There are many different models that can be used for planning a MEEC event, but the basics are the same. First, the purpose of the event and the desired measurable goals and outcomes must be created. This information will be communicated internally to potential attendees, and externally to hospitality and tourism suppliers that will be considered for being involved with the event. What is important here is that measures of success be clearly described; whether the MEEC event was a success or not is centered around the measurable goal and objectives. Next are the specifics related to the delivery of the MEEC event. Dates, time schedule, budget, and service quality must be clearly stated for both attendees and suppliers. The sponsoring organization and its representative, a point of contact (if not the same), and the target attendees must all be identified. It is especially important for marketing purposes that the benefits an attendee will experience from attending the MEEC event be clearly stated.

Related to the purpose of the MEEC event and the benefits attendees will experience, the actual program must be developed. It could be a small event in scope, or a complex multiple-day event, such as a convention or exhibition. With the program, a theme and décor may be an important element of the MEEC event. The choice of a theme will influence the destination, venue selection, and budget for the MEEC event. Additional services and materials may be required from vendors based on the theme, speakers' bureaus may be contracted for keynote speakers, for example. As mentioned earlier, some of the MEEC event planning activities must happen in a sequential

1. • Event Purpose, Goals and Objectives
2. • Event Details
3. • People
4. • Program
5. • Destination and Venue
6. • Theme and Décor
7. • Suppliers
8. • Production Schedule
9. • Day(s) of Event Activity
10. • Post Event Wrap Up

Source: Jeffrey Beck

fashion; others will happen concurrently. The destination location and venue or venues must be selected before many other decisions can be made. MEEC planners, when selecting locations and venues, generally have options to consider, so that the best possible outcomes can be experienced as a part of the goal, objectives, and budget for the MEEC event. MEEC planners may work with various hospitality and tourism suppliers to achieve success for the planned event. Travel management companies can be used to assist with the development of requests for proposals (**RFPs**) for both destinations and venues.

The travel management company then contacts a destination management company (**DMC**) and other MEEC specialty suppliers to submit proposals for the MEEC event. Destination management companies perform a variety of services to accommodate the MEEC planner. Other MEEC planners do much of the work themselves; they have the expertise to craft RFPs, conduct

destination and venue evaluations, and work with the specialty suppliers. Some of the suppliers involved with MEEC events include:

- The local Destination Marketing Organization (also known as the Convention and Visitors Bureau)

- Venue Management Companies

- General Service Contractors

- Creative Design and Décor Businesses

- Equipment Rental Companies

- Cleaning Companies

- Security Companies

- Audiovisual Companies

- Catering Companies

- Insurance Companies

- Tour Guides

- Registration Suppliers

In this case, they will work directly with the hospitality and tourism suppliers to achieve the desired outcomes of the MEEC event. The success of a MEEC event also depends on the production schedule; the EIC describes this schedule as the event specification guide, or the **ESG**. It is a comprehensive document that provides the who, what, where, when, and how of the MEEC event. The ESG conveys information clearly and accurately to MEEC venues and suppliers regarding all requirements for an event. This guide provides all products and services required during the day or days of the event. Because it is given to all suppliers, consistent communication occurs among all service personnel for the MEEC event. Finally, a post-event evaluation is performed to determine success, return on investment, and performance by the various hospitality and tourism suppliers for the MEEC event. A post-event report, or **PER**, also developed by the Events Industry Council, provides a documented record of the MEEC event for future reference by all stakeholders involved with the event.

There are three industry segments that support the hospitality and tourism industries. Food distribution is the most well known in hospitality and tourism; there are very large national distribution companies, and smaller regional companies. These food distribution companies, such as SYSCO, Gordon Food Service (GFS), and US Foods, are involved in the marketing, sales, and distribution of food products, dining room utensils, kitchen equipment, and miscellaneous supplies to lodging facilities, food and beverage establishments, healthcare facilities, and educational organizations. These companies also provide such products on a wholesale level to hospitality organizations that provide food service, such as Aramark and Sodexo. Food manufacturers, such as PepsiCo, General Mills, McCormick Spices, and Wayne Farms, employ sales professionals to develop business-to-business sales opportunities with various hospitality, tourism, and retail organizations. Hospitality amenity and equipment manufacturers comprise the third segment. The companies manufacture and sell equipment; produce and distribute amenities for lodging facilities; and manufacture, sell, and distribute furniture, fixtures, and equipment for hospitality and tourism organizations. Companies such as Ecolab, William Roam, Hospitality Designs, and Advance manufacture and distribute kitchen and lodging cleaning chemicals and equipment, guest room amenities, guest room furniture, and floor cleaning equipment for internal and external use. Each of the companies listed have sales and marketing organizations to sell and service hospitality and tourism businesses, both large and small.

What YOU will learn from this Book

The focus of this book is on professional selling in MEEC and the allied industries of hospitality and tourism. This book is designed to give you, the

© Billion Photos/Shutterstock.com

student, a very real experience in professional sales. **Hospitality sales is not a career for everyone, but everyone in hospitality sells.** Whether you are a guest service agent at the front desk, a server in the restaurant, a convention service set-up person, a human resources staff member, or a supervisor in housekeeping, you are selling a product or service, an idea, or yourself.

Many students realize that, after taking a class in sales where real scenarios are experienced, they have a better appreciation of what sales is, and are better prepared for interviews, regardless of their career choice. This book will be an excellent reference for your future career because it is not a book of theory; rather, it is a practical handbook. Many students have a misconception of what hospitality sales really is; many have images of "used car salespeople." Interestingly, after learning the sales process, students become interested in sales as a career. Many have said that they are better prepared than their colleagues for a career in sales after taking the course.

The Outline of this Book

This book has been designed to provide a review of the marketing process; the original concept of sales evolved into what we now know as marketing. **Marketing**, as a strategic function, seeks to develop products and services that satisfy customers' needs. The marketing function for a guest's experience can be likened to a road map; there are many different ways to arrive at revenues for the hospitality organization, much like there are many ways to get from point A to point B. **Chapter Two**, Mapping the Guest's Experience, provides an overview of the marketing function and how hospitality personal selling plays a role.

Chapter Three, The Sales Function for MEEC and Hospitality, outlines the differences between sales and marketing; it provides the student with a framework for how hospitality and tourism organizations "do sales." Sales organizational charts, job descriptions, and other information that describes how the hospitality sales office is organized is described in this chapter. **Chapter Four** provides information on how successful hospitality salespeople develop themselves. Ethics, time management, communication techniques, along with other knowledge for personal development, are covered. New hospitality salespeople are exposed to the various activities that will help them develop into sales professionals in hospitality. **Chapter Five** covers the basics of communication skills for hospitality sales. There are various styles of communication; successful hospitality salespeople understand what their personal style of communication is, and how to identify the communication styles of their prospects and clients. This chapter helps students develop their own communication style and adapt to the style of others. **Chapter Six** describes the various markets to which hospitality salespeople sell. There are association, corporate, government, and social market segments. The buying behavior is very different for each segment based on the size of the segment,

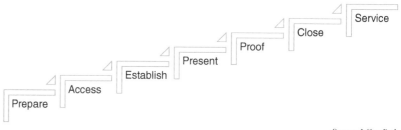

location, price sensitivity, and need. This chapter goes into the detail of the "sub-segments" within each of the larger segments.

Chapter Seven helps the student prepare for selling; product knowledge is paramount. Selling to the various market segments described in Chapter Six requires preparation; the selling process is just that – hospitality sales-people must be knowledgeable, well prepared, and practiced before they can be successful in a career in hospitality sales. **Chapter Eight** outlines the various methods and techniques hospitality salespeople use to identify prospects, communicate with prospects, and gain access through meeting with a prospect. **Chapter Nine** profiles the means by which the hospitality salesperson establishes or strengthens a business relationship with a current client or prospect. The sales dialogue is a well-crafted communication with the prospect with a specific objective as the goal. Sales dialogues have one (or a combination) of three objectives: to inform, persuade, or remind. The sales dialogue will be very different based on the objective of the communication. **Chapter Ten** highlights probably the most important skill a hospitality salesperson must have: the ability to ask questions that uncover the critical buying objectives of the prospect. The type, timing, and method for asking such questions is a skill that must be practiced and developed. Chapter Ten also describes the various methods for presenting hospitality products and services to prospects. **Chapter Eleven** describes the concerns that prospects and clients may have regarding the hospitality product or service. It is a rare occurrence that the hospitality salesperson gets the customer to say yes and sign a contract after their first attempt; more often, the hospitality salesperson must provide proof that the product and service the hospitality salesperson represents is the best option to satisfy the needs of the prospect or client. **Chapter Twelve,** asking for the sale, outlines the various methods that hospitality salespeople use to "close the sale." Depending on the client or prospect, the type of concerns they have, and the complexity of the sale, various methods are used to get a signed contract. **Chapter Thirteen** explains the "after the sale" service. The on-property sales and service functions are described in detail, with the various activities that occur at the hospitality facility prior to, during, and after the event. **Chapters Fourteen and Fifteen** are written by MEEC professionals in a planning or sales capacity. These chapters offer insight into the realities of MEEC and the allied hospitality and tourism sales professions.

Finally, a role play workbook is included that offers a hands-on experience of selling a hotel to the two most common market segments to which hotels sell. It follows the process that has been described here and will be used throughout the book. All the necessary information is provided to "role play" as a hospitality salesperson. These role plays can be conducted live, although support is provided to use online software. Like any life experience, the student will only "get out of this class what they put into it." Take advantage of this opportunity by putting your head and heart into this class; you will find it well worth your effort.

SUMMARY

This chapter provides an overview of the hospitality, tourism, and MEEC industries. Thus, it provides a definition of the term MEEC. It goes on to outline the steps of the MEEC planning process and names the various companies and organizations that support MEEC events. Further it describes the three industry segments that support the hospitality and tourism industries. Lastly, what you will learn from the book is discussed along with details regarding the content of each chapter.

KEY TERMS

hospitality industry	conventions	DMC
MEEC	congress	ESG
meetings	bleisure travel	PER
events	business event	
exhibitions	RFP	

DISCUSSION QUESTIONS

1. Discuss the hospitality industry.

2. Define the term MEEC.

3. Outline the steps of the MEEC planning process.

4. Name the various companies and organizations that support MEEC events.

5. Describe the three industry segments that support the hospitality and tourism industries.

6. What is "bleisure travel"?

7. What does RFP stand for?

8. What does ESG stand for?

9. What is a DMC?

10. What does PER stand for?

CHAPTER 2

The Road-map to Sales: Marketing

Exterior signage is a form of marketing
© Cassiohabib/Shutterstock.com

LEARNING OBJECTIVES

- Define marketing and differentiate between marketing and advertising.
- Differentiate between marketing strategy and tactics.
- Outline the marketing process and describe the marketing mix.
- Explain the purpose of market research.
- Differentiate between internal and external marketing.
- Describe the different types of customers in the hospitality industry.
- Describe how customer behavior impacts marketing strategy.
- Define value.

Introduction

This book deals with the topics of selling and sales in meetings, expositions, events, conventions, and hospitality. The current chapter on marketing is placed here, early in the book, to provide context for much of what follows. A sales professional must understand the concepts of marketing in order to be an effective salesperson, even if they do not undertake marketing themselves. This chapter is meant to be an overview of marketing and marketing principles. More in-depth coverage of marketing is found in entire books on the subject of hospitality marketing. Further, the current text is not meant to focus on hospitality marketing, but rather on sales and selling.

Marketing Principles

To better understand what marketing is, it might be helpful to understand some of the accepted theories and principles of marketing. Marketing is typically thought of as the method of promoting and selling a product or service. In the hospitality industry that can include a hotel room, a banquet, a dinner, beverages, transportation, events, exhibitions, entertainment, and more: products and services.

The American Marketing Association defines **marketing** as: the process of planning and executing the conception, pricing, promotion, and distribution of ideas, goods, and services to create exchanges that satisfy individual and organizational objectives. Let's break this sentence down into its component parts.

Process can be thought of as a series of steps or a course of action.

Planning is the research and homework necessary to intelligently decide *what* to do. We know that *execution* means to perform a task, or *how* to do it.

When we *conceive* of something, we demonstrate creativity.

The *price* we set, hopefully, is what the customer is willing to pay.

Promotion is about spreading information.

Distribution in this context is the actual delivery of the idea, good, or service. *Exchange* is giving something in return for receiving something. In this context, exchange requires two parties: the individual (customer) and the *organization* (the hospitality business).

For the *individual*, the *objective* is to satisfy a need or want.

The *objective* of the hospitality business is to make a profit.

In a nutshell, we can say that marketing is satisfying customers' needs profitably.

Marketing is probably the most visible function of any hospitality organization, yet it is often the least understood. Marketing is not advertising! Marketing is not selling! Marketing is a strategic process for creating real and perceived value for the customer.

MARKETING STRATEGY

Marketing theorists have developed mnemonic devices that are techniques a person can use to help them improve their ability to remember something. The following are two mnemonic devices to help remember marketing theory. Marketing strategy is widely known and summarized through the following two mnemonic devices.

Ps of Marketing

When considering marketing, strategy is often divided into four commonly accepted categories. These categories are known widely as the P's of marketing, like so ...

First, is deciding on the **product**/service to provide.

Price is what to charge the guest for the product/service.

Promotion techniques include advertising, public relations, personal selling, and merchandising.

Deciding on the **place** and/or distribution is also important – the location of the business, or what internet sites are used to sell the product service are examples.

With hospitality products and services, there are three additional P's that help with memory retention.

The **people** (employees) impact the quality of service, and thus the marketing of the business.

Process refers to the development of a marketing plan and careful examination of the effectiveness of the communication to the audience. Process refers to the steps that are taken.

Finally, **packages** (combinations of products/services and pricing schemes) may be a key element to hospitality marketing success.

The following is another mnemonic device referred to as the C's of hospitality marketing.

1. **Communication**:

Not only is the method of communication important for your intended client, but the way in which things are communicated is important. The choice of words, the grammar and spelling, the design and graphic layout, all tell a story that needs to compel your client to buy. The sales professional must keep in mind (1) who is the client and (2) why are they buying the product or service?

2. **Consumer**:

By focusing on how the hospitality product fulfills the client's needs and why the consumer should want to be there, the hospitality professional has better success at gaining interest in the hospitality produce or service.

3. **Convenience**:

This "C" refers to considering how easy it is to consume the product or service and how convenient it is for the client to get to the product or service. In the busy world today, convenience has become an important factor in a client's decision whether or not to buy the hospitality product or service.

4. **Cost**:

In deciding on a price to set, the hospitality professional needs to take into consideration both the income needed to produce the product or service and the client's perception of the value of the product or service to them.

Learning About Marketing Through Analogy

Consider that you (a customer) want to take a trip to a city 60 miles from where you are now. Let's say that you are very anxious to get to that city as soon as possible. If you were to use an internet-based mapping program to get directions, the first question you would be asked is your starting point. In another words, where are you right now, what is your current situation? That's a straightforward consideration most of the time – you would already know where you are. But if you were a hospitality owner/manager, you'd need to draw on research to really know your current situation – to better understand your customers, competitors, and the strengths and weaknesses of your establishment or department.

Next, you would be asked what is your goal, or, where do you want to end up? As a part of this, you would have options to take the shortest route in miles, avoid expressways, etc. Once you have a route with directions, you have a decision to make on what method of transportation to use. Then as you start the trip, you would track your progress. Finally, you would know if you arrived at your destination when you saw the address of your original goal.

Along the way to your destination, you would face many options and be required to make numerous decisions. Hospitality owners/managers must do the same to be successful at marketing. They must assess their current situation by asking various questions, for example: Who are their customers, and what do those customers need and want? What does the manager's department or organization do well, and maybe not so well? Who competes with the business? What is the state of the general and local economy?

Once you knew where you were, the mapping software asked you where you wanted to go. You had to enter the name of a business or prominent landmark, or a specific address. Being able to evaluate if we've been successful requires that we are aiming at something from the start. Stating a specific, measurable goal is likewise very important when it comes to effective hospitality marketing. Stating a goal helps to suggest *how* it will be accomplished, along with a means to measure achievement. For the hospitality owner/manager, this could be increasing sales revenues, increasing guest satisfaction, keeping the same customers, acquiring new customers, or a combination of these sorts of things. So, in our mapping example, since the goal was to travel 60 miles as quickly as possible, a choice had to be made relative to the best means to actually get to the destination. The first stated need was to get to the destination *as fast as possible*. Different transportation modes would be the strategy element of achieving the goal. Those modes might include flying, trains, highways, or even boating. There could be options within each mode, a commercial airliner versus a private jet, a personal vehicle or a rental car, an Amtrak train or a bus, motorcycle, motorboat, or even walking! Your decision is based on what is of value or important to you (and/or others who might be impacted) and can be undertaken in an ethical manner. So, owners, vendors, customers, and employees can all have an interest in the outcome. Time, money, and convenience are typical considerations when marketing decisions are being made.

Based on your goal of getting to the city 60 miles away as fast as possible, you may have chosen to rent a speedy sports car. Your *strategy*, then, would be to drive via a highway to achieve your goal. The *tactic* would be to rent a sports car.

So, for the hospitality manager, depending on the goal, a variety of strategies could be used to achieve the goal. You might create a new product or service, change prices, advertise, use specific internet sites, or create packages. Along the way to your destination, you track your progress to ensure you are getting there as fast as possible (legally!). You check your map, your watch, mileage signs, and speedometer compared to your original goal. Since your goal is "as fast as possible," you would most likely use your watch to track your progress.

If you weren't getting to your destination as fast as you wanted, say because of traffic or construction, you might adjust the original route. The hospitality manager uses accounting statements, guest satisfaction surveys, and other marketing research methods to track progress and make changes based on the competition, the economy, and whether customers are behaving as expected. If you have a GPS, you can be more precise in your measurement of where you are along the way. You might even say, "If I had taken an airplane, I would have been there by now."

Marketing Research

Let's explore marketing research for a minute. Marketing research helps to answer questions in three different contexts: 1) planning, 2) problem solving, and 3) control. In planning, for example, the manager uses market research to identify what kinds of people use the hospitality product and service, where they come from, and how much they earn. For that kind of information, the manager might use information from the US Census (http://factfinder.census.gov/home/saff/main.html?_lang=en). In that case, he would be using information collected by someone else for another purpose. This is what we call SECONDARY data. On the other hand, if the manager collected the information from her company's database, this would be PRIMARY research. Thus, **primary research** is conducted to answer a specific question using specific techniques. **Secondary research** is research conducted by others for other purposes but can be used to answer the manager's question. Obviously, primary research is more complex and costly to undertake. Secondary research, however, may not answer all the questions the manager would like to answer.

In problem solving, the manager may have questions related to satisfaction with the product or service, whether prices are too high (or low!), or what advertising would work best. There are different ways the manager can collect this information. It can be done through surveys, whether internet, telephone, or mail. Or it can be done through small group interviews – also known as focus groups.

Women in a focus group

© wavebreakmedia/Shutterstock.com

A manager must also have data to control the marketing activities. Marketing data in this area might be the percentage of the market that uses the manager's hospitality organization versus a competitor. Mystery shopping is also a control technique to determine whether the employees are serving, and the food is cooked, according to the standards of the organization. Managers might also be interested in the customer's perception of the company.

So, you have arrived at your destination. You know it because you can see the address you entered into the mapping software. You look at your watch and see that you made it within 10 minutes of what you originally planned. Not bad. The cost of renting the sports car was worth it (*of value*). Hospitality managers take their reports and measure them against the goal originally planned. Did they achieve sales based on their efforts? Have they retained customers? Did they satisfy customers better than before? Do they have more sales than their competitors? These measures help to indicate whether the hospitality organization *provided value* to the customer.

Marketing Function

This trip analogy describes the basics of the marketing process but does not consider some of the details that go into the marketing function. First, and most important, is a description of current and potential customers. When we consider all current and all potential customers for our product, we have described our **market**. Customers can be classified based on various criteria; when we divide our current and potential customers into groups with common characteristics, we define this as **market segmentation**. Customers can be segmented in two ways: 1) based on the benefits the market segment receives from the product, or 2) based on some observable characteristics, such as: demographics (age gender, etc.), geography (where they are coming from), purpose (why they are visiting), and distribution (buying from the internet versus calling the resort directly). Once we have described these common characteristics, we must *qualify* the market segment to determine whether we should target that market segment. Do they have a *need* for what we have to offer? Do they make the final purchase decision? Do they have the money to make the purchase? Can we satisfy their needs at a price they are willing to pay?

Once we have identified those market segments we wish to target, we must communicate a *unique benefit* to that target market. This is defined as **positioning**, a concept developed by Al Ries and Jack Trout in 1972. To illustrate the concept, think of your favorite fast food establishment. What is the most important thing that makes it your favorite? Now think of your second-favorite fast food restaurant. What one thing makes it second favorite? The things that made your choices first and second are their *positions in your mind*, and the difference between the two is what we call *the points of differentiation*. Adding to our definition of marketing then, we wish to divide our individuals (markets) into homogeneous market segments and use a unique benefit to *position* our hospitality product and service in the collective minds of that segment.

Images can be an effective means to market a restaurant

P – PEOPLE

Another element of marketing that our trip did not address was the importance of *people* in the hospitality marketing process. You may have heard of Ritz Carlton's mission statement, *"Ladies and Gentlemen serving Ladies and Gentlemen."* Ritz would not be able to state this unless they attracted ladies and gentlemen to be employees. Further, it requires *internal marketing* on the part of Human Resources to communicate why it is important for employees to strive to achieve Ritz's mission. We recognize that not only is it the tangible product and the intangible service, but also the people providing that service that help the customer to experience real and perceived value. To clarify, **external marketing** is all that we do to communicate value and influence customers to purchase our products and services. **Internal marketing**, on the other hand, is all that we do to attract and retain employees as part of our hospitality organization (we'll explore the overlapping importance of external and internal marketing – aka: human resources management policies and practices – in an upcoming module).

BRAND

So far, we have covered all the main elements of marketing except one: What is a brand? What if every lodging establishment in the country was just named "hotel"? How would you know which "hotel" you wanted to stay at? How would you know if one was different from another? How would you compare a hotel you stayed at before with a hotel you are planning to stay at? Thus, the reason for brand names as a means to differentiate one product offering from another. A brand is more than just a name, however. A brand name can communicate a benefit of doing business with that organization, a characteristic of the organization, or a phrase that is easy to remember (this could be an object as well).

Logos such as this one for McDonalds are a form of branding and marketing

MARKETING VS. ADVERTISING

What is the difference between marketing and advertising? It is hoped that our discussion so far has helped you to distinguish between the two. But to help you out, advertising is an *element of marketing*. Marketing strategy planning requires a one to five year time span. Marketing tactics planning typically require a planning window of eighteen months or less. More to the point, marketing is *what* to do (or strategy), and advertising is an example of *how* to do it. That "how" is what we call tactics. Other examples of tactics include personal selling, sales promotion, and public relations.

STRATEGY AND TACTICS

Table 1 puts forth a grid aligning the P's of marketing.

To better illustrate tactics, let's go back to our map example. Our goal was to get to our destination as fast as possible. We rented a sports car (strategy) and drove (tactic) to our destination within 10 minutes of our stated goal. We can use different tactics based on a similar goal. The selection of the tactic is based on the quality of the market research collected, and the decision-making ability of the manager. For example, let's say that there is increasing competition for our restaurant and our goal is to keep our sales level constant (also called retaining market share). We could 1) advertise more, 2) advertise in different media, 3) advertise a different message, 4) offer discounts, 5) change the menu, 6) add items to the menu, 7) change the service style (buffet versus by the plate), etc. These examples are only a few of the options; the tactic undertaken would be based on research, the costs involved, and the likelihood we would achieve our goal of retaining market share.

TABLE 1. STRATEGY / TACTIC MATRIX

Price	Promotion	Place	People (employees)	Packaging	Product
Highest	Advertising	Websites	Demographics	Combination with other related products within business	Keep same product
Higher than most	Personal sales	Physical Location	Knowledge	Combination with other related products outside business	Keep, but change appearance
The same as competitors	Merchandising	Multiple Locations	Skills	Combination with other related products outside business	Keep but improve quality
Lower than most	Public Relations	Intermediaries	Attitude / Personality	Combination with unrelated products outside business	Keep, add additional products or services
Lowest	Interactive				Innovate, creating new product
	Sales Promotion				

Marketing Tactics

IDENTIFYING TARGET MARKETS

Two critical elements in planning a successful marketing strategy are to identify the target audience and to use the right marketing to reach them. Knowing who the desired clientele is helps the hospitality professional determine what type of marketing to implement.

By understanding a little bit about the consumer behavior of their target market, the hospitality professional can identify the best way to reach them. The hospitality professional needs to become part psychologist, part sociologist, and part economist.

In the initial planning stages of the marketing process, the hospitality professional should outline who the event stakeholders are. A stakeholder is someone who has stake in an enterprise.

Some of the areas to consider when researching the consumer behavior of these stakeholders are:

Demographics of Stakeholders

These are the vital statistics of a specific population. What is their age? What is their marital status, their sex, their income, and their education level? What is their cultural or racial make-up? What profession and industry do they work in? What is their professional status?

Psychographics

These are the personality traits of your stakeholders. What are their values? What interests them? What is their lifestyle? What are their delights, persuasions, attitudes, and perceptions? What is the personality of the company?

By analyzing the stakeholders, the potential attendees' demographics, psychographics, and their desired outcomes, the event manager and event professional will be able to create a target audience profile to help them gauge the best types of marketing for the hospitality product or service.

REACHING YOUR TARGET AUDIENCE

Once the hospitality professional has analyzed who their target market is and where to locate them, they need to ascertain the best way to reach them. In marketing, the term **reach** is the estimated number of the potential customers who will see a specific type of promotional or advertising campaign. In some cases, the reach of the campaign will be determined by the limitations of the mail, email, or calling list. The hospitality professional needs to analyze the extent of the reach to determine if that specific marketing promotion will be the most effective for their target audience.

TYPES OF MARKETING TACTICS

Direct Marketing

Direct marketing is marketing by means of direct communication with consumers. The term "consumers" refers to your potential buyers or clients. Some of the more common forms of direct marketing for events include:

Mail:

Before the internet, direct mail was the preferred marketing technique. This entailed sending materials directly to an individual through the postal service. It is a costly and time-consuming method of marketing, but it can still be effective.

The target audience must be well defined since the success of a direct mail campaign is dependent upon which mailing lists are chosen. Statistics show that a 3% response from a customer or mailing list is typical (therefore, to enroll 300 attendees, it would be necessary to mail 10,000 invitations).

Email:

Email marketing has become the more predominant technique for direct marketing of hospitality services and products. The cost effectiveness and ability to reach a wide audience makes email marketing very appealing. There are several good software programs that can help an event professional with bulk email distribution.

When using personal email accounts, the hospitality professional needs to consider the recipients' concern about receiving spam emails and getting computer viruses. They also want to make sure the email reaches the recipient. Some items for consideration:

- A "catchy" but clear subject line that lets the recipient know what the email contains and piques their interest in opening it.
- Using the BCC (blind carbon copy) address feature or the group email feature on an email program helps the recipient emails remain confidential to the others in the emailing list.
- Most email recipients have a spam-blocker on their email program that blocks emails from bulk email senders. Sending emails in individual small batches of 20 – 30 recipients will help circumvent the spam-blocking feature. (The software programs that help manage bulk emails do this automatically.)
- The sender's name needs to be clear. Most email recipients will delete and not open emails from email senders whose names they do not recognize.
- Most ISPs (Internet Service Providers) have a limit of no more than 70 – 90 names in a single outgoing email.
- Most email recipients are hesitant to open attachments, especially from unknown senders. Ideally the invitation information should be in the body of the email.
- If attachments are necessary, most event professionals prefer to send PDF (Adobe Acrobat) files instead of Microsoft Word documents. PDF files are less likely to be altered.
- The size of the email (and any attachments) should be no more than 1 MB (Megabyte). High resolution graphics and photos can increase the email size to very large files that will stall, and sometimes stop, the receiver's email system. Graphics and photos should be reduced in file size before being included on an email.

The telephone is still an effective marketing tool

© Dmytro Surkov/Shutterstock.com

Telephone:

The telephone remains one of the best ways to connect with people on a one-to-one basis and response *statistics* far exceed the response success of either direct mail or email. Some hospitality professionals organize a telephone tree, which involves having several volunteers divide up a phone list to make direct phone calls to lists of contact names. Some hospitality professionals use third-party tele-marketing companies or internal sales reps (ISR's) to help make phone calls.

For a telephone calling campaign to be successful, hospitality professionals create a phone script for those who will call the target audience. A phone script helps callers use compelling language that will resonate with the potential guests. This phone script also functions as sales pitch to help those making phone calls remember all the critical details of the product or service.

Advertising:

© Scott Maxwell LuMaxArt/Shutterstock.com

Human wearing a sign

An advertisement is a public notice. In most cases, advertising refers to paid forms of commercial advertisements (also called "ads"). The most common forms of commercial advertising are print media ads, such as newspapers and magazines; broadcast media ads, such as television and radio commercials; and online media, such as ads on websites and on search engines, ads on social networking sites and web video commercials. Commercial advertising may also take many other forms, from billboards, to mobile telephone screens, bus stop benches, aerial banners and balloons, humans wearing signs (called human billboards), bus and subway train signs, and much more.

Because advertising can be expensive, hospitality professionals should target their advertising dollars to the people most likely to buy the product or service. Ads might be placed in relevant trade magazines, journals, or publications in order to provide exposure.

Some media outlets offer trade-out advertising in exchange for a service that the event organization can provide. For example, a restaurant sales manager might offer free meals in exchange for an advertisement in their publication. A radio or television station might be willing to become an event sponsor to give them marketing exposure at the event in exchange for free advertisements on their radio or television station.

Indirect Marketing

Also known as word-of-mouth marketing, **indirect marketing** is promotion using non-traditional and innovative means. Whereas direct marketing is marketing directly to your target audience; indirect marketing involves indirect communication about the product or service to create a "marketing buzz" about the event. Buzz is the sound that humming bees make; marketing buzz expresses the idea of people passing along the word about a brand, product, or in the case of event marketing, an event.

Social Media:

Social media refers to all types of internet communications. Interactive discussions on online news sites, blogging, online discussion communities, micro blogging, mobile technologies for communication, and social networking sites are all forms of social media. In prior decades, word-of-mouth marketing for events meant one person calling their friends and telling them about something they were planning to attend. These days, word-of-mouth marketing tends to involve social media as well.

The worldwide web has become an effective way to connect people. The hospitality professional might create a Facebook page, a Twitter feed, a LinkedIn discussion board, or any other social media platform, and then send a notification to others encouraging them to pass the word along to their friends. Social media marketing has become such a phenomenon that many companies hire staff to manage social media platforms and to monitor social media dialog about the companies' products or services.

Viral Marketing

Viral marketing is thought of as a marketing activity wherein insights about a product or service is disseminated on the internet; just like a virus that spreads from person to person. The goal behind a viral marketing campaign is to get people to tell each other about something, and then have those people tell even more people. Viral marketing for events can be difficult to implement, and, once begun, they can quickly develop inertia. Some of the most successful campaigns are those that get people to create something.

Guerilla Marketing

The term "guerilla marketing" evolved from the concept of guerilla warfare which refers to individuals who, as an independent unit, carry out harassment and sabotage during wartime. Guerilla marketing relies on unconventional and unusual approaches, usually in public places, to get attention. Examples of guerilla marketing might include: a costumed character's offering sample promotional items to the public; a random public performance; an unusual sign or billboard or a Flash Mob (a group of people summoned to a designated location at a specified time to perform an indicated action, such as a dance, before dispersing).

Guerilla marketing can be a fun and effective way to gain media attention. However, hospitality professionals need to be careful about city laws and restrictions. The very nature of guerilla marketing is rebellious and non-conformist. However, when it comes to city zoning and ordinances, some guerilla marketing tactics could backfire. For example, there have been cases in San Francisco and New York City where the city has fined organizations for not having a permit for their creative chalk art advertising on sidewalks.

Publicity

Publicity is an action that brings someone or something to the attention of the public through the use of non-paid communication methods. For example, a public guerilla marketing technique, like a flash mob, might be great way to get publicity. However, someone needs to notify the media that the guerilla marketing stunt is going to take place. A person who manages and generates publicity is called a **publicist**. A good publicist makes a living by getting to know the press and making valuable personal contacts that help their clients gain publicity. It often takes years to develop a good press list of names and contacts that can be depended on to give exposure to their clients.

Public Relations

Public relations (or PR) is the art of convincing the public to have an understanding for and goodwill toward an organization, person, or event. Many large-scale producers hire public relations (PR) firms. Even an untrained person can learn how to garner some of this press publicity. Some of the more common PR activities include:

Press Release - Sometimes the best kind of publicity comes from newspapers, magazines, or the internet. Print and online news media do not have enough staff or resources to be aware of all the possible news stories, so they rely on press releases to keep them informed about activities within the community and fill them in on news items that their reporters might not be able to cover. Press releases can also be sent to bloggers and other news reporting sources. Third party media distribution agencies can serve as a distribution channel to the media, or the event manager can create their own press list for distribution.

The press release should also include the name and contract information of the person sending the release. A press release has three parts: a headline, the body of the press release, and boiler plate. The headline should be succinct and interesting to get their attention. The body of the press release expands on the details and should be written as factual news, just as a journalist might write it. Some publicists or event professionals like to use a boiler plate. Boiler plate is a section of the press release after the story that tells about the organization or event. Boiler plate is an old news term that refers to standard text that is used repeatedly on multiple pages of a newspaper. Check with each publication to find out what medium is preferred for photographs (color, black and white, jpg, tif files).

Press Invitation - The media (including newspapers, magazines, radio, and online news) is typically looking for newsworthy subjects—so the more compelling the event is to them, the more likely the press will be to attend. Hospitality professionals or publicists need to send the first invitation to the media two to three weeks prior to the event and follow up with another invite two days beforehand.

Public Service Announcement (PSA) - An additional source of free publicity is the Public Service Announcement, also called a PSA. This is a written script distributed to broadcast media for their newscasters or radio announcers to read on the air. In the United States, the Federal Communications Commission (FCC) mandates rules for the licensing of radio and television stations. One of the mandates of the FCC is a requirement for them to broadcast a certain number of PSA's. They will accept them in written form or in pre-recorded form, such as an audio or videotape. They should be recorded in :20, :30, & :60 second "spots" and should be sent to the station two to three weeks in advance of the broadcast date. PSA's should be written so they can be easily read aloud.

WEB ANALYTICS IN MARKETING

As the discipline of online marketing has evolved, so has the sophistication of systems (or analytics) to determine its effectiveness. When deciding where to purchase advertising, the hospitality professional considers where they are most likely to reach their target audience. In commercial advertising the analytics to determine reach are important. The number of subscribers, the types of subscribers, and the publication distribution channels provide the basis for the reach statistics in print media. Broadcast media uses rating systems to determine how many people are watching or listening to their broadcasts on any specific time or day.

The use of web and media analytics to locate target audiences on the internet has become very advanced in recent years. There are often tools built into online advertising technology that can tell when a person has looked at a website. Internet tracking cookies are commonly used to measure an internet user's search engine browsing history and the keywords used. Keywords are the words used by an internet user when they do an internet search. When purchasing search engine advertisements, the event professional can select the keywords associated with their ad or their target audience. They can then have their ad appear on the internet user's search engine when the keyword on the specific defined category is searched.

For example, if an internet user types in "hotels" and "Rio de Janeiro," the online advertising that particular internet user will see will likely be about hotels or travel in Brazil. Internet advertising sellers can also give statistics about how many people looked up specific keywords. Most internet advertising is charged on a "pay-per-click" basis, meaning the advertising purchaser pays a fee for every time that someone clicks on the link to their advertisement. Because the costs can be difficult to control, many event professionals set a pre-determined maximum limit on the number of "clicks" that they will purchase from the online advertising seller.

SUMMARY

Marketing is a combination of science and art. It requires research to understand the customer and the marketplace. But it also requires creativity in decision making and communication so that the organization's product and/or services are attractive to the consumer.

There are two mnemonic devices that can help people remember key concepts in marketing: the P's and the C's. The hospitality professional must be able to define marketing and differentiate between marketing and advertising. They must differentiate between marketing strategy and tactics. It is critical to understand the marketing process and the marketing mix. It is also important to know the difference between internal and external marketing.

One cannot be an effective sales professional without knowing the different types of customers in the hospitality industry and how customer behavior impacts marketing strategy.

KEY TERMS

distribution	planning	publicist
market segmentation	positioning	reach
marketing	price	strategy
packages	process	tactics
people	promotion	

REVIEW AND DISCUSSION QUESTIONS

1. Explain the P's of marketing.

2. Explain the C's of marketing.

3. Define marketing.

4. What questions does marketing research help to answer?

5. Explain the difference between primary and secondary research.

6. How can customers be segmented?

7. Explain positioning.

8. Discuss what a brand is and what it accomplishes.

9. What is the difference between marketing and advertising?

10. What are some of the areas to consider when researching the consumer behavior of stakeholders?

CHAPTER 3

Introduction to Sales for MEEC and Hospitality

Salespeople and clients meeting in hotel lobby
© Kzenon/Shutterstock.com

LEARNING OBJECTIVES

- Describe the sales process in MEEC and hospitality.
- Define sales.
- Describe the responsibilities of MEEC and hospitality salespeople.
- Describe the various sales positions within the MEEC and hospitality industries.
- Discuss the job descriptions and job specifications for hospitality sales.
- Articulate the differing jobs and salaries in hospitality sales.

Introduction

We all sell in the world of hospitality. Whether we are influencing customers to select a particular menu item, convincing vendors to deliver needed supplies at a moment's notice, or persuading staff members to deliver high levels of quality service, every hospitality professional is a salesperson. Certainly, there are members of the hospitality management team who have the responsibility of selling to prospective customers, but all MEEC and hospitality workers sell something. The former are referred to as **sales professionals**.

Selling is about helping people solve their individual or organization's problems. Identifying what's important for that customer or that organization and responding with solutions that help to solve those problems is the primary role of the sales professional. They do this through **personal selling**. Personal selling can be defined as a process where person-to-person communication takes place between a salesperson and a current or prospective customer. Salespeople seek to understand the customer's wants and needs and satisfy them by presenting the customer with a hospitality product and/or service that satisfies that want or need. In selling for MEEC, salespeople use oral, written, and electronic communication for the purpose of informing about product/service options, influencing prospects to select those product/service options, and/or reminding prospective customers of the product/service offerings as they consider their options before making the final buying decision.

The Nature of MEEC and Hospitality Sales: Different Responsibilities

In order to be successful, MEEC and hospitality salespeople must take on the duties and develop the skills that help connect MEEC customers with product and service offerings that satisfy their needs. These duties and skills include: knowledge of the sales process, seeking new customers, stimulating additional sales from current customers, collecting information, providing advice, managing personal selling time and other resources, managing customer relationships, and providing creative solutions to customers' problems.

The **sales process** can be thought of as a step-by-step approach; each step of the process must be thoroughly addressed for the sale to be accomplished. The sales process includes looking for new accounts, making contact with these contacts, confirming that the prospect has a need for the MEEC product or services, presenting what the MEEC organization has to offer, overcoming objections, and closing the sale. Each step in this process relies on the steps before it; the sale cannot be made unless each prior step has been fully dealt with.

When sales professionals collect information, they are working like detectives to get as many facts as they possibly can about the customer. This information can include facts about the prospective customer as an individual and his or her company, the reason for the potential purchase of MEEC or hospitality products and services, and information about previous MEEC or hospitality purchases that provide insight into the prospect's buying process. Sales professionals also collect data about the economy, the competition, and other events and activities that can positively or negatively affect sales success. Prospective customers appreciate salespeople who are knowledgeable and have "done their homework."

When salespeople have done their homework about the competition and the prospective customer, and they know their own product well, they are poised to serve in a consultative capacity with their prospect. While some MEEC and hospitality consumers are knowledgeable and don't require much advice, others look to the salesperson as a consultant to help recommend product and service options that will help satisfy the prospect's needs. To provide advice, it is very important for the salesperson to be able to ask good questions; questions that help the salesperson collect information that could not otherwise be collected somewhere else. Having this information helps the salesperson provide customized advice based on unique facts. When the salesperson is well prepared, they bring an impression of confidence that evokes trust in the prospective customer. This is where the old adage comes from: "People buy from people they like, and people they trust."

One of the most important tasks of the MEEC or hospitality salesperson is to keep looking for potential customers. Research suggests that it takes a salesperson at least 7 hours of prospecting for new customers to achieve one appointment with a potential customer. In addition, the average MEEC organization loses between 10% and 30% of their customers each year. MEEC salespeople spend time networking and getting to know people who could be potential customers, or who know others who might become potential customers. One primary method of meeting potential clients is though attending and/or exhibiting at national conventions of professional associations. In MEEC these might include gatherings organized by the Professional

Convention Management Association, Meeting Professionals International, Destinations International, the International Association for Events and Exhibitions, IMEX, and others. The IMEX convention held in Las Vegas in October each year now draws almost 10,000 attendees: all MEEC related. Keeping the "pipeline" full of potential clients (prospects) is essential for a sales professional's success.

The old adage, "time is money" applies aptly to the hospitality sales professional. Allocating time to selling activities, keeping track of time spent on various activities, and using their time wisely help MEEC and hospitality sales professionals to be effective and efficient in finding new customers, developing relationships with potential customers, communicating with current customers, and closing the sale with customers who are ready to buy. None of these activities can happen without personal time management.

Salespeople work as the link between their organization and the customer. As such, salespeople must manage the relationship with customers in such a way that a "win-win" association takes place between the customer and the MEEC organization. Early in the sales process, the salesperson is getting to know what the customer's needs are, and the customer is learning whether the salesperson and the organization can satisfy those needs. Once a relationship has started to develop, the relationship progresses to one of establishing trust. Once trust has been established, the salesperson truly becomes the business partner that the customer is seeking.

The intangible nature of MEEC and hospitality product and service offerings require salespeople to be creative in how they present and what they offer prospective customers as solutions to customers' needs. Customers receive many communications from MEEC and hospitality organizations (and others); therefore, sales professionals need to be creative to make presentations that are memorable to the prospective customer. Customers are always looking for new and unique products and services. As a result, salespeople must work with their operations counterparts to provide those exceptional offerings that set the MEEC or hospitality organization apart from their competitors. Finally, MEEC and hospitality salespeople are successful when they can maximize the use of the space, products, and services they sell. Being creative results in satisfied customers.

MEEC and hospitality salespeople serve as the connection between the hospitality organization and the customer. For many customers, the salesperson IS the hotel, restaurant, conference center, convention center, or other MEEC organization. As a result, MEEC and hospitality salespeople must be customer-relationship focused and use data analytics to determine market segment potential, develop sales strategies, and uncover intelligence that helps to set their MEEC organization apart from the competition.

Various Roles of the MEEC Salesperson

Salespeople in the world of meetings and events take on various roles. These roles include demand creator, delivery personnel, organizational champion, technical specialist, and customer service representative. While each of these roles requires different responsibilities, the roles played align with the various steps of the sales process. Typically, newly graduated hospitality professionals are assigned a customer service representative or order taker role before moving into a demand creator role. Depending on the complexity of the meeting or event, there may be separate individuals filling each role. In other situations, these roles might overlap.

The **demand creator** is also known as the "hunter." The sales professionals in this role, as the name implies, spend much of their time seeking out: 1) new business, 2) additional business from existing customers, and 3) new business from existing customers. Much of the time of the demand creator is spent on the telephone or computer contacting potential prospects or making in-person sales calls. Demand creators are autonomous; they are very good at time management and independently determining the best course of action in order to close the sale.

Delivery personnel are just that; they are the on-site individuals who follow through with the contract created by the demand creator. Delivery personnel can be considered the service after the sale. For example, if the event includes meal service, catering or event managers would be responsible for working with the customer to develop menus and service styles. Depending on the venue, deliverers may represent the venue or a third-party organization such as a catering company.

The **missionary sales role** is typically taken on by the demand creator or a sales professional tasked with reminding the prospective or current customer of the products and services the MEEC organization has to offer. Further, the missionary sales role is designed to develop the relationship between the organization and the customer. Missionary salespeople work to develop goodwill with the customer; the objective of their contact is to inform the customer of new product or services offerings. The information that they provide is typically directed to the final decision maker.

In the MEEC world, the technician sales role is typically a third-party vendor position. As the description implies, technical salespeople have specialized skills and offer services such as audiovisual, electrical supply for displays, staging and booth setup, carpentry services, and décor. The two largest service contractors in the MEEC industry, GES and Freeman, have sales professionals and sales offices located throughout the world. Although the technician sales role is typically a third party in the MEEC industry, some facilities have staff members who fulfill the role of technician sales representative, especially in larger convention and event centers. Coordination is important between the MEEC organization and the third-party vendor, so that the customer has a seamless experience when holding a meeting or an event in the facility.

Customer service representatives are also known as "gatherers." An **"inside" salesperson**, this role is typically the equivalent of being an order taker. In most situations, the gatherer responds to inquiries from prospective customers. In hotels and similar venues, this customer service role focuses primarily on catered events such as weddings, anniversaries, small conferences, and other simple meetings and events.

Different Job Opportunities

There are multiple sales job opportunities in the MEEC industry. MEEC sales jobs that sell the *facility and services* can be found in hotels, convention centers, and restaurants. Sales jobs that sell the *destination and services* include destination marketing organizations (DMOs) and convention and visitors bureaus (CVBs). There are sales positions that sell services to trade show organizers and exhibitors. Destination management companies employ salespeople to sell services to event organizers and groups. Professional association salespeople sell exhibit space to vendors for trade shows related to the association.

There are many travel and tourism sales jobs. There are opportunities to sell tour packages to groups. Corporate travel companies and incentive companies sell tour packages to corporations and professional associations. There are bus tour companies that sell to groups. Airline sales positions sell seats on flights to corporations and groups. There are business-to-business (B2B) sales jobs: Equipment, cleaning, and guest supply companies selling products to MEEC facilities. Food distribution companies and beverage supply companies have sales representatives that sell food and beverages to MEEC facilities. Finally, third party/online travel companies (OTAs) have sales representatives who work with hotels to list hotel rooms on the OTA websites.

EXAMPLES OF SALES CAREER OPPORTUNITIES

There are probably more job opportunities in MEEC and hospitality than most people realize. AND they are some of the highest paid positions in the industry. The following are just a few:

- Sales positions in Hotels: they sell products and services that the facility has to offer.

- Sales positions in DMOs/CVBs - they sell the destination to groups of all sorts.

- Sales positions in Convention Centers - they sell exhibit space, services, and catering to trade shows and consumer shows.

- Sales positions with Service Contractors - they sell services to trade show organizers and exhibitors.

- Sales positions with Destination Management Companies (DMCs) - they sell services to event organizers and groups.

- Sales positions in Restaurants - they sell products and services to small groups. Every outlet of the chain Maggiano's Little Italy has at least one group salesperson (Banquet Sales Manager) on staff.

- Sales in Professional Associations - they sell exhibit space at their association's trade shows.

- Sales positions in Tour and Travel - they sell tour packages to groups.

- Sales positions with Airlines - they sell seats on flights to corporations and associations.

- Sales positions with Bus Tours - they sell package bus tours to groups.

- Sales positions with Food Service Companies - they sell food goods to hospitality businesses.

- Sales with Liquor Companies - they sell beverages to hospitality businesses.

EXHIBIT 1. SALARY BREAKDOWN FOR A HOTEL SALES REPRESENTATIVE (In 2017 dollars)

Salary $25,668 - $81,480

Bonus $197 - $30,360

Profit Sharing $0.00 - $19,793

Commission $980 - $74,506

Total Pay $30,325 - $107,266

EXHIBIT 2. SALARIES OF RELATED JOBS

Account Executive	$42,000 - $75,000
Account Manager	$41,000 - $70,000
Account Manager Sales	$45,000 - $80,000
Business Development Manager	$58,000 - $101,000
General Operations Manager	$40,000 - $81,000
Inside Sales Representative	$35,000 - $50,000
National Sales Manager	$71,000 - $120,000
Regional Sales Manager	$70,000 - $112,000
Sales Associate	$19,000 - $24,000
Territory Sales Representative	$43,000 - $71,000

Salaries for sales professionals vary by location. For example, in New York City, sales manager base salaries are about 44% higher. Organizations in other major cities, such as Houston, Washington D.C., and Boston, pay their sales managers 19%–25% more than the national average.

Job Descriptions and Career Overviews

HOTEL SALES

Hotel sales managers are responsible for bringing in guests and making the hotel money. They may work with senior sales managers or owners to plan sales promotions, set sales goals, and train staff. These professionals not only seek out business with individual guests but also typically meet with larger groups such as churches, traveling executives, and family reunions to encourage them to stay with their hotel. Agreements with large groups allow for successful repeat business, which generates sales for the entire company.

A hotel sales manager also sells prospective and current guests on the hotel's services, such as dining options, swimming pools, and exercise rooms, and notifies them of room upgrades. Possessing complete knowledge of all of the services the hotel offers is important for making a successful sale.

Many hotel sales managers start in hotel support positions, and then receive promotions after having been with the company for some time. Hotel sales managers have the option of venturing into public relations, marketing, or convention sales within the hotel industry. Upscale and luxury hotels typically require a college degree and extensive experience in hospitality.

Job Requirements

Working irregular and long hours on both weekends and evenings are commonly required of hotel sales managers. Sometimes, they must work longer than the traditional 40-hour week. Traveling locally, regionally, and nationally to meet with prospective guests and other sales managers to discuss business is often necessary. Transfers from one office to another are also common in this career, so hotel sales managers should be comfortable with relocating if needed.

Employers look for hotel sales managers who are flexible, decisive, motivated, reliable, and creative. Due to the potential pressure to generate sales, hotel sales managers should be able to handle and manage stress appropriately. Creating and maintaining mutually beneficial relationships with customers can close sales and lead to repeat business.

The following are examples of actual job posting for sales in hospitality:

SALES MANAGER - BUSINESS TRAVEL, LARGE HOTEL IN A LARGE CITY

We are seeking a creative, innovative Business Travel Sales manager, eager and excited at the opportunity to shape the market position for the BRAND-NEW *Large Hotel*, opening summer 2018! This is a unique chance to be a part of a hotel opening and have direct influence on the development of the property's personality. Ideal candidate must wear multiple hats and is ready to hit the ground running to penetrate the Business Transient Market. This position reports to the Director of Sales and Marketing.

Located adjacent to the main metro station in the *large city*, the hotel will offer 367 luxurious rooms and 23,000 SQ FT of flexible and unique meeting space—all just steps from the best *Large City* has to offer!

Job Duties:

- Responsible for soliciting and servicing transient business accounts in accordance with the marketing plan
- Generates a high profile and quality perception in the market place
- Responsible for generating guest room and other revenues as described by the Director of Sales & Marketing
- Responsible for maximizing profitability and ensuring overall guest satisfaction
- Participates in the marketing plans, promotions and services
- Meet or exceed pre-determined booking goals for guest room revenue; meet or exceed budgeted costs and revenue on a monthly average with the liberty to negotiate as needed on individual functions within established guidelines yet maintaining the overall revenue goals
- Compiles lists of prospective clients for use as sales leads based on information from newspapers, business directories and other sources
- Solicit new and repeat guest room and meeting business
- Determine the guest's needs, space availability, and meeting details
- Utilize site inspections and on-site luncheons to book business
- Monitor pricing, service levels, facilities and function activities at competitive facilities to ensure the Hotel remains in a competitive position
- Evaluate a potential piece of business for profitability and overall benefit to the Hotel
- Negotiate transient rates with clients on an annual and on-going basis
- Follows up on the progress of clients booked, such as room night pick up, with the Group Housing Coordinator to ensure maximum occupancy
- Represent hotel in community affairs and industry related events
- Make outside sales calls and telemarket to obtain business
- Maintain active liaison with competitors regionally through personal contacts, professional and industry associations
- Have acquired knowledge with the ability to upsell clients, while promoting a level of service parallel to the luxury stature of the facility
- Determine the requirements for and the follow up on special groups, VIPs, etc.
- Follow supervisor's instructions and completes other duties as directed or assigned

Job Requirements:

- Minimum 3 years of experience as a Hotel Sales Manager in a 3-5 star property required
- Bachelor's degree preferred or equivalent combination of education and experience. Hospitality Education a plus.
- Prefer experience with Delphi Software

- Prefer experience with Hotelligence Data
- Ability to effectively present information to employees, management, clients and the public in one-on-one and group situations
- Understand the mission, vision and game plan of the hotel
- Ability to understand Guests' service needs
- Ability to converse calmly with irate Guests', co-workers or supervisors in sometimes tense situations
- Ability to work cohesively with co-workers and other departments as part of a team
- Ability to meet or exceed productivity and performance standards and complete tasks as assigned by supervisor or manager

NATIONAL SALES MANAGER, LARGE CONVENTION CENTER IN A LARGE CITY

Here at the *Large Convention Center* we offer fulfilling and sensational careers on a campus which includes one of the world's largest domed structures; one of the largest convention centers in the United States; and the site of an Olympic Games. Every year the *Large Convention Center* campus accommodates over one million visitors for sporting events, concerts, and conventions and entertainment events hosted in the heart of downtown Large City. Our mission is to promote and facilitate events and activities that generate economic benefits to the citizens of the State and the City as well as enhance the quality of life for every citizen of our state.

The Large Convention Center is currently seeking a National Sales Manager to join our team. The National Sales Manager shall be responsible for implementation and management of their assigned segments of the Center's national convention and trade show, corporate, public and special markets. Performs functions of the Director of Sales in the absence of the incumbent of that position. This position reports to the Director of Sales. Good communication, strong organizational skills and the ability to work effectively with other team members is of utmost importance. A thorough understanding and conformance with convention center policies and procedures is also essential for this position.

Our ideal candidate will be a transformational leader with a passion for innovation. Successful employees at the Large Convention Center embody our four core values—to be one, to be honest, to be stewards, to be dynamic—and share our vision to be the #1 convention, sports, and entertainment destination in the world.

Essential Duties and Responsibilities

- Contribute to the development and implementation of a yearly action plan for assigned national and international accounts, as well as the corporate, public and special market accounts. Ensure Sales Executives are knowledgeable of the marketing plan.
- Assist the Director of Sales in assigning daily work assignments to the Sales Managers and Executives based on the marketing plan. Assist in monitoring sales efforts and make adjustment. Recommend changes to the marketing plan.

- Interview and recommend selection of Sales Managers and Executives.
- Supervise, counsel, and train Sales Managers and Executives regarding administrative procedures, policies, and operational procedures.
- Prepare monthly and quarterly sales reports for assigned accounts.
- Execute specific marketing plans relating to major events, using support of advertising, specialty advertising, and other related functions as directed.
- Entertain customers at facility hosted events, while making sales calls or hosting customer site visits and other local events, baseball game, concerts, special events, etc.
- Maintain liaison with the Large City Convention and Visitors Bureau and local hotels and suppliers by taking an active part in all facets of the industry. Attend Director of Sales meetings at the Convention and Visitors Bureau in the absence of the Director of Sales and Marketing.
- Travel throughout the United States to make sales calls or attend industry meetings.
- Develop and control sales program through evaluating staffing, training, and performance.
- Work with Public Relations in expanding public relations opportunities.
- Such other duties, functions, special projects and responsibilities as assigned by the Director of Sales.

Knowledge, Skills and Abilities
- Ability to prioritize tasks and to manage workload using own initiative
- Ability to multi-task and work under pressure with limited resources
- High degree of integrity and compliance
- Ability to build and maintain customer focused relationships with internal and external customers
- Thoroughness in task approach, follow-up and completion;
- Excellent computer skills
- Self-awareness
- Assess, weigh and manage risk in the face of uncertainty
- Ability to demonstrate an aptitude for developing sales principles and techniques
- Ability to communicate effectively and to handle multiple tasks simultaneously.

NATIONAL SALES MANAGER, NATIONAL DMC

Company: Started in 1981, National DMC is an award-winning, full-service destination management company providing clients with a professional service resource in designing and executing destination programs. We currently have 25+ offices throughout the United States. Our services include Special Events, Transportation, Activities, Sightseeing Tours, Program Logistics, Team Building Events, Decor and Entertainment Options. Office environment is friendly, relaxed, progressive and challenging.

Our Values and Culture:

Act with Humility Deliver with Intensity Own Our Results. This is who we choose to be, and how we show up every day. Whether wowing our clients, working with other members of our teams, or maintaining strong relationships in our communities and with our partners, these core values set the stage for how we do business.

Our challenge to every employee is to be a person who is passionate about what they do, working with a team focus, and leaving a positive impact on everything they touch. This is not easily lived out, but it is the National DMC expectation of excellence.

Apathy need not apply here. We're making waves and only want wave makers.

If this excites you and you're up to the challenge, then National DMC just might be a right fit for you.

Summary of Position: We are looking for a truly unique and dynamic professional who has proven high-quality sales abilities.

Essential Duties and Responsibilities

- Maintain and sustain client relationships, while building new client connections
- Develop internal and external leads
- Arrange client meetings, presentations and site inspections
- Manage assigned hotel relationships
- Promote National DMC through sales calls, sales trips and industry relations
- Provide progress reports on a regular basis
- Develop, manage and guide sales activities for the organization
- Assist in the design and execution of the sales strategy and sales plan
- Propose and execute policies and programs to achieve maximum sales volume potential for services
- Act as main point of contact for client through sales process to include brain-storming event ideas, manage creative proposal development and revisions as well as contracting; create and edit proposals and contracts if needed
- Work in conjunction with an Associate Director of Events to manage a team of Event Producers through the planning and operations phases of client program and attend events as needed to manage client relationships and ensure operational success
- Obtain complete and thorough knowledge of National DMC's policies, products and services
- Attend industry events and be familiarized with the industry, hotels and suppliers
- Comprehensive understanding of the proprietary National DMC software and systems
- Qualifications
- College Degree BA or equivalent

- Excellent writing skills and grammar
- Experience working with budgets
- Highly proficient in Word, Excel and PowerPoint
- Ability to promote National DMC and its product to clients, suppliers, staff and the general public
- Excellent interpersonal and communication skills
- Ability to build strong bonds with Event Producers to foster open, honest and candid communication
- Ability to work flexible hours; weekends, evenings, holidays and to travel to venue and sales trip locations as needed
- Possess a professional manner and appearance when representing National DMC with clients and supplier/partners

Work Environment: The work environment characteristics for this position are typical of those an employee encounters while performing the essential functions of this position. Reasonable accommodations may be made to enable individuals with disabilities to perform the essential functions. The noise level in this office is moderate.

Salary Range & Benefits: Appropriate with experience; Company sponsored Medical, Dental, Vision Package, 401K Plan, Healthy Paid Time Off Plan.

Sales Manager, National Food Service Provider (such as Compass Group, Aramark, or Sodexo)

National Food Service Provider is in the customer service business across food, facilities and uniforms, wherever people work, learn, recover, and play. United by a passion to serve, our more than 270,000 employees deliver experiences that enrich and nourish the lives of millions of people in 22 countries around the world every day. National Food Service Provider is recognized among the Most Admired Companies by FORTUNE and the World's Most Ethical Companies by the Ethisphere Institute.

National Food Service Provider's leisure group specializes in lodging, recreation, conference centers and meeting services. The scope of our operations includes lodging, conference and meeting space, houseboats and other marine activities, retail merchandise, casual and fine dining experiences, and interpretive tours in some of this country's most pristine protected lands and national parks. We have been active partners with the National Park Service for over 20 years, providing high-quality visitor services in numerous locations across the United States. We are one of the nation's leading managers of conference centers with a strong focus on customer experience. We are considered a premier provider of professional services by clients and competition alike, committed to providing high-quality recreation, hospitality and authentic experiences to clients and visitors from all over the world.

Job Description:

- Solicit, negotiate and confirm new and repeat business through various efforts (outside sales calls, telemarketing, referrals, tradeshows, sales missions, internet prospecting, etc.). Prompt and competent follow-up on leads/referrals, use of reader board analysis, and networking in order to maximize room revenue to meet and/or exceed individual and team sales and revenue goals.
- Develop and continually enhance relationships with key accounts, business and travel industry accounts, community organizations and professional associations to maintain high visibility and increase market share. Responsible for building Relationship Strategy and driving customer loyalty by delivering superior service throughout each customer experience. Able to successfully close profitable business and achieve revenue targets.
- Conduct property site inspections with potential customers. This involves walking client throughout property and grounds while performing an oral presentation of facilities and amenities. Be aware of hotel features and benefits, operations and competitive strengths and weaknesses to assist customers in their buying decisions.
- Identifies and anticipates market trends and volatility. Recommends alternative options and solutions to improve sales.
- Lead, develop, train and coach respective team members within the sales and catering discipline.
- Develop and implement creative sales strategy by analyzing historical, current and future hotel/market/account trends.
- Directs the implementation and follow through of all sales standards and initiatives according to National Food Service Provider guidelines and Standards of Operation.
- Ensures the assignment of all groups and functions, as well as the accurate and timely communication of event needs to conference planners and operations team.
- Increases account revenue and/or operating profit contribution by promoting ancillary spend and creating other opportunities for growth. Upsells and makes creative suggestions to clients.
- Maintain accurate, legible records and files consistent with sales and catering system. Create and distribute effective internal and external communication (written and verbal). Prepare and maintain sales related reports.
- Responsible for developing and implementing revenue and yield strategies related to group and transient rooms, group sales, meeting room rental, local catering sales and related revenue. Focus on market segmentation, pricing, direct sales, marketing and other strategies to maximize profitability for the property.

Accountable for achieving targeted performance relative to market, budget, forecasts and guest satisfaction scores. Direct and manage all group, transient, and catering sales activities and resources to maximize revenue for property.

- Regularly visit and shop the competition to stay abreast of their rate strategies, clientele and any changes in facilities, services and market position

Qualifications:

- Demonstrated oral and written communication skills
- Planning, organizing and effective time management skills
- Experience with computer applications including but not limited to: Microsoft Office, Maestro, Opera, Springer Miller System or other property management systems. Other experience with sales-based CRM applications
- Professional appearance and demeanor
- Ability to work effectively under pressure and meet established goals and objectives
- General financial acumen

The Relationship of Sales to Marketing

As we look at the evolution of marketing as it pertains to hospitality, sales as an era of the hospitality marketing profession began in the 1940's and progressed into the 1950's when franchising was initiated by Kemmons Wilson of Holiday Inn. At that point, sales in MEEC led toward the development of marketing departments, greater understanding of consumer behavior, and a movement toward marketing activities that would provide potential clients and sales activities that would consummate the sale. Marketing, then, became more of a strategic activity focused on brand development and sales activities that were tactical; let's get "the heads in the beds." Destination marketing developed even earlier. In 1895, the basis of today's **destination marketing organizations (DMO)** that are also called **convention & visitor bureaus (CVBs)** was put forth when journalist Milton Carmichael suggested in *The Detroit Journal* that local businessmen get together to promote the city as a convention destination, as well as represent the city and its many hotels to bid for that business. Shortly thereafter the Detroit Convention and Businessmen's League was conceived to do just that. Carmichael was the head of the group that later evolved into the Detroit Metro CVB that is now labeled VisitDetroit.

The role of CVB's (now referred to as Destination Marketing Organizations or DMOs) has changed over time. As in Detroit, most began by trying to attract only conventions and business meetings to their community. Later, they realized leisure visitors were an important source of business and added the "V" for visitors to their name. Today, virtually every city in the United States and Canada, and many cities throughout the world, has a DMO or convention and visitors' association (CVA). Many DMOs have now evolved to not only market but help develop and manage tourism in their destinations. Most recently, the term "DMO" is being used in place of CVB.

Marketing is defined as the activity, organization, and processes for creating, communicating, delivering, and exchanging offerings that have value for customers, partners, and society at large. Marketing seeks to gain the prospective customer's attention, and stimulate interest in the MEEC or hospitality organization's product and service offerings. Marketing activities are considered long term; branding and image are key elements to marketing the MEEC organization. The strategic elements of marketing include the characteristics of the product and services the MEEC or hospitality organization offers, the prices the organization charges for those products and services, where and how those products are offered, and what promotional strategies are used to communicate benefits to the customer. What is important for salespeople to understand as it relates to marketing is the phenomenon of consumer behavior. Customers have needs to be satisfied. Those needs are translated into wants, which are how people communicate their needs. These wants are described in terms of objects or actions that satisfy those needs.

Marketing strategy drives how the sales process is undertaken. Personal selling is an immediate activity; it involves oral and written communication that communicates the essentials of the MEEC or hospitality brand, persuades the customer toward purchase, and prompts the customer to understand how the MEEC organization is the best alternative among the competition for selection. Successful MEEC salespeople create a positive image of their facility and communicate that image through the characteristics they present. This technique is known as positioning, and it is used to help keep the MEEC facility at the "top of mind" with the customer.

The Sales Organization in MEEC

The sales and marketing mission within the MEEC facility guides the activities of each sales staff member. The mission of the sales organization is to bring revenues to the facility that exceed the planned budget. In order to achieve that mission, the culture of the sales organization requires a coordinated effort by all sales personnel on four activities. First, salespeople and staff must respond to all inquiries, whether they are via telephone inquiry or electronically via the internet. Next, salespeople should work to develop new accounts in targeted growing markets. As mentioned before, salespeople work to service their accounts in a manner that exceeds expectations. Finally, salespeople must work with the financial managers of the organization to ensure that forecasting is accurate, revenue is optimized, and the emphasis is on profit for the organization.

Many of the marketing activities of a MEEC organization are included in the sales unit of the organization. One of the most important activities is revenue management. Sales managers focus on customer's preference for *dates*, what prices they are willing to pay, and how many rooms and how much meeting space they need: commonly referred to as dates, rates, space – you can only have two of the three. However, there is now an emphasis on revenue potential for the entire organization, fitting business to dates of need by the organization, and how much of the facilities' capacity is required. As a result, more evaluation of the customer's potential to bring business to the MEEC organization is done BEFORE the business is booked.

Every MEEC or hospitality organization has a sales department that is the key revenue producing unit of the organization. The size and complexity of the organization affect the structure of the sales department. The sales efforts of smaller organizations are less specialized; sales managers handle all sales calls and types of business. In larger organizations, sales managers are more specialized based on the type of business, market segment, and geographic location. Regardless of the size of the organization, the sales function must be structured so that profitable business is acquired and maintained.

The Sales Organization

In the MEEC organization, a representative of the sales team is the first person the event planner will come in contact with. Obviously, every member of the sales staff should be hospitable, seeking to establish a positive relationship and making a great first impression of themselves and the MEEC property. The positions within the MEEC organization include: the director of marketing, director of sales, sales managers, sales coordinators, event sales managers, and sales assistants.

The **director of marketing** oversees all sales and marketing efforts in the MEEC organization. This position is strategic in nature, involved in setting prices, determining distribution strategy, creating promotion strategy and programs, and developing packages. The director of marketing, working with the director of sales, creates the goals and objectives that guide the sales effort. The director of marketing reports to the general manager or vice president and is typically a member of the MEEC organization's executive committee.

The **director of sales** is responsible for coordinating and directing the sales team in carrying out the marketing action plan for the MEEC organization. This position is more tactical; the decisions made are a result of the goals and objectives created by the director of marketing and the senior executives of the MEEC organization. The director of sales has many areas of responsibility that affect the sales managers and coordinators whom they supervise:

- Which markets to work with and how they are assigned

- Geographic territories to work with and how they are assigned

- Conducting sales staff and other operational meetings

- Revenue goals for each market and geographic area

- Coaching sales managers and coordinators

In addition, directors of sales are involved in the promotional activities of the organization that have an impact on the sales function:

- How advertising will be carried out

- Public relations and community service activities

- What tradeshows and sales events will be attended

- Developing sales brochures and other selling materials

The director of sales position is usually considered a department head position, and typically reports to the director of marketing. The director of sales, as the department head, is responsible for the budgeting, human resources, and day-to-day operation of the sales department.

The **sales manager** position is the "lifeblood" of the sales effort. Sales managers are the individuals who conduct the activities we will describe later in the chapter and throughout the remainder of this book. Like all of the sales staff, but most importantly, sales managers must be knowledgeable, professional, great communicators, and great at working autonomously. The sales manager position can be deployed in different markets, such as conventions, groups, and special events. Many large MEEC organizations, such as the major hotel brands and convention destination cities, complement their in-house sales staff with regional and national sales offices or representatives. Marriott, for example, has "cluster" sales offices in each of the major cities in the United States. The value of these offices is the capability of optimizing the product options based on the customer's needs. For example, with multiple hotel types and brands available in a particular city, the cluster sales manager can offer options that best meet the needs of the customer. A small meeting space at a select service property such as a Courtyard by Marriott may be a better option than the same size meeting space across the street at a Renaissance Hotel. The major brands also have national sales managers based out of the corporate office. These national sales managers represent the brand to major companies like Google, Microsoft, and Coca-Cola. Cities such as Orlando, Washington, D.C., Miami, Las Vegas, and Chicago have sales managers located across the United States, and in some cases around the world, to represent that destination and its MEEC facilities.

Convention service managers (CSM), as the title implies, provide the services of a convention sales manager contracted with the customer. Convention service managers represent the customer with all other departments in the MEEC facility by following through on the agreed-upon contract and managing the details to ensure a successful meeting, convention, or event. CSMs may seek to upsell products or services to the customer before the event takes place.

Sales coordinators provide the administrative support, customer service, and sales leads for the sales team. For many MEEC organizations, the competition is intense! Because of this, the sales office cannot function without coordinators to respond to the inquiries that arrive electronically and via the telephone. Like the other members of the sales team, coordinators must have a complete knowledge of the products, services, amenities, and promotions of the MEEC organization. Coordinators produce reports associated with the sales team's activities related to appointments, calls made, and business leads.

Sales Meetings

There are a number of meetings that the sales team must participate in. In hotels, revenue management meetings are a priority. There are weekly sales meetings, pre (and post) convention meetings, and one-on-one meetings with the director of sales or marketing.

Revenue management meetings in hotels are held daily, and, depending on volume and complexity, also weekly or bi-weekly. This meeting addresses past and future performance in guest rooms, food and beverage, function space, and other revenues. Revenue managers work with the sales team to maximize revenues through pricing strategies, space allocation, and group and convention evaluation. This evaluation of potential business entails a review of size, spending history, impact on revenues in food and beverage outlets, and impact on other revenues, such as audiovisual, recreational facilities, business services, etc. In convention hotels, this business review can be based on conventions that may not occur for as many as 6 years in the future and, in the case of major convention centers, upwards of 20 years in the future.

Weekly sales meetings are designed to update all members of the sales team on the MEEC organization's status on key metrics. Such metrics can be: occupancy/space in use; conventions in/out; financial results for the month and year-to-date; a review of the conventions, groups, and meetings in house during the current week; along with promotion and other marketing initiatives. These meetings are also used as an information-sharing vehicle, so that sales managers can share their call schedules, important visitors, and other important information of which all staff should be aware. Finally, Saturday office coverage is expected for any walk-in or telephone inquiries that may occur. In addition, depending on the size and complexity of an event, a convention service manager would be expected to be on site for any event or events that occur outside of regular business hours.

Pre-convention meetings are meetings held with the event planner and appropriate vendors and operational managers 24 to 48 hours before the event. Typically, the pre-convention (**pre-con**) meeting is coordinated by the convention services manager of the MEEC facility. The pre-con meeting is used to review the specifications of the event; these details include arrival and departure patterns, attendee profiles, billing, rooming lists, event space requirements, signage placement, and other special requests.

PRE-CONVENTION (PRE-CON) MEETING ACTION PLAN

First Steps
- Outline what will be covered. Plan to discuss important information about the meeting, including the sponsoring firm's expectations.
- Set a date and time. A pre-con typically takes place 24 to 48 hours prior to the event.
- Pick a place. Most pre-cons are held at the facility where the meeting or event will occur. At this time, planners also should be able to conduct a final walk-through of all facilities being used.
- Involve all relevant parties, including key members of the planning team, convention services manager, managers from each department servicing the meeting (such as housekeeping, catering, security, and A/V) and any suppliers instrumental to the meeting's success.

What to Bring
- Business cards
- An organizational chart of the company's attendees and/or pictures of VIPs, if available
- Sample signatures of persons authorized to approve charges for the master account
- An updated reservation list
- A contact list for key members of the planning team

Talking Points
- Overall company profile/mission statement
- Group demographics (age, gender breakdown, etc.)
- Guest attendance (including children)
- Rooming list and arrival times (including early arrivals)
- Likes and dislikes of the group in general
- Service expectations
- Inclusion of green/sustainable practices
- Special needs of individual participants, including VIPs
- Security/labor issues
- Equipment-loading issues
- Parking and coach-loading
- Distribution of room amenities and welcome packets
- Room upgrades

- Banquet event orders
- Packages (and air bill numbers) sent to the property
- Communications between hotel staff and planners
- Other groups in house, and the nature of their events
- City events, traffic, or weather that might affect the group
- Emergency drills/medical numbers
- Anticipated peak activity times for bell-desk, valet, or front-desk personnel
- Daily time for the meeting planner and billing department to review bills and discuss any specific billing issues

Format
- Begin with who's who. Typically, the conference services manager introduces the planner, who introduces the others on the planning staff. Venue staff introduce themselves. They should provide business cards, contact numbers and back-ups, as well as indicate their hours of operation and the responsibilities of their departments.
- Planners should present a synopsis of the organization, VIPs, purpose of the meeting, expectations, special needs of the group and expected emergency/security procedures.
- The planner and convention services manager present should summarize expectations and key points. Usually a member of the planning staff stays after the pre-con to discuss specific issues with the catering or food and beverage (F&B) manager.

What to Take Away (The client)
- Keys to meeting space
- Contact list of key facility staff
- Map of facility

Meetings are also held after the conference or convention, and are called post-convention meetings (**post-con**). Normally, these meetings are held with the convention services manager and the finance manager. This meeting focuses on bill review for accuracy, items for follow up, and a critique of the convention/conference/meeting. For large reoccurring conventions or conferences, this meeting might also include operational departments that were impacted both positively and negatively.

One-on-one meetings between the sales manager and the director of sales are designed to discuss revenue goals for the current month and future months. In addition, the sales manager is expected to cover their action plans for achieving the stated revenue goals. Directors of sales are expected to work with sales managers if the sales manager is finding it difficult to achieve the goals. This meeting provides the director of sales with "market intelligence" from the sales manager; for example, if there are reasons why a prospect is not booking the hotel, or there are competitive challenges affecting the marketplace. Needless to say, this meeting is very important for the director of sales to ensure the success of each sales team member.

Individual Sales Manager Organizational Activities

Each sales manager must organize their accounts to be efficient in the sales process. Accounts can be separated into four categories. The first type of account is the future prospects. These accounts call for occasional contact to remind the prospect of what the MEEC facility has to offer. The next type of account is tentative bookings; these accounts require regular follow up until the contract is signed. Big revenue accounts need regular communication from salespeople to develop and maintain solid relationships. Accounts who have signed contracts with the MEEC facility should be met with regularly.

Additionally, accounts should ranked based on their revenue potential and the amount of contact they require. These rankings may include company size, revenue, service level required, profitability, growth potential, and likelihood of retention. The nomenclature for ranking varies; ranking can be by letters or numbers, by stars, or by color codes. For our purposes, we will use letter rankings and three ranks. A-ranked accounts are those that have the highest potential; they command the most attention from the sales manager. These accounts should be communicated with at least once a month or more over the course of a year, whether it be in person, by telephone, or email. B-ranked accounts have medium potential either as new accounts or as solid current customers. These accounts require less attentiveness, but because of their potential should be contacted every other month. C-ranked accounts do not require much time or communication. Most visits to C-ranked accounts occur as part of visits to other, more productive accounts.

SUMMARY

We all sell in the world of hospitality, but the people directly responsible for selling are referred to as sales professionals. Most commonly selling is accomplished through personal selling and through the use of the step-by-step sales process. Salespeople work as the link between their organization and the customer.

Salespeople in the world of meetings and events take on various roles. These roles include demand creator, delivery personnel, organizational champion, technical specialist, and customer service representative. While each of these roles requires different responsibilities, the roles played align with the various steps of the sales process. These roles require diverse knowledge, skills, and abilities. Correspondingly, there is a vast array of sales positions in hospitality with an equally wide range of salaries, commissions, bonuses, and benefits.

The sales and marketing mission within the MEEC facility guides the activities of each sales staff member. Many of the marketing activities of a MEEC organization are included in the sales unit of the organization. Jobs include: sales representative, sales coordinator, sales manager, director of marketing, and convention services manager. This team meets on a regular basis to conduct sales meetings and with clients for pre-con and post-con meetings.

KEY TERMS

sales professional
personal selling
sales process
demand creator
delivery personnel
missionary sales role

customer service
  representative
inside salesperson
destination marketing
  organization (DMO)
convention & visitor
  bureau (CVB)

convention service
  manager (CSM)
sales coordinator
pre-con
post-con

REVIEW AND DISCUSSION QUESTIONS

1. Describe the sales process in MEEC and hospitality.

2. Define sales.

3. Describe the responsibilities of MEEC and hospitality salespeople.

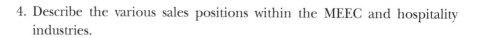

4. Describe the various sales positions within the MEEC and hospitality industries.

5. Discuss the structure of the sales organization.

6. Become aware of job descriptions and job specifications for hospitality sales.

7. Articulate the differing jobs and salaries in hospitality sales.

8. Discuss how to run a pre-con.

9. Define and discuss personal selling.

CHAPTER 4

Professional Development in Hospitality Sales

Professional Development Helps a Hospitality Sales Professional Achieve Maximum Career Potential
© donskarpo/Shutterstock.com

LEARNING OBJECTIVES

- Define the term hospitality sales professional.
- Describe the four elements of the thirty-second commercial.
- Answer the questions necessary to develop a personal selling philosophy.
- Explain what makes for a great hospitality sales professional.
- Differentiate between business and communication etiquette.
- Describe the key elements of professional attire.
- Define ethics for the hospitality sales professional.
- List the six obstacles to managing time.

Introduction

The hospitality sales professional is a person who engages in the pursuit of business for a hospitality organization in a professional manner. Hospitality sales professionals make a personal commitment to develop and improve their knowledge and skills in the highly specialized world of hospitality sales. These professionals work to keep themselves updated on the latest trends in the industry and to learn new techniques to address the needs and concerns of their clients and future clients or prospects. They are serious about the work that they do, and as a result are continually working to improve themselves. Hospitality sales professionals are competent and can be counted on to achieve results. They are reliable and concentrate on finding solutions for the benefit of their clients. Hospitality sales professionals are trustworthy and are honest in their dealings with clients, peers, and superiors.

Accountability is another characteristic of the hospitality sales professional. Linked to personal integrity and ethics, hospitality sales professionals hold themselves accountable when a mistake has been made. Hospitality sales professionals demonstrate a high degree of emotional intelligence. **Emotional intelligence** is the capacity to be aware of, control, and express one's emotions, and to handle interpersonal relationships judiciously and empathetically. This self-regulation allows them to be respected by their peers and clients, and by the executives who lead them. Finally, professional hospitality salespeople are polished, well groomed, and dress the part for any situation. Because of their appearance, they emanate an impression of confidence, which goes a long way with clients and prospects. They recognize that hospitality sales is a noble profession, and career advancement through hard work is very possible.

SALES & MARKETING CREED: THE INTERNATIONAL CODE OF ETHICS FOR SALES AND MARKETING

Your pledge of high standards in serving your company, its customers, and free enterprise

- The hospitality sales professional must acknowledge accountability to the organization for which they work and to society as a whole to improve sales knowledge and practice and to adhere to the highest professional standards in their work and personal relationships.
- The concept of selling includes as its basic principle the sovereignty of all consumers in the marketplace and the necessity for mutual benefit to both buyer and seller in all transactions.

- The hospitality sales professional must personally maintain the highest standards of ethical and professional conduct in all business relationships with customers, suppliers, colleagues, competitors, governmental agencies, and the public.
- The hospitality sales professional must pledge to protect, support, and promote the principles of consumer choice, competition, and innovation enterprise, consistent with relevant legislative public policy standards.
- The hospitality sales professional shall not knowingly participate in actions, agreements, or marketing policies or practices which may be detrimental to customers, competitors, or established community social or economic policies or standards.
- The hospitality sales professional must strive to ensure that products and services are distributed through such channels and by such methods as will tend to optimize the distributive process by offering maximum customer value and service at minimum cost while providing fair and equitable compensation for all parties.
- The hospitality sales professional shall support efforts to increase productivity or reduce costs of production or marketing through standardization or other methods, provided these methods do not stifle innovation or creativity.
- The hospitality sales professional believes prices should reflect true value in use of the product or service to the customer, including the pricing of goods and services transferred among operating organizations worldwide.
- The hospitality sales professional must acknowledge that providing the best economic and social product value consistent with cost also includes: (a) recognizing the customer's right to expect safe products with clear instructions for their proper use and maintenance; (b) providing easily accessible channels for customer complaints; (c) investigating any customer dissatisfaction objectively and taking prompt and appropriate remedial action; (d) recognizing and supporting proven public policy objectives such as conserving energy and protecting the environment.
- The hospitality sales professional must pledge that their efforts to assure that all marketing research, advertising, and presentations of products, services, or concepts are done clearly, truthfully, and in good taste so as not to mislead or offend customers. They must further pledge to assure that all these activities are conducted in accordance with the highest standards of each profession and generally accepted principles of fair competition.
- The hospitality sales professional must pledge to cooperate fully in furthering the efforts of all institutions, media, professional associations, and other organizations to publicize this creed as widely as possible throughout the world.

From www.smei.org/creed. *Reprinted with permission.*

What Makes a GREAT Hospitality Sales Professional?

Great hospitality salespeople have a number of things in common. Foremost is a positive attitude. The possibility of rejection is very strong, and the hospitality professional is resilient to such possibilities. Hospitality salespeople who think positively are more inclined to set performance goals and achieve them. Having a positive attitude also leads to better mental fitness and well-being. Linked to this positive attitude is a confidence in the hospitality organization and the products and services it offers. This confidence translates to the client and prospect, because they sense the confidence, and acquire the same when making the purchase. Hospitality salespeople are knowledgeable about their products and services, their organization, the market in which their organization resides, and the industry. People in hospitality sales must have ample knowledge in order to be able to offer product and service options to prospects. Confidence is a personality trait that great hospitality salespeople have taken the time to develop in the course of their careers.

Great hospitality salespeople are customer focused. They seek to become solvers of client's problems, and a partner whom clients and prospects can rely on for up-to-date information and advice that will provide the best possible solutions to customers' needs. When working with clients and prospects, they are polite and show good manners to everyone they come into contact with. Successful hospitality salespeople must have persistence; many prospects will say no or resist meeting with a salesperson. It is important that the hospitality salesperson resists discouragement when snubbed. Because of the possibility for failure, hospitality salespeople continually seek to improve by learning from the failures they encounter. By developing new skills, sharpening existing skills, and staying fresh on trends in the hospitality industry and the market in which they sell, great hospitality salespeople minimize the likelihood of rejection or lack of success.

Developing a **personal selling philosophy** requires the hospitality salesperson to answer the questions that follow. When they start every day, what do they want to *do as it relates to selling?* What, as it relates to selling, directs their actions and decisions? After a day in the selling environment, what gives the hospitality salesperson satisfaction? Why are beliefs related to sales important? The ethics of hospitality sales must be a part of the personal selling philosophy. How does the ethical philosophy of the hospitality salesperson correspond with the individual's personal selling philosophy?

Outstanding hospitality salespeople develop a personal selling philosophy that includes the following items. With the customer focus that a hospitality salesperson maintains, they become a trusted advisor and partner for their clients and prospects. This means that they provide the resources and support that their clients need. They ask many questions to understand clearly what the client needs. Hospitality salespeople deliver on their promises at a level that exceeds expectations. They demonstrate a passion for the hospitality products and services they sell, and a desire to help clients achieve their buying objectives. Finally, their personal selling philosophy drives how they manage themselves, their time, and their relationships with others.

Management of Self

It takes several years for hospitality sales professionals to development **self-management skills**. This means that, through practice and contemplation, and with experience, individuals can become successful hospitality salespeople. Self-management includes a number of topics. Hospitality salespeople work to know themselves; what strengths and weaknesses they have and what personal values they hold. Goal setting and developing plans for the years ahead prevents "busyness" that does not take the hospitality sales professional anywhere. Developing **emotional intelligence** and achieving emotional stability helps to improve functioning in all areas of business and personal life. **Time management** is not just about prioritizing activities, but also using time wisely. Avoiding procrastination and staying focused on what needs to be done through perseverance leads the hospitality sales professional to success. The beginning of self-management begins with a positive attitude, a confident outlook, and a willingness to learn and improve.

Business Etiquette

Business etiquette is defined as the established protocol of behavior in business settings. The hospitality sales professional is adept at displaying appropriate etiquette in client meetings and communications, including email, telephone, and face-to-face. When proper etiquette is used, everyone involved in the situation feels comfortable and everything goes smoothly. Appropriate etiquette is the foundation for establishing a business relationship. The hospitality sales professional who demonstrates proper etiquette also establishes straightforward and honest dealings with everyone, which strengthens the business relationship.

When meeting the prospect for the first time, the hospitality salesperson displays a number of techniques to allow for a great first impression. When it comes to attending a pre-set appointment, the hospitality salesperson makes a point of being early. There is an old saying, "being ten minutes early is like being five minutes late." The hospitality salesperson who will be late makes a point of contacting the meeting attendees to alert them to the tardiness. Before the meeting is to begin, introductions may be required. When a hospitality salesperson is introducing themselves, they look the other person in the eye, use a firm handshake (more about that later), and demonstrate self-confidence. If the hospitality salesperson is introducing others, the client or guest outranks everyone and should be introduced first.

Introducing a Client or Guest

1. State the name of the client or guest (Ms. Smith).

2. I would like to introduce (Mr. Jones).

3. Refer to some details about each individual ("Ms. Smith is considering having her event in our ballroom; Mr. Jones is our director of catering").

At that point, or during introductions, all parties involved should shake hands. Shaking hands is gender neutral; that is, women and men should shake hands in identical ways.

Shaking Hands During Introductions

1. If seated, rise to shake the other person's hand.

2. Stand no closer than 3 feet from the other person.

3. Extend the right hand, thumb upward and fingers together. Use eye contact and smile while extending the hand.

4. Be sure the hands are web to web, middle of the hand. Do not squeeze beyond normal pressure, and do not grab the fingers.

5. Shake up and down (pump) no more than three times, maintaining eye contact.

Handshakes can be an indication of communication styles, which can assist in understanding how to adapt to the client or prospect. Strong handshakes may indicate a desire to be controlling; handshakes that contain energy may indicate an outgoing nature. Weak handshakes (that also may be sweaty) may indicate anxiety in meeting other people. The hospitality salesperson knows to have dry hands, keep handshakes brief, smile, and use eye contact throughout the introduction.

Hospitality salespeople focus on the client. They NEVER use first names during introductions and initial meetings, UNTIL they are given permission to use a first name. With introductions come business cards. Hospitality sales people ALWAYS have business cards; many keep cards in all of their business clothing so that they have them at the ready. Cards should be presented with two hands with the card lettering facing the receiver. Hospitality salespeople look for cues/body language from the prospect as a means of understanding communication style as well. Simple gestures such as knowing how to say please and thank you are a part of the basic etiquette that never goes out of style. Cell phones should be turned off and not looked at during sales conversations.

Communication Etiquette

Business relationships rely on good communication. **Communication etiquette** is vital to the success of the hospitality salesperson. Whenever the hospitality salesperson meets or communicates with the client or prospect, he or she must respect the time of the person with whom they are meeting. It is always best to be upbeat and enthusiastic, while also demonstrating humility. Later in this chapter, creating an opening statement that captures the client or prospect's attention will be discussed. Hospitality salespeople are good at asking questions; customers love to talk! As a result, listening skills are imperative and must include eye contact. Polite hospitality salespeople ask permission to take notes; this simple request demonstrates a respect for the client. At some point in the sales conversation, it is also respectful to ask how the client prefers to communicate—face to face, email, telephone, or regular mail. When speaking with the client in person, the hospitality salesperson maintains eye contact 70% of the time and matches the voice volume of the client.

When using the telephone, the hospitality salesperson uses appropriate volume. During the call, the hospitality salesperson removes all distractions to ensure full attention to the client. Gum, candy, and beverages are not conducive to good conversation. When leaving voicemail, the hospitality salesperson speaks slowly, states his or her name and telephone number to be returned, the reason for the call, and finally repeats the name and telephone number to call back. By doing so, it is easy for the person receiving the call to take notes, and not have to waste time replaying the voice message. When the hospitality sales professional will be out of the office, he or she should record a voice message that includes the day or days they will be out of the office, instructions on how to leave an urgent message, and when the caller can expect to receive a reply.

When sending emails—or traditional letters for that matter—the hospitality salesperson seeks to be brief and to the point. If possible, regular letters should be no more than one page in length. Emails are best when there is no need to scroll down on the screen. Emails should be answered as soon as possible; no later than three days after being received. Especially with business emails, emoticons and exclamation marks should be avoided. Business emails should have a clear subject line; hospitality salespeople avoid subject lines that may indicate junk or spam emails. A signature with all contact information should be at the end of the email. Like introductions, the receiver's last name should be used with "Hello" or "Dear." Because most sales communications are based on prior conversations, the hospitality salesperson rarely uses one-line emails, since the client or prospect receiving the email may have forgotten the topic.

Sales Letter Writing

Written sales communications, both regular letters and email, are written for a variety of reasons. Letters may be written to prospect or search for new clients.

Letter Format Basics

- Use Letterhead
- Date
- Address of Recipient
- Salutation
- Body of Letter
- Close / Signature
- Enclosures

Sales Letter Format Basics

- At Least Three Paragraphs
  - Attention
  - Interest
  - Benefits
  - Action
- Short Sentences
- "I" is inappropriate

Written communications can be used for providing information, persuading the customer to take action, and to remind the client about previous communications or about outstanding requests for action. Written communications are also used for follow-up. Thank you and apology communications can be written; the hospitality sales professional determines when a telephone call or a face-to-face visit is warranted in place of a written form of communication.

Sales letters should be customized for the reader; use of the client's name within the letter helps in that regard. When writing, it is always best to proofread; the hospitality sales professional does not rely on spelling and grammar checking software. Humor is rarely warranted in sales communications. The written sales letter can be outlined similar to a sales presentation; the letter should capture interest in the first or second paragraph, followed by wording that further generates interest. The body of the letter should include specific statements of how the reader will benefit by acting. In this section, the hospitality salesperson takes the time to emphasize the value of working with the hospitality organization. Finally, the last paragraph should ask the reader to act. The last sentence should indicate how the hospitality salesperson will follow up.

Research indicates that Tuesdays and Thursdays are the best days to send emails. Email messages should be kept to a length of no more than 25 lines;

attachments can be referred to, in order to shorten the length of the message. The end of the email should be signed as it would be in a regular letter, with a closing such as "thank you" or "best regards." Standard fonts in black are best, especially if the client wishes to forward the email. The hospitality sales professional who will be out of the office for more than one day should set up an automated out-of-the-office reply. When sending messages from a smartphone, it is unwise to include a signature that says "sent from XYZ smartphone."

Professional Appearance

Professional appearance is critical to the hospitality salesperson's success; prospects buy both the hospitality organization and the individual representing it. By having a professional appearance, the hospitality salesperson gives the impression of being highly competent. Again, first impressions count, and the hospitality salesperson is judged by their attire. There will be different wardrobes for sales contacts, special events, and casual workdays (days when company policy allows employees to dress in more casual attire). In general, hospitality salespeople should wear well-fitted clothing. If the hospitality salesperson is unsure of what to wear, he or she errs on the side of formality. It is better to be overdressed than underdressed for the occasion. Clothing must be coordinated, and it is better to be conservative than trendy. All of these guidelines must also take into consideration the nature of the client's business.

Professional Appearance for Hospitality Sales Professionals	
FOR MEN	FOR WOMEN
• Fresh hair cut	• Skirt suit—dark blue, gray, or charcoal
• Shined shoes (laced)	• Blouse—Crisp white
• Crisp white shirt	• Shoes—Black or brown (flats or 2" or less heels)
• Conservative Tie	• Jewelry—limited, appropriate
• Accessories (limited)	• Cosmetics—not too bright
• Neatly groomed—Hair, moustache & beard	• Grooming—neatly manicured
• Cologne—optional & applied sparingly	• Perfume—a little goes a long way
• Suit or sports coat & slacks—Dark blue, gray, or charcoal	

The dress of the hospitality sales professional indicates their level in the organization, how they are perceived, and how they perceive themselves. Today, the business environment is embracing a more casual culture. At the same time, research indicates that what is worn can have an impact on behavior. Area of the country, seasonality, and the organizational culture of the hospitality organization should also be considered as part of personal appearance.

Time Management

Many individuals consider time management as the same as self-management because they don't management time, but they manage what they do with their time. It seems that people who manage their time are more productive and have more time to do things that bring them pleasure. Learning how to manage time is one of the most sought-after skills by hospitality sales professionals. By learning time management skills, the hospitality salesperson increases his or her effectiveness and efficiency. Managing time helps to determine the activities of the day, week, and month.

There are many obstacles to managing time. Some of the major obstacles in managing the hospitality salesperson's time include:

- Lack of organization

- Procrastination

- Reacting to dilemmas/emergencies

- Meetings

- Attending to customers

- Lack of delegation

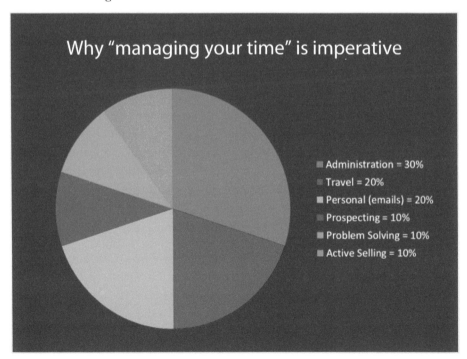

These obstacles can drain the energy of any hospitality salesperson and keep them from having the capacity to serve and sell to clients and prospects. Therefore, having techniques to avoid the time wasters is imperative to success. A big problem with the success of time management and scheduling plans occurs when interruptions occur and hospitality salespeople allow themselves to procrastinate to the point that not only are their short-term goals compromised, but also their intermediate and long-term goals as well. Hospitality salespeople set specific and definable goals for themselves. Accordingly, a calendar that reflects the selling schedule, along with all the activities they are responsible for on a weekly basis, becomes part of a daily to-do list that is prepared each day for the next work/selling day.

Lack of organization is the biggest time trap. The desk and files of the hospitality salesperson are organized so that the highest priority tasks are easily found, and all other materials are out of sight. Hospitality salespeople take the time to review paperwork so that details are covered and problems are avoided. When things are done correctly the first time, mistakes are prevented, and rework is minimized. The hospitality salesperson doublechecks paperwork, emails, and other communications to prevent angering clients, the boss, and co-workers. Paperwork and emails should be handled only once; starting a pile or folder of items read previously only causes disorganization.

Next on the list of time wasters is procrastination. **Procrastination** occurs when the delay or avoidance of an issue facing the hospitality salesperson arises due to the fear of making a mistake or of calling an angry customer, or when other activities provide immediate gratification over activities that must be done in a timely fashion. When the hospitality salesperson is in a productive mode, procrastination is avoided, and self-satisfaction and accomplishment are felt. So, bundling unpleasant tasks with pleasant tasks is one method of reducing procrastination. Reviewing reports while working out would be one example. Meeting an angry client at a favorite restaurant might be another instance of procrastination avoidance. Another means of reducing procrastination is making the task more achievable. Small measures of headway on large projects help to make continued action easier. Furthermore, when a task is completed earlier in the day, the more productive the hospitality salesperson feels.

Emergencies can and do happen in the hospitality industry. Efficient time planning can keep these urgent situations to a minimum. A back-up plan should be in place for completing high-priority tasks when a crisis occurs. By having such a plan, the schedule of the hospitality salesperson, as well the schedules of others, are less likely to be interrupted. These emergencies can cause anxiety; a well-executed time plan allows the hospitality salesperson to be calm in stressful situations.

Meetings are a necessary part of the business life. Hospitality sales professionals must attend revenue strategy meetings, staff meetings, and meetings with clients. If a meeting can be avoided, or it can be conducted electronically, all the better. Client meetings, especially when conducted over a meal, should last no more than two hours. If the meeting is one that a sales assistant could easily attend, the hospitality salesperson should delegate such tasks. When attending meetings, the hospitality professional is prepared with an agenda and the necessary materials to contribute to the meeting; not being organized for meetings is a big-time waster, angering all in attendance.

Customer service prior to, during, and after an event are a necessary responsibility of the hospitality salesperson. Appointments can be made prior to and after events, but attending to the client during an event can lead to interruptions. When these occasions occur, the hospitality salesperson assesses the degree of urgency of the client, and addresses the issue, or delegates to the appropriate staff member. When customers are angry, the hospitality salesperson addresses the issue immediately. After the problem or complaint has been resolved, a five-minute break is often the best way to recover from what was likely a stressful experience.

Delegation is an important skill for hospitality sales managers to learn. Sales reports, expense reports, and other documents that can be completed by sales assistants are just a few of the activities the hospitality sales professional can delegate. Answering telephone calls and emails are examples of other delegated activities. Many times, hospitality sales professionals take on activities that would be better completed by someone else. No, although difficult for a hospitality salesperson to say, sometimes is the appropriate answer to a request for time.

Finally, there are times when the hospitality salesperson can multitask; the commute to work, during a workout, or other down times can be perfect for reading, listening to audiobooks for self-improvement, or completing other tasks that are relatively unimportant to the business, but important to the individual. This chapter is titled "Professional Development in Hospitality Sales"; the successful hospitality sales professional sets aside time to improve his or her skills by scheduling time for self-improvement opportunities.

Networking

Networking can help the hospitality sales professional expand business opportunities. The interesting dichotomy about networking events is that, by giving of yourself at a networking event, you have the opportunity to grow your business, your potential clients, and referrals to other business opportunities. So, it is important to develop personal connections first by focusing on building friendships. Smart hospitality salespeople know that being genuine in building relationships, regardless of the business opportunity in the future, is best. People want to feel that they are being listened to; hospitality salespeople listen and ask questions rather than monopolizing the conversation. Networking events can be intimidating and full of pressure; trying to make a friend can minimize the anxiety.

Hospitality salespeople who are great networkers plan in advance. They research who will be in attendance, and who they would really like to meet – not only for the business they can do, but for what they can *learn*. Hospitality salespeople make the best impressions when that impression appears effortless. This happens when a plan is in place to decide what questions will be asked, what information (personal and professional) will be shared, and how the hospitality salesperson can help the people they are meeting. It is important not to be too aggressive, nor to "butt into" conversations already underway. Hospitality salespeople at networking events share what they have to give, not sell what they are offering. Having a helpful attitude is the best way to enter a networking event. Obviously, any offer to help must be followed up on. Nothing will hurt the potential for a long-term relationship more than not following up on promises made.

In a networking setting, having an authentic smile is an invitation to engage. Smiling communicates a state of mind that makes others want to communicate with the hospitality salesperson. Smiles have an implicit message of trust; research indicates that people who smile appear more likable and competent. The best part of smiling is that it improves the mood of the smiler when it is authentic, and smiling is contagious to others. When joining a conversation that others are having, it is polite to listen first before speaking. Listening first makes for a good first impression. By blending into the conversation, the hospitality salesperson adds to, rather than stops, the conversation. When introducing themselves, hospitality salespeople have a personal, memorable sentence or brief story that is a personal description of who they are or what they do. For example, "My name is Janet Smith, Smith is a common last name, but I am anything but common." The brief story can be crafted into what is called an elevator speech or thirty-second commercial.

The Thirty-Second Commercial

The **thirty-second commercial** is a clear-cut and succinct message or "commercial" about the person who is delivering the message. The central theme of the message is how the hospitality salesperson can help the other person. Also called an **elevator speech**, it is thirty seconds in length, which is typically the amount of time it takes to ride an elevator from the bottom to the top of a building. The scheme behind the thirty-second commercial is that the hospitality salesperson has a message prepared that can be delivered anytime, anywhere—even on an elevator.

The thirty-second commercial format is outlined below. After writing their commercial following this framework and practicing it several times, the hospitality salesperson will appear natural, and the commercial, or parts of it, will be second nature when meeting other people in any setting.

FORMAT FOR THE 30-SECOND COMMERCIAL

Who Are You?
- The hospitality salesperson opens with a statement or a question that captures the attention of the person they are meeting.
- The hospitality salesperson then describes themselves and the hospitality organization they represent.
- The hospitality salesperson then describes what they do as part of their key skills (e.g., problem solver, facilitator, change agent, etc.).

What Do You Bring to the Table?
- The hospitality salesperson can describe their core temperament (e.g., fun loving, serious, positive, supportive).
- The hospitality salesperson can then describe how a problem was approached and how it revealed an outstanding part of their character.
- Finally, what is the hospitality salesperson interested in finding out about the listener?

What Is Your Unique Selling Proposition (USP)?
- The hospitality salesperson describes the product or service that they can provide and how they are unique to other offerings.
- A description of how the listener will benefit must be included.

The Call to Action
- The thirty-second commercial or elevator speech always contains a request for action.
- This call to action may be for an appointment, a business card, and/or a referral.

- Write down all the things that come to mind about the individual (you).
- Use short, powerful sentences to describe yourself; avoid slang or jargon.
- Ensure a smooth, natural flow for the thirty-second commercial with the following structure: introduction, presentation, and call to action.
- Be sure that key points are clear and easily memorized.
- Always present in terms of the listener. Too many "I" statements will turn off listeners.
- It is always a good idea to have different versions for different occasions.
- Demonstrate an enthusiasm or passion that is contagious and leads the listener to take action.

In preparing the thirty-second commercial, the hospitality salesperson has practiced and memorized the speech, so it comes off as natural and authentic. A thirty-second commercial lasts no longer than 35 seconds. This equates to approximately 100 words, or 10 sentences. Most importantly, it is crafted to limit the use of the word "I"; the hospitality salesperson always refers to "you" or "your company." By doing so, the "give" referred to in the last section on networking is implied, and the receiver is more open to the message.

Ethics

Business ethics are rules, standards, and codes that provide guidelines for morally correct behavior and truthfulness in business situations. This is ethical behavior is that is "right" or "good" in the context of the code of conduct of the hospitality organization. Ethical dilemmas occur when a situation happens that has potential benefits but is unethical.

FIVE SITUATIONS THAT CAN BE CONSIDERED UNETHICAL

The first is **paternalism**, where an individual's autonomy is in conflict with the consumer's welfare. Environment issues relate to the **physical environment**, such as lakes, oceans, and the air we breathe. **Coercion and control** situations arise when threats, the use of power, or other means are used to affect a decision. **Conflict of interest** situations occur when a hospitality salesperson has more than one interest which if engaged in may result in harm to another individual or the hospitality organization. A circumstance involving **personal integrity** occurs when the decision presents issues of conscience.

A review of the SMEI Code of Ethics presented earlier in the chapter helps illustrate some of the unethical sales behaviors that can occur. Many of these behaviors fall into the category of personal integrity:

- Passing blame onto others for actions for which the hospitality salesperson is responsible

- Selling unneeded products or services

- Withholding or falsifying information

- Exaggerating benefits

- Falsifying testimonials from customers.

Hospitality salespeople are in unique situations that can lead to ethical dilemmas. First, they are advocates for both the hospitality organization they represent, as well as the client to whom they are selling. As a result, they have loyalties to both sides that have different expectations and interests. Hospitality salespeople have some degree of autonomy in their jobs, which can lead to unethical behavior. The pressure to make sales goals, pressure from customers, and pressure from superiors can lead to unethical behavior.

When an unethical situation might exist, the hospitality salesperson has questions to ask:

- What is the situation, and are ethics questioned?

- What are the facts?

- What are the options for deciding?

- Are these options

    - Legal

    - Correct

    - Beneficial to all involved

- Based on the decision made,

    - How would his or her family feel about the decision?

    - What if the public found out about the decision?

- Make the decision/take action

Ethical Guidelines for Hospitality Sales Professionals

- Use factual information
- Seek to educate your client
- Do not make decisions outside your purview
- Limit conversations with competitors

- Be consistent in your dealings with all customers
- Do not disparage the competition
- Avoid promises you cannot honor
- Review all sales materials for misrepresentations

The hospitality salesperson must avoid misrepresentation at all times by using factual information. They must educate the client by offering strengths and weaknesses of various characteristics of the hospitality organization and its products and services. It is better to refer to a higher authority than to make decisions that are outside the given responsibility. It is illegal to discuss rates, occupancy, and other performance statistics with individual competitors. Collusion is a given. All clients and prospects must be dealt with fairly; hospitality salespeople are wise to consider the consequences of unequal treatment. A well-respected hospitality salesperson never criticizes the competition. In all dealings, the hospitality salesperson must be honest, and consider all situations for legal and ethical correctness.

SUMMARY

This chapter explored the activities an aspiring hospitality sales professional must undertake to succeed. First a review of the ethics required for sales professionals was covered with the SMEI Creed for Ethics in Sales and Marketing. Next, an outline of the various characteristics for great hospitality sales professionals highlight the fact that hospitality salespeople are customer focused. Successful hospitality sales professionals develop emotional intelligence, time management, business etiquette, and oral and written communication skills to enable trust with potential clients. Hospitality sales professionals are well groomed, and represent their organizations well. All hospitality employees, especially hospitality sales people should develop a "Thirty second Commercial" or "elevator speech" that describes who that person is, and how they can help their audience. For example, hospitality students networking for their internships and first job should craft a message that in thirty second or less describes what makes them unique and a attractive candidate for a job opening. Finally, ethics is an important facet of hospitality selling. Students should be aware of the various issues that hospitality sales people face as they represent their organizations to the client, and the client to their organizations. Ethical dilemmas may occur.

KEY TERMS

accountability
personal selling
  philosophy
self-management skills
emotional intelligence
time management

business etiquette
communication etiquette
casual workdays
procrastination
delegation
networking

thirty-second
  commercial
elevator speech
unique selling proposition (USP)
paternalism

REVIEW AND DISCUSSION QUESTIONS

1. Define the term hospitality sales professional.

2. Describe the four elements of the thirty-second commercial.

3. Answer the questions necessary to develop a personal selling philosophy.

4. Explain what makes for a great hospitality sales professional.

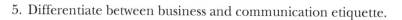

5. Differentiate between business and communication etiquette.

6. Describe the key elements of professional attire.

7. Define ethics for the hospitality sales professional.

8. List the six obstacles to managing time.

9. Describe the 30-second commercial or elevator speech.

10. Explain emotional intelligence.

CHAPTER 5

Communication Skills for Sales

Communication
© Marijus Auruskevicius/Shutterstock.com

LEARNING OBJECTIVES

- Define the concept of communication style as it relates to selling in hospitality.
- Describe the four types of communication styles.
- Explain the forces that affect the buying decision.
- Describe the four types of buying objectives.
- Discuss the three theories of buyer behavior.

Introduction

The best salespeople do their homework before they communicate with their prospective or active client. **Adaptive selling** describes the process by which salespeople adapt their communication styles to meet the style of their clients. Communicating hospitably, communication styles, and adapting to the communication styles of others are all important parts of the hospitality sales process. In future chapters, we will talk about buyer behavior and, specifically, how the various market segments of hospitality behave as they relate to meetings and events.

The Sales Relationship: Communication Styles

Your communication style is the *you* that is on display every day—the implicit communication style or pattern of behavior that others see. If your style is very different from your client's, it may be difficult for the two of you to develop a rapport and a long-term selling relationship. We understand that everybody has a different type of style, and that personality styles and communication styles tend to be stable—especially personality styles. But as we gain understanding of who we are, and as we become more skilled at reading others, we become more adept at adjusting to others. Voice patterns, eye movement, facial expressions, and body language are components of communication style. That is a preferred way of using the abilities one has. A **communication style** refers to how someone likes to communicate. We learn as we mature, but the style we use tends to be stable throughout our lives.

The **hospitality salesperson** must be "on the same wavelength" with the people they communicate with. The analogy you want to remember is two tuning forks that are the same frequency, so they sync with each other. When you sync your phone, it means your phone is talking to whatever device its syncing with. When we hit a tuning fork, and we have a tuning fork with an equivalent pitch or frequency at another side of the room, the forks will sync. It is important for the sales professional to focus on developing the ability to adapt to other people's communication style.

There are similar behaviors that people exhibit, but by combining descriptors four style types emerge. People have a tendency to be either controlled in their behavior, or responsive. People who are controlled tend to be reserved in their behavior, movements, and how they speak with people. People who are responsive are more open and assertive in their behavior, movements and how they speak to others. So being controlled or responsive is part of the communication equation.

The second part of the equation is whether a person tends to focus on getting the job done as quickly as possible, or whether they focus on the process of getting the job done. Using these two opposites, we can come up with a very simplistic type of communication style. Let's talk about what we mean by these communication styles. There are four types of communication styles: analyzer, controller, persuader, and organizer. Each one of those types falls into a quadrant in terms of whether they're controlled or demonstrative in their demeanor and whether they are motivated by process or expedience in completing the task.

Analyzers. If you had to translate that into what an analyzer customer wants, they want the numbers more than anything. They want strictly the facts. You can try to schmooze with them, but analyzers are truly about the facts. So, what's the implication of that relative to a salesperson? If you're working with an analyzer customer and that customer wants facts and information, what does that mean for you as the salesperson? The answer is to give them more details. You must give them more details, which means you'd better know what? You have got to know everything you possibly can about your product—absolutely everything. So, analyzers tend to work toward perfectionism. Analyzers deal with the facts, with the logic, with the details. No detail is too small. In hospitality in general, we tend to be very big picture, we want to solve problems, but we don't always look at the details. We tend to take the view that the answer is yes, now what's the question? With analyzers that doesn't work. So, we must be sure that if we're going to try to sync with them, we want to have as much information and detail as we possibly can. Analyzers tend to be slower to make decisions because first they're going to try to acquire as much information as they possibly can. Therefore, they are slow to decide. These individuals are not risk takers. Analyzers tend to be reserved; they tend to be controlled in their emotions, and they tend to be more about the process by which the work is completed. But because they look for as much information as they possibly can, when you meet with them, they may already have all the information and they're looking for you to add more detail that they weren't able to collect on their own. So, analyzers do a lot of research behind the scenes. Because they tend to be controlled, they're not always going to show their emotions. As a result, they tend to keep their emotions and beliefs hidden from the salesperson. In summary, salespeople should use a thoughtful, well-organized approach with analyzers. Information should be presented in a deliberate, step-by-step manner. Documentation or "proof" should be provided. This documentation can be data, customer comments, performance statistics, or other information that helps the analyzer make a decision. Analyzers should never be pressured for quick decisions.

Organizers. With this group, there's a place for everything and everything in its place. Analyzers tend to follow a schedule. As the name would suggest, organizers tend to be organized. With this type of person, there is an expectation that a project or activity will follow a process as well. In that regard they are like analyzers but are more responsive or emotional. The organizer tends to be the type of person who relies on friendships and relationships. People are very important to the organizer. They like to get involved in community activities and do things in teamwork settings. You'll find that organizers tend to be the soccer mom or the coach of the Little League baseball team. Organizers, as you can imagine, are very good at handling multiple tasks. They can have a lot of things going on at once. For example, an organizer may have a lot of pictures on the wall about a variety of activities. They may talk on the phone while working with somebody in their office. Organizers are the kind of people we we see as meeting and event planners. They are very controlled and organized in how they do things. They are very good at time management. When dealing with organizers, you want to be sure that you're bringing the facts to them as well. They are very concerned about the feelings of others. They're very adept at understanding. If they're a meeting planner, especially for associations, they're very adept at understanding what their attendees and their members want. Until they really get to know you, you will not find that organizers speak their minds freely. They'll tend to hold their opinions to themselves until they trust you, get to know you, and understand what you're about as a salesperson. Because they're so focused on the process, if you criticize them for something that didn't happen the way you thought it would, or an attendee or group of attendees criticize an organizer, their feelings get hurt easily. Hospitality salespeople should listen carefully to their opinions and feelings. Salespeople do well with organizers when they provide assurances for the organizer's viewpoint. Organizers take a little more time to work through the information. Thus, hospitality salespeople need to have patience and give them time to comprehend the sales information being presented to them.

Persuaders. This is the kind of person who wants to draw attention to themselves. They want answers quickly, and are more likely to "solve the problem, then figure out how to do it." How are you going to communicate with them? You should use a high-energy approach that supports their ideas. If they want something that's relevant to them and appeals to them, focus on that item. Another way is to capitalize on something they said to you. You're definitely going to want to spend a lot of time finding out what their needs are. But with these kinds of people it's all about relationships and selling yourself. That's what the persuader is like, you want to use high energy. You want to find out what's important to them. You want to ask all kinds of questions to get them speaking. Persuaders like to be in the spotlight. You might use a statement like "Your members will love you for it." That kind of positive reaffirmation is the type of communication persuaders appreciate. Selling to persuaders requires the hospitality salesperson to be enthusiastic, not stiff or formal. In most cases, persuaders want you to take the time to establish goodwill. Relationships really matter!

BUILDING SALES RELATIONSHIPS USING THREE BASIC TECHNIQUES

There is an old sales adage: "People buy from people they like." There is a meaningful body of social science research that supports this concept.

When you have a strong relationship with a customer, you tend to have more influence with that customer. That means the customer respects your experience and advice. They are more likely to value your contribution to the decision process and there is a greater chance of the customer becoming a long-term customer.

One of the quickest and most effective methods for building sales relationships is building rapport. Rapport enables smooth communication because it allows people to be at ease. Sometimes rapport happens naturally—you might instantly hit it off with someone. This is often how friendships are started. At other times, you must be more deliberate in building rapport with someone.

Three basic techniques to help you quickly develop rapport with your customers are: mirroring and matching, finding common experiences, and active listening.

1. Mirroring and Matching

Mirroring and matching are based on the powerful concept that people like people who are similar to themselves. Conversely, when people are not similar, it is more difficult to have a relationship with that person. You can quickly develop rapport with a customer by mirroring and matching:

Body language: For example, if the customer sits down and crosses their legs, you do the same. This sends a positive subconscious message that you are paying attention to all of their communication (nonverbal in this case), making them essential, and signaling that you are on their side.

Voice: The same rationale for mirroring and matching body language also applies to mirroring and matching the pace and volume of someone's speech. Of course, be careful not to unconsciously mimic their accents.

Communication/processing style: People communicate and process information in different ways. Some people are action-oriented and results driven; these types of customers want to get down to business. While other customers may have an emotional communication/processing style and so they welcome a substantial amount of rapport-building chit chat before getting down to business. Some customers are analytical and focused on data; these customers want the facts and don't value lots of small talk. Recognizing your customer's communication/processing style and adjusting how you communicate is critical for building rapport.

It is important to note that mirroring and matching techniques work at the subconscious level. Obviously, a customer will not do business with your hotel just because you are mirroring and matching their body language during a meeting. However, they may be more "comfortable" with you and as a result more open to learning more about your solution.

2.   Find Common Experiences

Another successful rapport-building technique is to find common experiences with the customer and then bring those up during the conversation. This is something we all do when we first meet someone, such as talking about the weather, sports, or current events. This is a fast way of building rapport. But be sure that you don't focus only on this step — if you don't mirror and match your customer, the customer won't feel that your rapport building is natural or sincere.

Social media (LinkedIn, Facebook, Pinterest) has now made it easy even for inside sales reps (who don't have the benefit of visiting the customer in person) to uncover common experiences with the customer quickly. With social media, any salesperson can promptly research their customers and find potential common experiences such as career background, current work situation, education background, hobbies, etc.

3.   Active Listening

The last strategy for building rapport is active listening. Did you know that research suggests that we only remember 25% to 50% of what we hear? That means that we miss up to 75% of what the customer is saying! Active listening is a fundamental sales communication skill that is important not only for building rapport but for all other aspects of selling as well.

Active listening isn't merely hearing. Hearing is the physical process of transmitting sound waves to the brain, while active listening means that you're really suspending your thoughts and you understand what you hear. When a customer perceives that you are actively listening to them they feel important, understood, appreciated, and respected.

In order to be a good active listener you should listen with the intent to understand. This means that as a seller you should change your focus from "pitching" your product to a mode where you are genuinely trying to understand the other person. You should focus completely on listening—no multitasking! The word active means that you are so engaged in listening to another that you really can't send an email, check your phone, or anything else. You should ask questions. You inquire to be sure that you're really understanding the speaker and to demonstrate that you are listening. You should summarize. This technique, above all, sets a great listener apart from others. It is one thing to be able to repeat the key points of what was said – and that is important—but when you reflect what it means back to the speaker is when the speaker feels heard and understood at a deeper level.

Building a strong relationship with a customer is foundational to successful selling, and a great relationship begins with developing rapport. Remember these three simple techniques to help you build rapport on your next sales call: mirroring and matching, finding common experiences, and active listening.

Persuaders. When dealing with a persuader, the hospitality salesperson must spend extra time on the nonverbal skills related to active listening. While maintaining eye contact, nodding the head to show understanding, and paraphrasing statements to show understanding are all examples of the actions a salesperson should perform with any client, they are especially important with persuaders.

Controllers. They are authoritarian. They take control. What are the implications of working with controllers? They are very results oriented. You must let them talk. They have probably already made up their mind about you and your product(s). They might even tell you what you need to do about a situation. They like to provide guidance to others. They think their answer is the correct one – they think they are always right. Controllers can appear to be really pushy. If you're an organizer and you must work with a controller, you'd better make sure that you've got a thick skin. Controllers can very easily upset an organizer, just based on their style. Controllers might be CEO types, where they're very demanding of themselves and others. Controllers can be highly self-critical. They move toward perfectionism as well. But where an analyzer tends to sit back and be reserved, a controller is more critical and will let you know it. The analyzer will keep an opinion or idea to himself or herself, a controller will not. Controllers might be described by this statement: "Resent those who waste time with idle chit chat." You're a sales manager. You're coming to meet with a controller. In summary, selling to controllers means keeping the relationship businesslike. The techniques used by the hospitality salesperson include efficiency, being respectful of the controller's time, and being well organized with sales materials and the meeting agenda. With controllers, asking specific questions and carefully noting their responses is important because they want to make sure you are providing accurate information. It is important that the hospitality salesperson understands, and clearly demonstrates, support for the goals of the meeting planner who demonstrates the controller communication style.

You want to develop relationships with all of your clients. If you develop relationships the right way, you're going to make sales and generate the revenue. When we go into a sales call with a controller, probably the last thing we want to do is spend time asking, "How's your family? How's your business going?" Instead try, "Ms. Businesswoman, the reason I'm here today is to talk to you about the Kellogg Center Hotel. Do you have some time to spend with me? Fantastic." The latter approach might be characterized as cutting to the chase. The salesperson has told them what the agenda is and they have confirmed that because his time or her time is important. We want to confirm that we have their time and their undivided attention. Which, in fact, we will have.

But it's simply a start to developing an understanding of what you're about and what other people are about. It's important for you to understand the characteristics of people and that they have certain communication styles and techniques. And third in all of this is looking to manage not only your style but also to manage it in the context of the people with whom you're working. We look at individuals and we identify with them on certain levels, but we also want to understand them for what's important. For our purposes, **artifacts** can be defined as the items and other things that people surround and adorn themselves with. Examples include how they decorate their offices, what they wear, and how they present them-selves. Examining the artifacts of the people we are selling to will help us understand their communication style in a way that helps us understand what is important to them and motivates them to buy.

With controllers, prior to a sales meeting, you should focus most of your preparation on the content. You should get your product in your head, with all the details and with everything complete and just

The unique elements in this office are examples of artifacts

in the back of your memory. But when you're in the sales meeting, your focus should turn to the delivery; that is, to reading the person and delivering the information in a way that they'll understand and appreciate. When we get into a setting where it's a little uncomfortable for us because it's new, what do we tend to do? We tend to focus more on what we know. Ideally, you should already know the hospitality product you are selling, and you already understand what the product has to offer in terms of benefits for the customer. Unfortunately, what typically happens is, because we're in a setting that is new to us or we are with new people, we tend to focus less on the delivery and more on trying to understand the communication style of the prospect. In interacting with controllers, for example, salespeople should spend more time saying, "Let me show you. We've got this and we've got this. And we've got this." We focus on our portfolio or we focus on our tablet presentation or whatever information we brought with us. We tend to hang onto or use as a crutch something that we know for certain and try to go that direction. However, when you are thinking about the delivery, it's almost like you're at a different level. It is hard to describe it until you experience it. But as a sales-person sits down and starts talking to somebody, they are thinking about what content they want to talk about, while at the same time trying to understand what the customer is trying to tell the salesperson. This "dual-focus" can be difficult to achieve, and young sales managers can become uneasy and fall back on the things that they know the best. That's why practicing, spending time and focusing on conversations with others, is really what the salesperson should do to become a great sales professional.

When the salesperson is talking business with a prospective client and they are meeting them the first time, they want to have something to work from.

That's why we look at the artifacts. We do this not only to try to understand the person's communication style, but also to help us develop a relationship.

Do not be inflexible based on what you see. Be a detective. If you see something, confirm what you believe by asking a question. If you're wrong, that is OK. Remember that you are trying to develop a relationship. This can be additional information about this particular customer or prospective customer that can be of use later. Again, the more the sales professional can understand about that potential customer, the better off they are.

TIPS FOR EFFECTIVE COMMUNICATION

1. Practice active listening

2. Read body language and control your own body language

3. Pay full attention

4. Master the nuance of voice tones

5. Be empathetic

6. Understand what's not being said

7. Speak in specifics

8. Be a subject matter expert

9. Be genuinely curious

10. Don't act like you know everything

11. Assume good intent

12. Always be honest

13. Don't make assumptions

14. Be persistent, not pestering

15. Be comfortable with silence

Types of Communication

There are several types or methods of communication. One that humans experience from birth is verbal communication. This includes not only the words that are used but the speech's tonality, loudness, softness, speed, etc. Another common form of communication is written. This can include words placed in an email, placed on hard copy, texted, faxed, etc. Still another type of communication is visual. Visual communication includes images on hard copy, transmitted electronically, projected, etc. Visual communication can also include hand movements, as in the use of sign language with those who are hearing impaired.

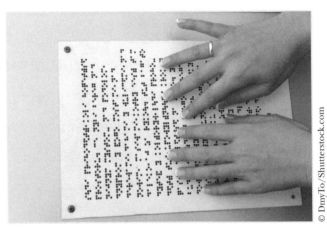

© DmyTo/Shutterstock.com

Braille can be used to communicate with people who are visually impaired

It is critical for the sales professional to ascertain as quickly as possible the methods of communication the client prefers. Not all people prefer email: some prefer phone calls. Further, the preferred method may vary based on the interaction taking place. Using the example above of the association, the buyer may prefer communicating via email for most of the communication with the sales professional but may require a face-to-face meeting to finalize the buying decision.

STYLES – VERBAL AND NONVERBAL

The two major types of communication are verbal and nonverbal. Verbal communication can take the form of the spoken word or transmission of language. **Nonverbal communication** refers to communication that is not verbal. The most common form is body language. This takes place in face-to-face communication and includes shaking hands, patting the back, hugging, pushing, or other kinds of touch. Other forms of nonverbal communication are facial expressions, gestures, and eye contact. When someone is talking with another person, they notice changes in facial expressions and respond accordingly (e.g., movement of the body, hand gestures, eye movement, etc.). The sales professional needs to be constantly aware of the verbal AND nonverbal messages they are transmitting to the buyer, and vice versa.

SEVEN TIPS FOR EFFECTIVE INTERPERSONAL COMMUNICATION

1. Sincerely greet every client

2. Speak in a clear, pleasant, easy to hear voice

3. Ask questions and take notes

4. Never ignore a client

5. Never interrupt a client

6. Maintain direct eye contact

7. Have a firm handshake

Selling to the Hospitality Customer: The Customer's Buying Process

The basic buying process of the customer follows four steps: need recognition, Information search, evaluation of alternatives, and the purchase decision. First, the customer has a need. That need could be to hold an event, reserve hotel rooms, or add audiovisual to a scheduled meeting. In many cases, the need is clear. The hospitality salesperson will ask few questions, as the stated need will be direct. Next, the prospective customer will seek out additional information. They may go to the internet. For example, they will acquire additional information and look at reviews from others. Research has shown that when customers are considering product and service options, they often seek advice from a trusted family member or a business associate. Meeting and event planners regularly reach out to their peers to get additional information about potential locations or potential businesses that they are considering. Once they've got all this information—and remember some communication styles take a great deal of time doing research—they reduce the number of potential choices to two or three. Once the choices have been fully evaluated, a buying decision is made. The time it takes to go through this four-step process may take days or weeks for events that are simple and months for events that have an emotional component or are more complex.

FIGURE 1. BUYING OBJECTIVES CLASSIFICATION

Internally Driven	Externally Driven
emotional	devotional
rational	product objectives

The first stage of the buying process can be translated by the hospitality salesperson into what objectives the prospective customer seeks to address by selecting the hospitality product or service. A buying objective is then, "An aroused need, motive, drive, or desire that stimulates behavior to satisfy that aroused need." While the prospective customer may have many objectives or motives, what is most important to the hospitality salesperson is to ascertain the three-to-five characteristics of the hospitality product or service that dominate the purchase decision. These buying objectives can be classified into four different categories: emotional, rational, devotional, and product or service. The emotional and rational buying objectives can also be classified as internally driven, while the devotional and product objectives are guided by external forces.

This four-step buying process, the customer's buying objectives, and the time it takes to decide yields a type of buyer who can be classified into two types: the **transactional buyer** and the **relational buyer**. The transactional buyer tends to be focused on simple purchasing decisions that emphasize efficiency. Simple, small meetings or events that require little customization and are typically planned in the short term are transactional in nature. The hospitality salesperson has an immediate solution, and little understanding of buying motives is required. The term "one-stop shopping" applies here. On the other hand, relational buyers are looking for the hospitality salesperson to be an expert consultant who will guide them to a purchase that will be the right choice for them. In this case, then, the hospitality salesperson must develop a relationship with the buyer, and foster trust in the prospective customer. The term "salesperson as consultant" applies here.

The Hospitality Customer's Buying Objectives

People are motivated to buy for a variety of reasons. They may have emotional reasons. If the purchase is for a special event or has high importance to the client, the buying decision will be affected by the emotional aspect of the purchase. The hospitality salesperson may use the joy emotion for the special event or the emotion of trust for the event that has high importance. Other emotions that the salesperson can appeal to include, fear, surprise, and anticipation. It is important that the hospitality salesperson connect with the right emotion, especially when the customer is considering two hospitality products or services that are quite similar.

Those people who are motivated to buy for rational reasons are acting on logic and judgment. These buying decisions are comparatively free of emotion. This type of purchase decision typically involves a purchasing manager or committee with a clear set of specifications that must be addressed. The hospitality salesperson should ensure that as much data and information as possible is provided to the rational prospect. It must be noted that there are things such as requests for proposals (RFPs) and site visits that take place for larger events and conventions or conferences where a rational buying motive prevails.

Another buying motive, which might be combined with an emotional or rational motive is the devotion to a specific hospitality operation. Typically, this devotion is based on a past positive experience with the product or service of that operation. The hospitality salesperson who emphasizes superior service, excellent product quality, and a commitment to providing outstanding sales support is successful in appealing to this buying motive. What is important to emphasize with this motive is that it is linked to a specific hotel, venue, or restaurant. For example, there may be two hotels of the same brand located near each other, but this motive would suggest that the buyer would select one over the other because of a positive prior experience.

Sign language can be used to communicate with people who are hearing impaired

The last buying motive is a broader motive related to brands and product quality. This motive tends to be based on loyalty toward a brand, and the belief that the brand is superiority in quality, price, design, and service level. This is an example of the adage "the brand sells itself." The prospective customer uses this buying objective as a filter when evaluating information. Much like the devotion to the operation, this motive relies on prior experience of the buyer, or the experience of others he or she relies upon for recommendations. The hospitality salesperson, in this case, appeals to the buyer by emphasizing the consistent superiority of the brand.

Customer Buying Theories Applied to Sales

There are three theories that are commonly applied to the sales process. The first is the Need Satisfaction Theory for selling. This approach relies on effective communication between the hospitality salesperson and the customer. As the title implies, the salesperson seeks to understand what buying motives or needs dominate the customer's buying process, then develops a sales strategy which addresses the buying motives in a way that the customers realize value. The need satisfaction approach requires that the hospitality salesperson systematically ask questions, confirm an understanding of the need of the customer, and arrive at a conclusion by proposing a solution that will address that need and provide the customer value (see graphic above). If the hospitality salesperson is successful in this approach, the theory indicates that customer trust and loyalty will result.

The second theory pertinent to the sales process is the Buyer Resolution Theory. This theory emphasizes that a customer's purchase behavior is dependent upon the buyer's mental steps that surround five issues that must be decided to complete the purchase. Each one of the five issues are summarized in the graphic above. Ultimately, the customer must have answers to five questions: Why should I buy? What should I buy? From whom should I buy? What is a fair price, what is the best value? Finally, when should I buy?

It is important that the salesperson works with the customer to answer each of these questions, from the customer's point of view. The question, "why should I buy," is most important because it confirms that a need exists. If the customer does not indeed see a need, there is no reason for the salesperson to advance to the next mental step. The next question, "what should I buy," gives the hospitality salesperson the opportunity to present various options to the customer. This is also an opportunity for the salesperson to highlight special product features that satisfy the needs identified in the first question. The third question, "where should I buy," gives the hospitality salesperson the opportunity to make the case for why his or her organization will provide a superior product, service, and experience. For a meeting planner, this question is probably the most important. The fourth question, "what is a fair price," is probably the second most important question for meeting planners. A positive answer to this question comes only when the price offered is competitive and the perceived value is apparent. The last question, "when should

Source: Jeffrey Beck

Source: Jeffrey Beck

I buy," has two elements. First, is there an immediate need to consummate the purchase? It could be that the meeting planner has other people to consult with, or there is no perceived value in purchasing immediately. The second element pertains to the planner's flexibility around purchasing. For example, the dates of a conference may not coincide with the space the hotel or venue has available. Therefore, if the planner has flexibility, different dates may be selected and that choice will have an impact on the purchase decision.

The third theory or approach to sales involves the **outside influences** which impact the buying decision. The theory suggests that there are four interpersonal buying influences: economic, user, technical, and coach. This approach has been very popular with Marriott International as it has helped hotel salespeople understand what other influences have an impact on major buying decisions. The economic buying influence refers to who has control of the budget. The person who will "pay the bill" is the economic influence. A simple example would be the father of the bride who is paying for the wedding that the bride is planning. In this example, there is only one economic buying influence, the father. The user influence is the person who will experience the product or service. In our example, the bride and groom would be the user influence. The technical influence asks for options. The technical influence can say no to a specific product option, possibly because there are better choices. In our example, a venue may be rejected because of its distance for the family of the groom. Finally, the coach is someone who guides the process by adding information to help the hospitality salesperson sell (and the buyer to buy). In our example, the coach might be a family member or member of the wedding party who has a viewpoint that influences the buying decision.

SIX RULES OF THUMB WHEN WRITING A SALES MESSAGE

1. Write like you talk.

Sales messages are meant to be spoken. Even when somebody reads the message, you want readers to feel like you're talking to them personally. Therefore, whenever you write a sales message, ask yourself: "Does this sound like something I'd actually say to a real person?" If it is not, your message won't be effective.

2.   Get to the point.

When it comes to sales messages, fewer words are better. There's hardly a sales message that can't be tightened to remove extra words and phrases. Be sure to edit. If you lack the skill to write concisely, hire a professional editor.

3.   State facts rather than promises.

Promises are only meaningful to people who already trust you, and that list probably doesn't include prospects who aren't yet customers. In fact, most people view a promise from a stranger with skepticism if not outright suspicion. It's more effective to provide a quantitative, verifiable fact that creates credibility.

4.   Don't lie.

It's a terrible idea to start out a business relationship by telling a bald-faced lie. And that's what people try to do when their sales message says something like: "I'm not trying to sell you something."

5.   Use common words rather than jargon.

Unfortunately, when most salespeople sit down to write something, they start writing in gibberish, stuffing sentences full of important-sounding terminology that means little or nothing. The cure is to use simple nouns and verbs that have a precise meaning.

6.   Replace clichés with specifics.

Words like "guarantee," "no obligation," and "free trial" are red flags that convince the customer that both you and your firm are full of meaningless talk and nonsense. Everyone with a bit of common sense knows that:

*   Guarantees are meaningless.
*   A free trial costs time and effort.
*   A sales call implies social obligation.

Use specifics instead.

SUMMARY

Good communication is critical for a salesperson's success. A communication style refers to how someone likes to do something. The hospitality salesperson must be "on the same wavelength" with the people they communicate with. Based on the lettering that you see, there are four types of communicator: analyzer, controller, persuader, and organizer. The customer's basic buying process of the customer follows four steps: need recognition, information search, evaluation of alternatives, and the purchase decision. There are three theories that are commonly applied to the sales process. The first is the Need Satisfaction Theory for selling. The second theory pertinent to the sales process is the Buyer Resolution Theory. The third theory or approach to sales involves the outside influences which impact the buying decision.

KEY TERMS

communication style
hospitality salesperson
controlled
responsive
analyzers
organizers

persuaders
artifacts
nonverbal
   communication
transactional buyer
relational buyer

need satisfaction
   theory
buyer resolution theory
outside influences
site visit

REVIEW AND DISCUSSION QUESTIONS

1. What are the two types of buyer?

2. What is an RFP?

3. What is a site visit?

4. What is Buyer Resolution Theory?

5. Define the concept of communication style as it relates to selling in hospitality.

6. Describe the four types of communication styles.

7. Explain the forces affecting the buying decision.

8. Describe the four types of buying objectives.

9. Discuss the three theories of buyer behavior.

10. What do the best salespeople do before they communicate with their prospective or active client?

ACTIVITY: What is YOUR Communication Style? REQUIRES INSTRUMENT

ACTIVITY: Responding to a Sales Inquiry

CHAPTER 6

Market Segment Behaviors

Professional sports teams, such as this rugby team, are a hospitality sales market
© Paul D Smith/Shutterstock.com

LEARNING OBJECTIVES

- List the various hospitality market segments.
- Describe the characteristics of each market segment.
- Discuss the implications of selling to each market segment.
- Outline the hospitality sales process.

Introduction

In the previous chapter, we discussed the customer's buying process. The recognition of need begins the process. Next, the customer seeks information, so that product/service options can be evaluated. Third, the customer resolves any concerns they may have about the options they are considering. Next, the customer makes a buying decision and chooses the organization/product or service that best corresponds to the needs identified in the first step. Finally, the customer uses/experiences the hospitality product. Understanding this buying process is critical, as the hospitality salesperson must align the hospitality selling strategy to the customer buying process.

A customer selling strategy for hospitality concentrates on who the hospitality organization sells to, what products and services will be offered, and what selling techniques will be used. The first step in developing a customer selling strategy requires that current and potential customers be segmented into meaningful clusters that allows for a customized selling strategy. Next comes an understanding of what products and services are needed by that market segment. Finally, the hospitality sales process is undertaken, which is an organized flow of all the things the hospitality sales team must accomplish to do business with the prospective customer.

Who Are We Selling To?

In the hospitality industry, we sell both to individual consumers and to organizations. In the case of individuals, their needs typically concentrate on social catering and special events. The individual is actually representing a group of people who will attend the event. These events can include weddings, anniversaries, and other family-related events. It is important that the hospitality salesperson be sensitive and empathetic to the special nature of such events. When making such important decisions, individual buyers may take more time to evaluate alternatives and collect information. As we discussed in a previous chapter, the influences on the purchase decision must be considered as the customer buying process and the hospitality selling processes advance. Many times, recommendations from others and the reputation of the hospitality organization play a critical role in the final decision.

With organizations that buy hospitality products and services, there are many different needs and behaviors that affect the buying process. In most cases, more than one individual makes the buying decision. With some organizations, a committee may be involved in evaluating alternatives. Buying decisions can be a quick decision if the organizational need is not complex and the buyer has all the necessary information to decide on the purchase. This is the transactional sale discussed earlier. In this scenario, the hospitality salesperson is wise to facilitate making the sale as easy as possible by emphasizing service. In other more complex buying situations where an expensive purchase is being made, a greater length of time for decision making can be expected. As you might imagine, the hospitality salesperson should anticipate questions from the buyer(s) who are evaluating options and work as a trusted advisor to help the buying process move to purchase.

Major Market Segments in Hospitality

There are four market segments which hospitality salespeople encounter in their work: associations, corporate businesses, and incentive travel. Another market is **SMERF**, which stands for social, military, educational, religious, and fraternal. Within these categories are specialized groups that we will discuss in this and future chapters. Each one of these market segments has various needs and characteristics that affect the buying process that they undergo.

The Association Market Segment

An association is an organization of individuals who come together to expand their own knowledge of their profession or interest area and the guidelines under which they operate. These associations may fulfill their mission through research, government affairs programs, publication of books and journals, certification, or a host of other programs. Seven out of every 10 adults belong to at least one association. You probably know more about associations than you realize. You may participate in sports, belong to a college fraternity or sorority, volunteer for the Red Cross, or pay dues to an association of people who share a hobby with you. There are over 100,000 trade and professional associations in the United States. These associations educate, serve, train, manage, oversee, lobby, inform, and more. They affect our quality of life through their services, their guidelines, and their interactions with legal, regulative, and legislative processes.

Conferences, conventions, and seminars are the lifeblood of an association. On average, association planners organize 12 meetings per year, with the largest being the annual convention or conference that is also their largest revenue producer. According to the 2017 meetings market study by the Professional Convention Management Association (PCMA), 32% of the revenue for associations comes from conventions, exhibits, and meetings. That same survey also found 48% of the total revenue from most meetings comes from registration, while 21% comes from exhibit booth space sales. Because associations can be local, statewide, regional, national, or international, the meetings they sponsor can vary tremendously in type, size, and location.

Associations can be run by volunteers, while some associations have an individual or company professionally manage the association. There are two staffing options for an association: directly retaining an individual staff executive as an employee of the association or hiring an association management company to run the association. **Association management companies** (AMCs) can be hired to run the association and/or its events. They offer the expertise, staffing, and resources that allow smaller professional societies, trade groups, not-for-profits, and philanthropic organizations to manage day-to-day operations and advance their long-term goals. Chicago-based SmithBucklin is the world's largest AMC.

In either case, several individuals are involved in the hospitality buying decision-making process. The association director (can also be titled CEO), the president, the board of directors, and the chair of the conference committee can all play a role in the decision-making process. The president, board, and committee chair positions are all elected, and thus change personnel on a regular basis; the association director/CEO provides longer-term continuity to the association. Because of this continuity, the association director wields a great amount of influence on the destinations and hotels to be considered for association events. The president, board, and conference chair will have significant input on the final decision. For some scientific and educational associations, a local committee may request the opportunity to host the conference.

Associations hold many different types of meetings. First and foremost is the annual convention. As mentioned earlier, the annual convention is the main source of revenue for many associations. Typically held in conjunction with the convention are exhibit/trade shows, educational sessions, and association board meetings. This convention is typically held once a year, in rotating locations. If it is a national or international convention, destinations move geographically. For example, if it is a national convention, the destination may move from the East Coast to the Midwest, to the West Coast over a three-year time span. International conferences may rotate by way of the continents represented in the membership. Because the convention draws the largest percentage of the membership, attractive locations with easy accessibility to travel options are very important to the meeting planner. The destination must have the resources, such as quantity/quality of hotel rooms or amount of exhibit space, to meet the needs of the convention.

Associations hold other types of meetings that may be independent of the annual convention. The association board of directors meets on a regular basis. These meetings can be held at potential future convention locations, to allow inspection of the destination and venues being considered. They can also be held at locations where allied organizations are holding meetings or conventions, and most of the association members will be in attendance. For example, while the American Medical Association is holding their annual meeting, the board of a smaller association such as the American Thoracic Society may meet in the same locale. The size of attendance varies according to timing and the association; most board meetings have from 10 to 50 people in attendance.

THE FIVE BIGGEST ASSOCIATIONS

The five biggest associations in the United States have over 45 million members and budgets totaling $2.8B. Here are some more fun facts about them.

1.   AARP

Mission: Nonprofit, nonpartisan membership organization for people age 50 and over. AARP delivers value to members through information, advocacy, and service.

Number of members: Over 37 million

HQ: Washington, DC

Year founded: 1958

Board size: 21

Budget: $1.4B

2.   National Rifle Association

Mission: NRA advocates for the protection of the Second Amendment and the promotion of firearm ownership rights as well as marksmanship, firearm safety, and the protection of hunting and self-defense in the United States.

Photo: From NRA's annual convention held earlier this month.

Number of members: 4.5 million

HQ: Fairfax, VA

Year founded: 1871

Board size: 75

Budget: $256M

3. National Education Association

Mission: NEA is the nation's largest professional employee organization, representing elementary and secondary teachers, higher education faculty, education support professionals, school administrators, retired educators, and students preparing to become teachers.

Number of members: 3.2 million

HQ: Washington, DC

Year founded: 1857

Board size: 162

Budget: $371M

4. American Diabetes Association

Mission: Prevent and cure diabetes and to improve the lives of all affected people. ADA funds research, publishes scientific findings, and provides information and other services to people with diabetes, their families, health professionals, and the public. The ADA also advocates for scientific research and for the rights of people with diabetes.

Number of members: Over 441,000 people with diabetes and nearly 16,500 healthcare professionals.

HQ: Alexandria, VA (Soon to be Arlington, VA)

Year founded: 1940

Board size: 18

Budget: $228M

5. American Chemical Society

Mission: ACS is the world's largest scientific society and one of the world's leading sources of authoritative scientific information. A nonprofit chartered by Congress, ACS is at the forefront of the evolving worldwide chemical enterprise and the premier professional home for chemists, chemical engineers, and related professions around the globe.

Number of members: Over 161,000

HQ: Washington, DC

Year founded: 1876

Board size: 16

Budget: $523M

Depending on the association, educational events, such as seminars and workshops, can be held during the annual convention, or separately in various locations in the association's territory. These events are important for associations whose members rely on continuing education. Regional meetings or meetings of subgroups within the larger association may be held at quarterly intervals. Other meetings that are affiliated with the association are held as needed.

Selling to Associations

There are many motives that impact the buying process for associations. Associations can be characterized as a group of people united by a common interest or goal. As such, the criteria for destination and venue selection vary with the characteristics of the association. There are two things that all association meetings have in common: attendance by members at association events is voluntary, and registration and all travel expenses are paid for by the attendee or their institutions. As a result, associations require affordable room rates, reasonable food and beverage prices for the location, and other amenities that appeal to attendees. In addition, destinations and venues must be attractive, to facilitate high attendance percentages by association members. If the association is regional or based in a single state, the organization is typically limited on where it is able to hold its meeting to within the region or state that it is based in.

Associations use many different types of meeting venues. Downtown hotels with large exhibit hall space are most popular for conventions, since the exhibit space is a revenue generator for the association. Resorts with extensive meeting space, convention centers, conference centers, suburban hotels, and airport hotels are also used by associations. Other unique venues, such as gaming facilities, golf resorts, and university conference centers may be used, depending on the goal of the meeting or event.

Chacko and Fenich (2000) identified several attributes that are important to site and venue selection for conventions. One important buying motive for the association is an adequate number of guestrooms in the lodging facility or destination. Many large state associations are restricted in the locations that can be selected because their memberships are higher than the number of guestrooms the hotels in the destination contain. Other buying motives are the availability of rooms on dates and at room rates that the association desires along with the amount of exhibit and meetings space available in the destination.

In summary, the hospitality salesperson should emphasize the attractiveness of the location, the quality of the facilities, and the value received by attendees. Associations are cost conscious and rely heavily on the annual convention to retain members and generate revenue.

The Corporate Market Segment

Corporations and businesses rely on people and processes to generate income; businesses produce and distribute goods and services to make a profit. Because of these activities, meetings and events are held to communicate. There are five reasons why people communicate within a business. The most common reason is to inform people—internal or external stakeholders, or both—of a message. Another reason businesses hold meetings is to educate employees; the production and delivery of quality goods and services require training. Businesses hold meetings and events to improve teamwork and employee morale. Achievements are celebrated, and presentation of the goals of the business can inspire the organization. Especially in corporations, business strategy meetings with high level executives are held to decide the future of the business. Holding the meeting off company premises frees those involved from distractions and allows them to focus on what's important – resulting in better decisions and better plans. Finally, a special set of circumstances beyond what can be considered a normal business problem requires a meeting of all those able to help solve the issue in a discussion of ideas and solutions. Whatever the purpose of the meeting, it is important for the hospitality salesperson to stay focused on those meetings that are held outside the companies' offices – at a hospitality facility.

WHAT IS A CORPORATION?

A **corporation** is a firm that meets certain legal requirements to be recognized as having a legal existence, as an entity separate and distinct from its owners. Corporations are owned by their stockholders (shareholders) who share in profits and losses generated through the firm's operations. Corporations have three distinct characteristics: 1) Legal existence: a firm can (like a person) buy, sell, own property, enter into a contract, sue other persons and firms, and be sued by them. It can do good and be rewarded and it can commit offence and be punished. 2) Limited liability: a firm and its owners are limited in their liability to their creditors and other obligors only up to the resources of the firm, unless the owners give personal guaranties. 3) Continuity of existence: a firm can live beyond the life spans and capacity of its owners, because its ownership can be transferred through a sale or gift of shares.

There are many types of meetings and events that corporations and businesses hold. National and regional sales meetings bring together the sales management and field salespeople for information exchange, updates, and networking. Product introduction/dealer meetings can be information dissemination, or an event to announce publicly new products. Professional and technical meetings, like the type that associations hold, are for maintaining the knowledge of scientific and technical staff. Training meetings are just that; meetings to train employees on a variety of topics. Management meetings are held for various levels of executives in the corporation. These may be strategy meetings that could include video conferencing to other locations. Incentive meetings are designed to reward top producers and are typically held at ultra-luxury hotels and resorts.

"Then, unfortunately, our market launch ran into a brick wall."

Selling to the Corporate Meetings Market

In general, the ten most important factors meeting planners consider when selecting a meeting location are: 1) location, 2) meeting room capacity, 3) layout of the meeting space and facility, 4) quality and capability of the AV equipment, 5) meeting room flexibility, 6) décor, 7) competent sales and service staff, 8) price flexibility, 9) quality food, and 10) guest satisfaction. Locations that have easy access to public transportation or are close to work locations are most attractive. Most of the meetings planned are for 100 to 150 attendees. Therefore, venues with meeting spaces of that capacity are most attractive. Planners want to be sure that attendees can easily locate the meeting space and that there is adequate space for networking outside the meeting space. State-of-the-art technology that is reliable and easy to use is another factor a meeting planner evaluates. Meeting spaces that can be subdivided and set up in various arrangements are important. Meeting locations must be clean and adequately furnished. The more professional and competent the venue's sales staff and service personnel are, the more likely a planner will select that location. Locations that demonstrate pricing flexibility are more attractive, as costs are an ongoing concern. Flexibility in menu options and production are becoming more important as health and last-minute dietary requirements are becoming standard practice among attendees. Finally, the quality of the guests' experience with the location plays an important role in whether the participant will attend another meeting. Three factors have emerged as most important to corporate meeting planners: price, design of the event space, and food and beverage quality.

Training meetings are the most frequently planned meetings in the United States. Training meetings typically involve no more than 50 people, require quiet locations within the venue, are set up in a classroom style, and require efficient (but not elaborate) food service. Training meetings can be the "bread and butter" for smaller hotels. Training managers are not seeking prestigious locations; locations that are convenient to attendees are more important. Training meetings last approximately two and a half days, and do not require room resets; cleaning and refreshing of beverage stations should be done on a regular basis.

Sales and marketing meetings held off site are the next most commonly planned meeting. With the dynamic nature of sales and marketing, meetings are planned and held in various locations throughout the world. The composition of the sales function requires both national and regional sales meetings. Sales meetings, on average, last approximately two and a half days. Attendance at such meetings varies; national meetings can have as many as 200 attendees and run four days. Regional meetings tend to be smaller, with between 50 and 75 people, and last between 1 and 3 days. As you might imagine, sales meetings have both business and social components. Attractive locations with amenities (contained or nearby), such as fine restaurants and sports activities, are popular with the sales and marketing staff planning the meeting.

Board of Directors Meeting

Management meetings, which include senior leadership and board meetings, generally have no more than 20 attendees and are held at the most exclusive venues.

Many times, these meetings are held under the promise of confidentiality by the hotel sales staff. Locations may be remote for privacy reasons. While these meetings are held regularly, special circumstances may require a meeting to be planned at the last minute. A strong relationship between the hospitality sales manager and the meeting planner is essential. The highest quality guestrooms, food and beverage, and service are essential for the success of such meetings.

Professional and technical meetings, which can be planned as conferences, seminars, or workshops, can last three days. These meetings can be on a variety of topics and may include many participants. Because of the educational nature of such meetings, a large amount of meeting space in the form of break-out rooms is required. The hospitality sales manager will often find that standard accommodations and food and beverage offerings will suffice for such events. With these types of meetings, individuals from outside the corporation or business may be invited to participate, lecture, and/or demonstrate to update technical staff on new trends that impact the industry the business operates within.

Corporate incentive meetings and special events can take on many forms. The purpose of the incentive meeting is to reward employees, distributors, salespeople, and customers for targets met or exceeded, or a job well done. These meetings and events are the most expensive on a per-person basis; corporations and businesses spare no expense. Incentive meetings last between three and five days at opulent resorts in exclusive and fashionable destinations. Hawaii is very popular for these incentive travel events. Special events can be defined as brand communication events, appreciation events, and company milestone events. The hospitality sales manager must understand that the venue he or she represents is also representing the corporation or business to its important stakeholders. Because these events are for recognition and communication, they tend to last no more than two days. High quality guestrooms and food and beverage service are expected. If all goes well, the hospitality sales manager can count on additional bookings.

Product launch meetings can be internal to inform all employees of the company regarding upcoming products. These may not require hospitality venues and services. Depending on the complexity of the product, the announcement might be combined with training or demonstration meetings that would require hospitality services. Public product launch events are most common for business-to-consumer (B2C) companies. These meetings are some of the most public meetings a company holds. They are designed to generate media coverage and create excitement. Depending on the company, product, and marketing strategy, these events can be small one-day affairs, or large "Las Vegas" style productions lasting multiple days and involving many subcontractors and logistics personnel. As with special events, the product launch meeting or event gives the hospitality salesperson the opportunity to showcase the venue he or she represents.

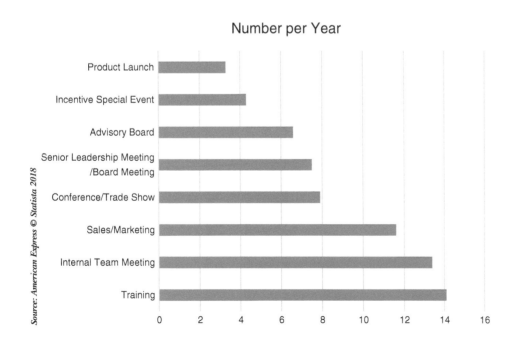

Number per Year

Source: American Express © Statista 2018

FIGURE 1. Average Number of Meetings Planned Per Organization in the United States by Type

Other Markets

Some of the most productive pieces of business come from what is known as the SMERF market segment. SMERF is the abbreviation for social, military, education, religious, and fraternal groups. Because of their nonprofit status, these groups tend to be price sensitive. As a result, they are attractive to all types and service levels of hospitality venues. They are flexible in their date and space selections, which helps the hospitality venue fill in open dates that are less attractive to other market segments. These groups also vary in size and room requirements. Most of the time these groups hold their events on weekends, which is perfect for hotels that primarily have a business clientele and do not attract the weekend leisure customer. The leadership and meeting planners for these groups are usually volunteers who change each year. Therefore, hospitality sales professionals really must take on the role of consultant to help the SMERF group make the decisions that will help make the event successful.

Social groups can be described as those organizations that share a common interest and a sense of unity with one another. The social market encompasses a variety of groups, such as weddings, civic and professional organizations, charity events, holiday celebrations, small interest groups like scrapbookers, organized fans of a sports team, hobbyists, people who are users of different types of software, and recreational athletic organizations. They may require event space for awards dinners, instructional sessions, or guest rooms and space for weekend sporting events. These groups can be local, regional, or national in scope. Many times, local organizations hold monthly meetings which can generate regular food and beverage revenue for the hospitality venue.

> As of 2018, the cost to put on a wedding in the United States had risen to over $30,000 — exclusive of guest travel and accommodations or the honeymoon.

Military meetings and events can be broken into military and volunteer auxiliary groups and reunions. Military business meetings tend to be most common near military bases and are likely to have between 25 and 100 attendees. Volunteer auxiliary groups, such as the US Coast Guard auxiliary and the

USAF Civil Air Patrol, are two examples that meet regularly and have annual state, regional, and nationwide conferences. Overnight accommodations are required, but not on a large scale. A very popular part of the military market is the reunion. The Alliance of Military Reunions represents over 650 military reunion groups (allmilitaryreunions.org). Members of these reunion groups tend to be older, with spouses who accompany them to events. Because they are older, they may have special dietary or medical needs. With the ongoing military actions around the world, younger veteran groups have been forming. According to the Alliance, over half of the reunion groups are centered around Navy ships. Most military reunions are held in the fall, with spring being the next most popular season. These events can draw between 20 and 300 attendees, staying anywhere from three to five nights. Although military reunions often select cities with military history, the annual reunions are in different cities each year.

Educational meetings and events are extremely diverse; they can be held for teachers and staff at the elementary, high school, and post-secondary levels. In addition, they can be affiliated with national extracurricular organizations, such as the Future Farmers of America (FFA), that benefit students. These meetings can be regional, national, or international in scope. Much of the time, educational meetings are held in the summer, although early fall and late spring are also popular. Because these events and meetings attract cost-conscious attendees, cities that are considered "second tier" by meeting planners are most attractive to educational organization planners.

Religious organizations are much like other SMERF organizations; the major point of emphasis is the diverse religious beliefs and attitudes the organization may hold. Hospitality venue amenities that attract religious groups are food and beverage outlets with good food and service, places for small groups to meet at the spur of the moment, and venues with simplistic service offerings. A major attraction of a religious retreat venue is the proximity to secluded areas, such as hiking trails, wooded areas, and places that allow for solitude and introspection. For the larger religious organizations, conventions for attendees of 10,000 to 40,000 are common. As a result, major locations that are appropriate for families are more commonly selected by religious organizations. The Religious Conference Management Association (RCMA) is the association for religious meeting planners; it provides hospitality salespeople a source for reaching out to and qualifying (ensuring that the sales prospect has the ability, authority, and budget to purchase a hospitality offering) these people who require hospitality facilities of all sizes and amenities.

The Last Supper of Jesus Christ is a religious event—AND—somebody had to plan it.

Fraternal organizations are commonly described as the **service organizations** within a community. Kiwanis International, Optimist International, Lions International, and the Fraternal Order of the Elks are examples of these organizations. There is also, however, the segment of Greek organizations known as fraternities and sororities. The purpose of such organizations can be educational, altruistic, communal, or a combination of all three. Like the other types of SMERF groups, attendees pay their own expenses and may bring family members to make for vacation opportunities. It is important to emphasize the venue's amenities that are attractive to these attendees. The hospitality sales professional is wise to consider joining one or more of these organizations in the local community; in fact, becoming a member of these organizations is a typical tactic of the SMERF sales manager.

Still Other Markets

Besides the association, corporate, and SMERF markets, there are other sub-markets that are worthwhile sources of customers for the hospitality sales manager. These markets include: government, financial/insurance, medical, sports team/event, and incentive. The Society of Government Meeting Professionals (SGMP) formed in 1981. SGMP is the national organization dedicated to government meeting professionals. The Financial & Insurance Conference Professionals (FICP) organization serves as a resource for meeting planners in the areas of education and experience related to meetings and events for the financial services and insurance industries in North America. Meetings Professional International (MPI) has begun a community tailored to meeting planners from the pharmaceutical, biotech, medical, life sciences, and healthcare industries. Hospitality sales professionals will find that professional, collegiate, or youth and adult recreational sports teams and tournaments can bring a great deal of business to their venues. The Society for Incentive Travel Excellence (SITE) is an organization that represents incentive travel professionals; while incentive travel is part of the corporate market segment, the unique nature of incentive travel requires that it be discussed as its own sub-market.

The government meeting market includes federal, state, and local government agencies of all types. There is such a wide variety of business opportunities with these agencies that it is challenging to summarize the needs of the government meeting planner. The most important thing to remember is that government agencies work from a *per diem* allowance. The U.S. General Services Administration (GSA) has set federal per diem rates for any official government travel. The federal per diem guidelines may change from year to year; the rates also vary for different locations. Locations that government meeting planners choose are in easily accessible destinations; lodging facilities must have an ample supply of rooms with two beds. Because of the political nature of government activity, government planners are price sensitive and select facilities that are more economical in product and services.

The financial and insurance markets are a sub-category of the corporate market. According to FICP, each company in the financial service and insurance industries planned approximately 95 events in 2011, and the average meeting budget for these companies was $3,000,000. As a result, planners and attendees are not cost conscious; they expect luxury facilities and outstanding service. Hotels and resorts are more popular with the insurance meeting planner, while conference centers devoted to education are more frequently chosen by financial service planners. The small insurance meetings are typically focused on training of the sales force; the smaller financial services meetings focus on training related to governmental regulations.

Medical meeting planners have an important responsibility when planning medical meetings. There are many complex activities that must be carried out. These include ensuring compliance with federal regulations, staying on top of trends, keeping up with advances in equipment and procedures, and providing pharmaceutical information. Health Care Providers (HCP) must stay up to date through continuing education. Continuing Medical Education (CME) encompasses educational activities to maintain and develop the knowledge, skills, and professional performance of physicians and HCP. Each state medical board has different CME credit requirements. While online education is available, the majority of HCP prefer face-to-face educational opportunities. Physicians and surgeons are the attendees of these meetings, so they have a very high level of expectation for quality venues and service. Medical meeting planners must demonstrate to their constituents that the event or meeting they will be attending will provide maximum value.

Professional sports teams and their fans can be great business for a full-service hospitality venue. Once the team has booked the property once, repeat business will occur provided they received quality service. It is important that the hospitality salesperson be professional and be attentive to the team's special needs and requests. Depending on the team and sport, guest rooms with two queen-sized beds or rooms with extended length beds are commonly requested (e.g., football teams). Meeting spaces for team meetings and meals are also required. Emphasizing the quality of the food and beverage staff can be a key buying motive for the team. Colleges and universities can provide a great quantity of room nights for their teams and fans as well. It is important for the sales professional to get to know the athletic director, sports information director, and coaches of the local college or university so that referrals can be given. Youth and adult teams and leagues can be an attractive segment. It is important to be linked to the local convention and visitors bureau (CVB) as they play an active role in attracting athletic tournaments and advising team officials of accommodations.

Like the insurance and financial services market, the incentive travel market is a sub-market of the corporate market. In fact, many incentive meetings and events are held for insurance and financial sales professionals. Incentive-based meetings and events are used to reward employee achievement, effort, and contribution to the success of the organization. Rewarding sales accomplishments is a typical reason for a company to host an incentive meeting. This segment has grown into a vibrant segment of the meeting/event industry. Because of the nature of reward for performance, unique destinations, venues, and amenities are always key buying motives for incentive travel planners. What is important to the corporate meeting planner is not always important to the incentive planner. Business meetings are kept to a minimum during incentive travel trips. In fact, many corporate planning offices outsource their incentive travel planning to third-party companies. Maritz Incentive Travel is well known as one of the largest incentive travel houses in the world. The buying motives of the incentive planner include the safety and security of the location and venue; hotels and resorts with golf courses and spas are popular and are frequently requested. The hospitality sales professional must be clear as to the make-up of the attendees when selling to the incentive planner. The sales professional must be sensitive to needs, personalities, and culture of the company the incentive planner represents. While the average incentive trip lasts up to five days, trip lengths are getting shorter.

The Hospitality Sales Process

The **hospitality sales process** can be defined as the steps a hospitality salesperson must follow to align with the customer's buying process. The hospitality sales process includes seven steps: 1) Prepare, 2) Access, 3) Establish, 4) Present, 5) Proof, 6) Close, and 7) Service. In the prepare stage, the hospitality salesperson prepares themselves to become a successful sales manager. To be successful, the hospitality sales manager must work on becoming a sales professional in their knowledge, skills, and attitude. The sales manager must learn as much as they can about the venue, product, or service they represent. They must become emotionally intelligent; they must develop the personal skills to work with and influence others, while developing the skills to manage themselves. Finally, hospitality salespeople must develop a positive and winning attitude. Nikos Kazantzakis, a renowned writer of Greek literature, once said, "In order to succeed, we must first believe that we can."

The first step in the hospitality process, which interfaces with the customer's buying process, is **access**. In this step, the hospitality salesperson is seeking to create interest on the part of the customer. This can include prospecting for potential customers, taking calls from customers, following up with people who have indicated an interest in the hospitality product or service offering, creating awareness, and providing information. The next step in the process

EXHIBIT 1: STEPS IN THE HOSPITALITY SALES PROCESS

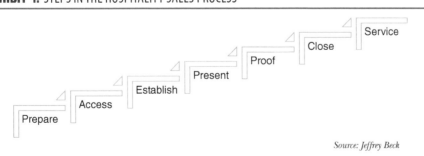

Source: Jeffrey Beck

is to establish and assess the customer's need. The activity of **qualification** is undertaken to establish that a prospect has the ability, authority, and budget to purchase. The salesperson explains the characteristics of the product or service they have to offer. Many questions are asked during this step, so that the hospitality salesperson can gain a clear picture of which buying objectives of the client are the most important. Once the buying objectives have been clearly identified, the sales process moves to the **present** stage of the sales process. In the present step, the hospitality salesperson makes the connection between what the hospitality organization has to offer and how the potential customer will benefit. A property site tour, a restaurant taste panel, and an equipment demonstration are examples of the present stage of the hospitality selling process, because they demonstrate what the hospitality organization has to offer. If asked by the prospective customer, the hospitality salesperson will compare what they are offering to that of the competition. A **proposal** which is customized to the specific needs of the customer is typically presented in this stage. Listening on the part of the salesperson is a very important behavior during the establish and present stages of the sales process. In the *proof* stage of the process, overcoming objections, negotiation, and persuasion take place. In this stage, any concerns are addressed and resolved. It is also in this stage that the hospitality salesperson will know if they have successfully established that the customer has a need, presented a benefit, and confirmed that the link between need and benefit is strong. Once all issues have been addressed, asking for the business in the **close** stage is undertaken. Developing the specific terms of the contract, asking for referrals, and thanking the customer for the sale are all part of the **close** step of the hospitality sales process. Finally, the **service** stage of the process moves the customer toward the actual meeting, event, or service delivery through planning. It is in this stage that the customer will work with onsite event or service staff to plan and execute the meeting, event, or service delivery the customer contracted for. It is at this point that opportunities for **upselling** or offering additional products or services can be offered. The remainder of this textbook will cover each of the steps necessary for the success of the hospitality salesperson.

SUMMARY

This chapter is on the hospitality sales process. The various hospitality market segments, such as association, corporate, government, medical, SMERF, professional sports, and others, were discussed as were the characteristics of each market segment. The implications of selling to each market segment were covered and the hospitality sales process was outlined. The hospitality sales process includes seven steps: 1) Prepare, 2) Access, 3) Establish, 4) Present, 5) Proof, 6) Close, and 7) Service.

KEY TERMS

customer selling strategy	management companies	hospitality sales process incentive meetings
association	corporations	SMERF

REVIEW AND DISCUSSION QUESTIONS

1. Describe the major hospitality sales markets.

2. Describe the other hospitality sales markets.

3. Explain the implications of selling to each market.

4. Explain the hospitality sales process.

5. How many steps are in the hospitality sales process?

6. What is the average cost of a wedding held in the United States?

7. What is the average number of events planned per year, by type?

8. What is the largest market segment for hospitality events?

9. Meet with a group of friends or classmates. Take turns discussing your wants and needs if you were to get married.

10. If you were to plan an incentive travel meeting/event, where would it be and why?

CHAPTER 7

Developing a Strategy for Selling the Product

The Hospitality Product Is Multifaceted
© nalinratphi/Shutterstock.com

LEARNING OBJECTIVES

- Outline the process for gaining product knowledge.
- Define the product levels that a salesperson represents to the prospect.
- Describe techniques for discovering the competition for your property.
- Outline the process for ranking the competition for your property.
- Describe how product features are linked to customer benefits.

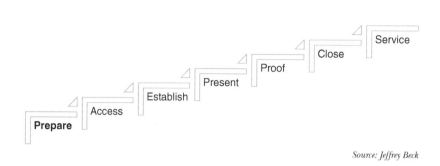

Source: Jeffrey Beck

The hospitality sales process includes seven steps: 1) Prepare, 2) Access, 3) Establish, 4) Present, 5) Proof, 6) Close, and 7) Service. The hospitality sales process can be defined as the steps a hospitality salesperson must follow to develop relationships, create trust with their customers, then present a hospitality product and service that will satisfy their needs, causing them to buy. There is an adage, *"People buy from people they like and people they trust."* In the prepare stage, the hospitality salesperson must prepare themselves to become a trusted sales manager through knowledge acquisition.

In this step of the process, the hospitality sales manager must work on becoming a sales professional in their general knowledge of the products and services they have to offer. Specifically, they must understand how these products and services satisfy customers' needs. Hospitality sales managers must be able to convince the customer how he or she will experience greater value when compared to the competition. The hospitality sales manager must also be in touch with what is happening in the marketplace, locally, regionally, nationally, and internationally as appropriate.

When it comes to the hospitality product you are selling, you want to know as much as you possibly can. Recognizing the strengths and weaknesses of the organization you represent helps you to become an expert in the eyes of your potential customer. Having that expertise helps you to develop the confidence necessary to present your hospitality organization in a positive light. It is almost like taking a test in school; when you know the material, you have answers to the questions before they are asked. When you answer questions confidently, you develop trust within the customer. Much of the information about your hospitality organization is easily accessible on the internet. Customers who are more focused on the transaction will have the information they need to make a buying decision. It is the information that cannot be found easily that you as the hospitality sales professional must become secure in your knowledge of. You then become more of a consultant, a trusted partner providing a solution for the prospective customer.

STRENGTHS AND WEAKNESS OF PRODUCT POSITIONING

Product positioning involves defining a relative position in the marketplace. A bakery, for example, sells cakes in a crowded market that includes competition from other bakeries' cakes and entirely different dessert alternatives. To set its cakes apart from all other options, the bakery must position its product in the minds of consumers as being uniquely suited to their needs.

COMPETITIVE ADVANTAGE

The greatest strength of effective product positioning is that it can create a competitive advantage. In other words, if a company can establish its products as uniquely valuable, competitors will find it difficult to make a compelling case for buying substitutes. For example, suppose a bakery uses well-guarded recipes that competitors can't easily imitate. That bakery's products might occupy a secure position in the marketplace because consumers recognize that no other options offer the same benefits. Similarly, a fashion designer's clothing might have a stylistic element that all other options lack, allowing the designer to command a high price in that market.

PERCEPTION

Another potential strength of product positioning is that the most important factor in consumer purchasing decisions can be perception, not necessarily reality. In other words, rather than create an objectively better product, a company can use a variety of marketing techniques to position its products favorably in the minds of consumers. For example, a skateboard manufacturer might use celebrity endorsements and vivid designs to establish its products as revolutionary and cutting edge in the minds of young skaters -- regardless of the actual merit of these claims. Similarly, a restaurant might use prestige pricing -- selling products at higher-than-normal prices to foster an aura of luxury -- to attract high-income diners. These techniques might fail, but when they work, they allow companies to set themselves apart from competitors without offering anything significantly different.

HIGH COMPETITION

A potential weakness of product positioning is that every company wants to position its products favorably in the minds of consumers, so there is usually a high level of competition. New companies, for example, often find it difficult to position their products in a market that has well-established competitors. Also, carving out a niche in a large and competitive market is often difficult for small businesses, so many newcomers focus on a very narrow segment at the start, building their brand identities before stepping into larger competitive arenas.

INEVITABLE CHANGE

Another weakness of product positioning is that maintaining a competitive position in a market is always difficult. Consumers might tire of a company's products, for example, requiring the company to freshen its image by developing new products or by significantly improving old products. This can be especially hard if the company has fostered a brand image that is starkly different from the new identity it wants to adopt. For example, a brand known for being a low-cost alternative will be difficult to market as a luxury item when a company adapts to meet the demands of a new market. In any case, the company must fight to maintain its competitive position, a task made more difficult if many other products are simultaneously competing for consumers' attention. Many other changes can occur, from economic distress to radical shifts in technology, all of which threaten to undermine a company's previously successful positioning techniques.

Four Levels of Product

Sales managers have four levels of product to consider when presenting their offerings to their prospective customers. These four product levels are called the core, facilitating, supporting, and augmented. As we go through this chapter, the reader will see how each level of product can be important to the sale. **Core products** are at the most basic level of hospitality offering. Of course, depending on the hospitality enterprise and the need of the customer, the core product can be different. Let's take a convention resort hotel, for example. For some guests, the hotel provides an overnight stay. For others, the convention center offers a location to hold multiple-day meetings. And for still others, the recreational facilities provide leisure. The hospitality salesperson must think of the core product as essential to the customer's purpose for buying.

All hospitality facilities must offer the following qualities for the guest or patron to be satisfied. Whether it is a hotel, restaurant, convention center, or other hospitality enterprise, all areas of the facility open to guests must be *clean*. Additionally, all hospitality facilities must be safe and secure. Those

O'Hare Airport in Chicago is an example of a facilitating product.

© Thomas Barrat/Shutterstock.com

hospitality facilities that add additional amenities to ensure the safety and security of their guests can emphasize that information, adding to the attractiveness of the facility. Internet or Wi-Fi access has become a "need to have." **Facilitating products** are those products or services that must be in existence for the customer to buy. Can you imagine a convention center without a loading dock? Restaurants must have a means by which the menu is delivered to the customer for selection. Destinations must have a means by which travelers and tourists can gain access (e.g., airports, train stations, bus depots, or highways). These are examples of facilitating products that can be used by the hospitality salesperson to confirm that the core product will meet the customer's needs.

Most important to the hospitality sales manager is the **supporting product.** Supporting products are defined as those products, services, or amenities that add value to the basic offering or core product. Supporting products, services, or amenities help to set the hospitality offering apart from its competition. According to Merriam Webster, the *secret sauce* can be defined as an element, quality, or ability that makes something or someone successful or distinctive. Think of supporting products as the secret sauce of the hospitality organization. For each hospitality organization, the secret sauce may be something different. What is most important to remember about support products, services, or amenities is that these items are not easily copied. As a result, the service culture of a hotel, restaurant, or conference center can be the reason why a customer selects one property over another. Frankenmuth, Michigan is well known as the "Little Bavaria" of Michigan. The city has a strong architectural presence that is similar to the Franconia region of Germany. Nearly fifty percent of the population are of German heritage; over three million tourists visit annually to the Bavarian themed restaurants, shops, and inns. While the core products of hotels, restaurants, and other attractions are in place, the Bavarian theme is presented by the Frankenmuth Convention and Visitors Bureau as their secret sauce.

Augmented products are those elements that add to the atmosphere, interaction, and experience of the customer. From the standpoint of the atmosphere, this includes the sights, smells, sounds, and physical sensations that the customer experiences. Salespeople can take advantage of these sensations to emphasize the experience the meeting planner's attendees will have. A well-known sales trainer, Elmer Wheeler, coined the phrase "sell the sizzle" to emphasize the experiential elements of the core and supporting products. With the intangible nature of hospitality products and services, being able to "sell the sizzle" makes it easier for the customer to understand how their needs will be satisfied.

Solution Selling

Solution selling is a selling methodology whereby the product and its characteristics are not at the center of the sales presentation. Instead, the hospitality salesperson focuses on the customer's problems and needs; then offers products and services that lead to problem resolution and satisfaction. **Transactional buyers**, that is those who know what they want, will have done much of the research necessary to request a proposal. The transactional customer will be clear on their budget, objective to be gained from the purchase, the date or dates they will consider, and what specifically they are looking for as solutions to their needs. For example, a simple meeting for 40 people with 10 guestrooms for one night and one meal does not take a lot of advice on the part of the hospitality salesperson. In this case, customized product offerings by the hospitality organization are less likely to be needed. Transactional buyers are less concerned about loyalty and are uninterested in an ongoing relationship.

The real starting point for a truly solutions-selling orientation is at corporate philosophy and culture.

1. Management needs to determine which segments they want to approach.

2. Next, management should be exploring and identifying how their products or services need to be changed, extended, or adjusted (if at all), to accommodate the expectations of the buyers in the sales segments. The key word here is "expectations." Compared to product-related selling, solutions selling extends the value delivered by satisfying both needs and expectations.

3. The next stage involves a serious re-think about the corporate philosophy. Companies need to be prepared to partner with other organizations in order to extend their flexibility.

4. Once these stages have been re-evaluated, companies can start looking at their sales teams. There are several activities that should be considered that dramatically change the way salespeople sell.

Product and service selling is based on the salesperson's ability to uncover a buyer's need and then introduce the benefits of a product or service that will most closely and effectively satisfy that need. And that is a noble calling. But solutions selling is vastly different. For starters, determining what solutions are required is based on value, not the features and benefits of the product or service. Secondly, whereas the sales organization defines the product features and benefits, buyers determine what an ideal solution is and its value. This makes the sales interaction more complex.

All of this means that salespeople need a broader business knowledge base, more industry expertise, and far greater analytical capabilities than salespeople selling products. They also need a different mindset and behavior.

Most of the solutions are usually some combination of products, services, and possible additions. A company that wants to increase its position in the market and make the shift to solutions selling must start with the way it thinks and builds its corporate and then its sales strategy. Simply giving salespeople some training and telling them to talk about solutions rather than products won't make the difference.

Relationship buyers are likely to be seeking to develop a relationship such that one buying experience will lead to many more. For a complex purchase, such as a multiple-day meeting, the meeting planner will want to have a trusting relationship with the sales and operational staff of the hospitality property for the expertise they have to offer. Relationship buyers may be less experienced in the selection of the hospitality product and service, therefore they are likely looking for a trusted partner to help them make the right choice. These types of buyers look to the hospitality salesperson to guide them toward the product and service options that will best satisfy their needs. But to sell a solution, the hospitality salesperson must have the knowledge that is acquired by studying the hospitality organization they represent. This knowledge includes geographic information, physical building information, experiential information, price information, amenities available, other services in-house or nearby, what awards or honors the facility has received, and what the guest mix of the hospitality organization is. It is important to note that successful hospitality salespeople do not persuade the customer to buy based on this information. What's important in developing this knowledge of the characteristics of the hospitality property is to learn how to offer them so that they are solutions to the customers' problems.

Geographic information about your property includes information such as address and general location within the city, the distance to airports and other transportation, local transportation offerings, and routes to the property from other nearby cities. The physical building information includes the

Smartphone apps are frequently used to locate hospitality products such as hotels.

© LanKogal/Shutterstock.com

number of guestrooms if it is a hotel, the number of seats if it is a restaurant, the number and type of meeting spaces and banquet facilities, and the age of the facility. For hotels, it is very important for the salesperson to know how many rooms contain various bed configurations. This includes how many king-bedded rooms, double-bedded rooms, and suites are available. The age of the facility also becomes important if renovations have been completed. Other physical attributes include square footage of guestrooms and meeting spaces, location of food and beverage services, and the number of floors or levels of the facility. For convention facilities, the number of loading docks, ceiling height, and spaces without obstructions can be other features of interest.

Experiential information can include the décor of the various public, meeting, and guestroom spaces, and how the guest interacts with such spaces. Further, the experiential information can include information about themed restaurants and bars, specialized sports facilities (in-house and nearby), and other attractions near the hospitality facility that could augment the experience the guest has in-house. Experiential information can also include services available. For example, at resorts, children's programs and recreational training classes are held for those interested in various athletic activities. Many restaurants offer a chef's table, where special guests or VIPs can be served themed menus prepared by the head chef. Price information includes room rates and meeting space rental rates, but also includes other information on how these rates are applied. For example, room rates for groups will be based on the size of the group, the total amount being spent, and other variables that are advocated by the revenue manager. This can apply to catered events; for example, if a minimum amount is not spent for food and beverage, meeting room rental is applied.

Describing the amenities available can include things such as the number of food and beverage outlets, the amount of parking available, including valet and covered parking where available, amenities in the guest rooms, and amenities in meeting spaces. Amenities in the guest rooms include the quality of linens, quality of bath products, technologies available (Wi-Fi, flat screen TVs, smartphone charging stations, and other newer technologies), in-room dining availability and menus, and other unique aspects of the guest rooms that could be attractive to the guest. Amenities in the meeting space could include the technologies available, the types of tables and chairs available for set-up, staging and lecterns, and guest comforts that would be appealing to customers. While many of the amenities described here pertain to hotels and resorts, restaurants and conference and convention centers include similar amenities or unique services that are attractive to the potential customer. Other services in-house or nearby can include business services such as printing, faxing, and email; child care; doctors on call; airport/city shuttle; laundry; and dry cleaning,

At the beginning of this chapter, we stated a common phrase, *"people buy from people they like and people they trust."* That goes as well for the hospitality organization they are buying from. Because there are so many hospitality organizations offering similar products and services, sometimes information about the organization itself can be a powerful and convincing influence. For example, local, regional, and national awards won by the organization help to present the organization as one with renowned expertise. The 21st annual "Fortune 100 Best Companies to Work for" recently listed Kimpton, Hyatt, Hilton, Marriott, and Four Seasons based on workplace culture. Kimpton and Joie de Vivre, among others, have been identified for their sustainability efforts. Kimpton, Hilton Garden Inn, Ritz Carlton, and others have been recognized by the J.D. Power organization for their top rankings in guest satisfaction. When customers know that the organization they are considering has values like their own, and has been recognized for high performance, there is a confidence that future performance will be equally as superior. The hospitality salesperson uses this information to make the case for why the prospective customer should choose the hospitality organization that the salesperson represents.

The Mobil Guide evaluates hotels using a system of one to five stars, with five stars being the best.

Hospitality sales managers can uncover their competition by asking their colleagues. General managers, sales coordinators, front office staff, revenue managers, service staff, and other sales managers can all be enlightening as to who the competition is. Of course, customers are the main source of information on the competitive marketplace. Competitors can be direct or indirect. **Direct competition** can have similar product offerings, ratings by third parties, pricing, and a nearby location. Resorts, convention centers, and destinations compete on similar features as described, even though they are not geographically close to each other. **Indirect competition** is typically in a nearby location, but does not offer identical services. For example, an

© Andrii Yalanskyi/Shutterstock.com

TABLE 1. COMMON HOSPITALITY PRODUCT / SERVICE / ORGANIZATION ATTRIBUTES

- Physical Property Condition
- Length of Time in Business
- Year of Last Renovation
- Property Décor
- First Impression (Curb Appeal)
- Lobby/Entry Area (Second Impression)
- Hotel Guest Room Quality
- Meeting Space Comparison
- Ceiling Height
- Lighting Quality
- Square Footage
- Ownership of Chairs, Tables, etc.
- Union versus Non-Union
- Service Personnel to Guest Ratios
- Property Location
- Accessibility (Airports, Other Transportation, Highways)
- Awards, Recognition
- Staff Quality/Awards
- Food and Beverage Quality
- Number of Food and Beverage Outlets
- Other Amenities (Recreational)
- Other Amenities (Convenience)

Airbnb would be an indirect competitor for a lodging property because they offer the same core product. Hospitality salespeople should consider the following questions when evaluating the top competition:

1. What other hospitality organization does our organization lose business to?
2. Where do we send customers whom we cannot accommodate?
3. Who do we monitor for daily performance?
4. Who is most similar in terms of product offering?
5. Who are we most fearful of in terms of a strategy change?

Other things that the hospitality sales manager should consider include what third party awards the competition have won compared to the organization the salesperson represents. In the case of hotels and restaurants, the brand can be a factor to consider. Ownership and management structure can also be a point of comparison. Another element of evaluation for competition is the amount of positive press they receive. If the competition has professional, energized management and staff, it can be an indicator of how hard the sales manager will be required to work to achieve success. Finally, how well does the competition negotiate? Do they match rates and product offerings? The table below considers some of the things a hospitality salesperson should evaluate about their competition:

Much of the information about competitors can come from other sources as well. For example, the hospitality salesperson can learn quite a bit just by looking online at the hospitality organization's website. Other online services such as TripAdvisor, Yelp, and Foursquare can be a means by which comments from customers can aid the sales manager in understanding the competition. Looking at the competition's marketing materials can help the hospitality sales manager to understand what the competition is focusing on. Finally, hospitality sales managers should "shop" their competition by taking a tour or sampling food and beverage services. Many times, the competition is eager to take competitor sales managers on property tours to show off their properties. Needless to say, competition in the world of hospitality is very keen. It is important for the hospitality salesperson to know the competition – it is just as important as knowing the prospective customer. Hospitality salespeople should not fear the competition, but rather welcome it; it helps the organization stay on its toes. Appreciating why customers like the competition helps the hospitality salesperson anticipate customers' needs and objections.

Hospitality salespeople should take all of the information they have collected and translate it into a **competition analysis worksheet** which compares the property the salesperson represents with those of the top three competitors. In rating the competition, the salesperson should identify those that are better than the property the salesperson represents, those that are the same, and those that are worse than the property the salesperson represents. Typically, the items of comparison are those that are most important to the customer but they can include the items listed in the table above. The table below is an example of some of the items that a hospitality salesperson might use to analyze the competition.

COMPETITOR ANALYSIS WORKSHEET

Competitive Attributes	Our Hospitality Organization	First Competitor	Second Competitor	Third Competitor
Product				
Room Quality				
Food Quality				
Service Standard				
Company				
Brand/Reputation				
Facilities				
Staff Quality				
Salesperson				
Knowledge				
Responsiveness				
Honesty/Integrity				

Positioning

Having knowledge of the competitors for the salesperson's hospitality products and services is another important element of the preparation process. Competitors are not always selling the same products; many hotels rely on wedding groups for overnight hotel room business. Airbnb has cut into that market segment by offering overnight accommodations to family members at more reasonable prices. Knowing who the competition is and distinguishing the strengths and weaknesses of their product and service offerings helps the hospitality salesperson differentiate and add value for the organization they represent. Known as **positioning**, such knowledge aids the salesperson in providing answers that build the case for why the represented organization is a better selection. The **value proposition** is the positioning statement that clarifies to the prospective customer what advantage they will gain by selecting the organization the hospitality salesperson represents over the competition.

To create the value proposition for the customer, hospitality salespeople work hard to understand what matters most to their prospective customers. Another way of looking at it is to remember that customers want to know what's in it for them. Hospitality sales managers use a **feature** and **benefit** approach to describe how a prospective customer will be satisfied with what the hospitality organization has to offer. While features and benefits are critical to the successful sale, benefits justify why the customer should choose the products and services the hospitality salesperson represents.

Features can be defined as the characteristics or attributes of the hospitality facility and organization. For hospitality products and services, this can be anything that the customer can see, feel, taste, hear, or measure. For example, in a hotel, the number of guest rooms, the square footage of the meeting space, and the type of restaurants would be considered product features. In a restaurant, the type of menu or cuisine offered, number of seats, and function space square footage would be examples. Examples in a convention center would be the square footage, ceiling height, number of loading docks, and the size of a space without columns. Product features are typically offered on websites, brochures, and other marketing materials. Young hospitality salespeople typically emphasize features, overloading the prospective customer with too much information. Savvy hospitality sales managers call this "feature puking"; it is seen many times as part of property tours where many amenities are presented, but never in relation to how the customer will benefit.

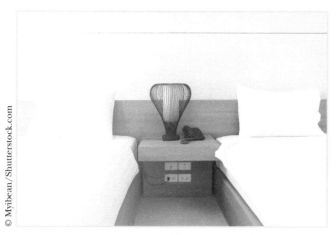
Hotel room with twin beds

Benefits are the result of what a hospitality product or service can do for the customer. Products and service benefits satisfy the needs and buying objectives that prospective customers are seeking. Benefits can appeal to emotions; for example, the appropriate guest-to-service ratio for banquets will help ensure that the wedding reception will go off smoothly. Benefits can also appeal to the rational buyer; the square footage of the meeting space will accommodate the multiple-day meeting. The number of guest rooms with two beds at this hotel will accommodate the large number of youth group attendees.

Features and benefits should not be confused with an **advantage**. Advantages describe what the feature does to benefit the prospective customer. For example, a high number of loading docks at the convention center will allow the trade show materials to be dropped off efficiently, which means that the trade show will be erected on time or early. A large number of guest rooms with two beds would help save youth group meeting attendees money through shared room rates. Advantages can be part of the sales materials, and salespeople should regularly bring them to the attention of the customer. Advantages are also called **general benefits**, because they are easily recognized and can be of benefit to any prospective customer. **Specific benefits** meet specific needs of the prospective buyer. Hospitality salespeople work to understand what the customer's **buying motivations** are in order to present the features and

TABLE 2. FEATURE BENEFIT WORKSHEET

Feature	Benefit (*this means...*)
High capacity high speed wireless internet in the meeting rooms	The large number of attendees will not experience slow service
All guest rooms have been renovated with the inclusion of 48-inch LED televisions	Guests will find the rooms clean, attractive, and comfortable
The hotel is centrally located on the university campus with free parking	Guests and visitors will be able to access all parts of the campus conveniently without costly parking fees
The restaurant has been recognized nationally for its cuisine for three out of the past four years	Guests will have an outstanding experience with appetizing meals
The convention center is LEED Platinum certified	Guests can be satisfied in knowing that the convention center reduces the carbon footprint

corresponding benefits of the product and services of the hospitality organization that lead to the sale. Buying motivations can be summarized as one of three general themes: fear, need, and greed. Below is a table that can be used to assess features and benefits.

When hospitality salespeople are presenting features and benefits to prospective customers, a statement that links the feature with the benefit is used. This statement assists the salesperson in helping the prospective customer connect the benefit they will derive with the specific feature that provides the benefit. Phrases such as "so that," "which means," "this means," and "as a result" are all examples of connector phrases that link features and benefits in a way that helps customers understand how they will realize a satisfaction of their buying motivation.

There are two components to presenting products and services. First, the salesperson can present the features and benefits that will address the customer's needs, greed, or fears. Second, the salesperson can differentiate their hospitality organization from to the competition. As previously mentioned, this is called positioning. What this means is that the salesperson must deliver a compelling idea that is as simple as possible for the prospective customer to understand. It is a must that the salesperson clearly understands what is most important to the customer, and then stays on message to ensure that the differentiating message is clear in the customer's mind.

Hospitality products and services can be positioned based on four basic ideas. A product or service can be first in the marketplace. Another positioning idea is that these products and services can be better than all competitors in the marketplace. A third idea is that the hospitality product or service can have the largest reach in the marketplace by being the biggest. Finally, hospitality products and services can be positioned as different than the competitors in the marketplace. Each of these strategies must be based on a simple idea that the customer can readily understand. Most salespeople use the different positioning strategies to distinguish their hospitality organization from the competition.

Using the "different" positioning approaches listed above, the salesperson can organize various ideas in such a way that the customer's needs and wants will be satisfied. While these approaches are different, they take advantage of the other primary approaches listed above. There are six means by which the hospitality product or service can be positioned in the mind of the customer. The table below outlines these six steps:

TABLE 3. POSITIONING

Positioning Approach	Positioning Example
Specific product features	Location, indoor swimming pool
Benefits or solutions to stated problems	Reduced travel time to and from airport (location) Relaxation for attendees (indoor pool)
Specific usage occasions	Facility provides ideal location for a wedding
User category	Facility is ideal for executive education
Against another product	This convention center has more square footage space than X competition
Product class dissociation	This restaurant and brewpub event space may seem of lesser quality, but it competes with the finest event spaces in the city

It ought to be clear that positioning should be focused on how the customer will benefit, receive value, or gain from purchasing from the hospitality service or organization that the salesperson represents. By emphasizing price as a differentiating tactic, salespeople weaken the opportunity to be considered *different*, which is the point behind positioning. Unfortunately, there are meeting planners and others who have fewer complex needs that entail a more transactional sale. In these cases, hospitality salespeople should emphasize product and service offerings in a way that helps to minimize costs and still provide quality products and services. With complex sales, more consultation is required on the part of the hospitality salesperson, and therefore there is more opportunity to provide value.

SUMMARY

This chapter focused on being prepared by understanding the hospitality product, service, and competition. "Prepare" is the first of the seven steps in the hospitality sales process. The chapter went on to discuss the four levels of product: core, facilitating, supporting, and augmented. Solution selling was also covered, and direct and indirect competition was reviewed. A competition analysis worksheet was developed. Lastly, positioning and positioning approaches were discussed.

KEY TERMS

core products	relationship buyers	value proposition
facilitating products	direct competition	advantage
supporting product	indirect competition	general benefits
augmented products	competition analysis	specific benefits
solution selling	worksheet	buying motivations
transactional buyers	positioning	

REVIEW AND DISCUSSION QUESTIONS

1. Discuss the difference among core, facilitating, supporting, and augmented products.

2. What is the difference between general benefits and specific benefits?

3. Discuss the difference between direct and indirect competition.

4. What is solution selling?

5. What is the difference between transactional buyers and relationship buyers?

6. How is a competition analysis worksheet used?

7. Discuss different buying motivations.

8. What are the seven steps in the hospitality sales process?

9. Provide examples of experiential information.

10. How can hospitality sales managers uncover information about their competitors?

CHAPTER 8

Gaining Access to the Prospect

Funnel of sales customers prospect vector
© Anatoir/Shutterstock.com

LEARNING OBJECTIVES

- Identify prospects for the hospitality sales organization.
- Describe sources of hospitality prospects.
- Describe the process for qualifying prospects and organizations.
- Explain the components of a prospecting plan.

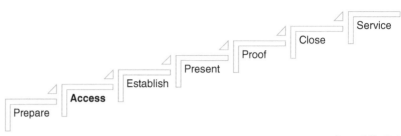

Source: Jeffrey Beck

Prospecting

Successful hospitality salespeople develop and maintain an inventory of prospects for their hospitality products. These prospects can be current customers, former customers, or individuals who have never done business with the hospitality organization. Prospects can also be organizations or accounts. The process of identifying prospective customers is known as **prospecting**. Prospecting is an important part of the hospitality sales process, for without potential customers (prospects) the salesperson cannot bring new business, or repeat business, to the hospitality organization. Believing that current customers will provide adequate repeat business is a very weak assumption by the hospitality salesperson. Prospective and current customers may have needs that change, find the competition to be more attractive, and become more sensitive to price. With changing market conditions repeat customers may purchase less. Customers who are dissatisfied may also leave, causing the need for new business. There are many reasons why potential customers avoid speaking with hospitality salespeople. These include 1) a lack of need because they don't plan events or don't require hospitality services; 2) the timing is off because they have already planned an event with another hospitality organization; 3) prior experience with the organization the hospitality salesperson represents was not positive; 4) the prospect does not perceive the value of the salesperson's product or service; and 5) the prospect is not familiar with the hospitality organization that the salesperson represents.

FIGURE 1. Why Hospitality Sales Managers Prospect

- Many customers have only a one-time need, such as weddings or anniversaries
- Customers change rotation patterns
- Competition takes clients away
- Companies go out of business
- Individual clients leave (promotions, etc.)
- Client dissatisfaction

It is important to bear in mind that prospecting does not lead to immediate sales; the hospitality salesperson must develop a relationship (gain access) before the prospect becomes a customer of the hospitality organization (See Figure 1). As a result, hospitality salespeople must be constantly prospecting to increase sales and replace sales lost. Although it is one of the most important functions of a hospitality salesperson, prospecting is rarely afforded the amount of time necessary to achieve success. Most importantly, salespeople have a fear that they will be rejected by prospects. This fear of rejection comes from a need for approval; at the first sign of "no interest" the salesperson gives up, rather than showing persistence. In most cases, it takes between ten and twelve contacts with a prospect before they become a customer!

New salespeople must remember that they should be spending seventy percent of their time seeking out new customers, and twenty-five percent of their time learning about the hospitality establishment they represent, the products and services they offer, and the market environment in which they find themselves. Therefore, if it takes ten or more strategically planned communications with a prospect, no wonder so much time should be spent on prospecting. In fact, many sales professionals suggest that the tenth sales contact with a prospect should be treated the same as the first; the result is that this **"need for approval" emotion** will subside. It is also important to remember that less than twenty-five percent of the leads that hospitality salespeople identify will become customers. Therefore, it is important for the hospitality salesperson to stay positive. The goal of the "hospitable salesperson" is to generate sales by developing new clients. Therefore, identifying prospective clients is paramount to long-term success in hospitality sales.

The first step in prospecting is to generate **potential prospects** for the hospitality organization. This is the broad market of companies or individuals who have a need for the hospitality product or establishment. As we mentioned in Chapter Six, there are many different markets which the

- Prospecting is about business, and nothing personal

- Block out time to regularly prospect with no distractions

- Set achievable goals

- Learn as much about the prospect as possible

- Have bullet points ready that can be used when leaving a voice message or when at a loss for words.

- Stay positive

FIGURE 2. Tips for Becoming a Professional Hospitality Prospector

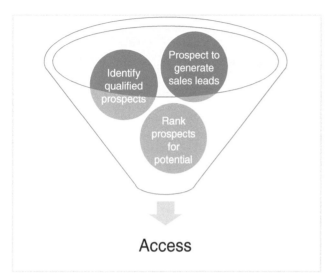

FIGURE 3. Tips for Gaining Access to Prospects

hospitality sales professional could seek out. Each of these markets has different needs, and it is important for the hospitality sales professional to understand what needs of the prospective customer can be best satisfied by what the hospitality product or operation has to offer. Some unique prospecting opportunities for an existing business are things like:

- Reviewing current files for repeat business opportunities

- Business that was lost to competitors in the past

- Business that was turned away because of high occupancy or low capacity

Effective hospitality sales professionals evaluate the leads that they possess to determine which prospects are most likely to buy from the hospitality organization. As mentioned earlier, the evaluation of prospects is what is known as **qualification**. Qualifying a prospect involves considering three elements:

- Does the prospect have a need for the hospitality product or service?

- Does the prospect have the budget or financial ability to purchase the hospitality product or service?

- Does the prospect have the authority or decision-making power to make the purchase decision?

Hospitality sales managers manage their time and sales efforts based on the answers to the questions above. Hospitality sales professionals who take the time to qualify their prospects on these three elements have a greater likelihood of success. Once the hospitality sales professional has addressed these elements with each prospect, a **profile** can be developed that ranks each prospect for the potential of a successful or bountiful sales relationship. Typically, these can be grouped into A sales prospects, B sales prospects, and C sales prospects. As one can see, hospitality sales managers should spend more of their time on A sales prospects than on C sales prospects.

SIX OPEN-ENDED QUESTIONS THAT WILL PRODUCE INSIGHTS WHEN CONDUCTING CUSTOMER INTERVIEWS

1. What do you think of this product?

This question is intentionally vague. While the question seems deceptively simple, it's what you're listening for that matters. The hospitality sales professional should listen to whether the customer talks about wanting to use the product or how it could be improved. Given how vague the question is, the former is positive, while the latter may be a sign that improvement is needed. Because it's so general, it's a good place to start.

2. What is the single thing I can do to make things better for you?

This question is asked as a way to learn, rather than to preach the views of the hospitality sales professional.

3. What should we discontinue doing?

As a hospitality sales professional, you are in the business of creating and improving. Sometimes, subtracting beats adding. Ask yourself, your customers, and your allies this question frequently to remain focused on core competencies. If you can't figure out what you should discontinue doing, it might be an early warning sign that you don't know what your strategy is.

4. Can you give me an example?

If you have an opportunity to drill down into the specifics of a concern, do it. These answers will give the hospitality sales professional hard evidence when they need to support or reject a feature idea.

5. Why? or Why not?

Asking "why" repeatedly might remind the hospitality sales professional of a small child's game, but it's often the way to get down into heart of a particular challenge

6. What bothers you the most about this product?

The sales professional should ask this question to understand the "pain points" of the customer. This is a good question to pair with a few "whys" — some customers may be hesitant to really share their frustrations, but don't let them off the hook. After asking and getting an answer to this question, the sales professional should end up really understanding what gives the customer grief.

Sources of Prospects

There are many different sources and means by which prospecting can occur. A great hospitality salesperson has many methods by which he or she can acquire prospective customers for the hospitality organization.

There are several different prospecting methods that can be used to identify potential hospitality customers. These include cold calling, referrals, introductions through networking, prospects from non-competing salespeople, company databases, and public sources such as the internet. **Cold calling** (making telephone calls to prospects without prior arrangement) is one of the most inefficient and most difficult methods used for collecting prospects. Because rejection comes so easily from cold calling, most salespeople are less likely to use this method than other methods. A popular form of cold calling used by hospitality sales professionals is what's known as a **sales blitz**. The sales blitz technique is less intimidating, because the salespeople drop off promotional materials when visiting office buildings targeted in advance. If hospitality salespeople have referrals that they can use during cold calling, the likelihood of success is increased. A **referral** is a sales lead that is collected from current customers. The most valuable referrals are those where the salesperson can use the name of the of the customer who provided the referral or is personally introduced by the referring person. Hospitality salespeople use various types of **networking** methods for prospecting. One of the most common methods used by hospitality professionals is to join civic and

FIGURE 4. Prospecting Sources

- Travel Agents
- Professional Organizations
- Social Organizations
- Reader Boards
- Convention and Visitors Bureaus
- Chambers of Commerce
- Trade Shows
- News Media
- Trade Publications
- Sports Venues
- Churches
- Funeral Homes
- Internet
- Company Databases
- Hoover's
- Social Media
- LinkedIn
- Facebook
- Geographic Canvassing

professional organizations, clubs, or fraternal organizations. These memberships offer the opportunity for hospitality salespeople to build relationships with other members who may then offer up business leads or business opportunities for the hospitality sales organization. When salespeople from destination marketing organizations (DMOs), also called convention and visitors bureaus (CVBs), offer sales prospects to hotel salespeople, this is an example of sales leads from non-competing sales professionals. Company databases, such as Hoover's, provide a large list of potential prospects. The challenge with company databases, however, is that specific names of individuals who purchase hospitality products and services are not usually listed. **Trade shows** can be an excellent source of prospecting, because the prospects that are collected are pre-qualified based on their interests. In a typical trade show, prospects stop by vendor booths at random, and they may or may not be the person with purchasing authority. A newer form of trade show developed by the IMEX group out of the United Kingdom is the **hosted buyer**. Here, the potential buyer or prospect pre-registers for the trade show and provides documentation that they are qualified to make purchase decisions. In return they are "hosted" by the trade show and receive reimbursement of airfare and hotel costs. In return, the prospect agrees, in advance, to participate in scheduled meetings with vendors who have products that can meet their wants and needs. Even though a hosted buyer trade show is more expensive for the vendors, they like it better than traditional trade shows because they know that they will be meeting with qualified buyers. IMEX America, which is held in Las Vegas, and IMEX Frankfurt each attract over 10,000 meeting and event professionals (See Table 1). Hospitality salespeople also visit their competition to view what businesses are holding meetings and events at their competitors' hotels; they can use this reconnaissance to identify businesses that they may be able to attract to their own hospitality organization.

A hospitality salesperson's plan for prospecting to gain access requires four elements: 1) time management, 2) recordkeeping, 3) confidence, and 4) monitoring. Contact targets must be at the center of the prospecting plan developed by the hospitality salesperson. These contact targets can be defined as the number of new prospects acquired over a period. By keeping good records, the salesperson is not only monitoring performance, but also identifying areas of success, which helps to develop confidence. As we spoke of in the last chapter, confidence is also acquired when the hospitality salesperson has thorough knowledge of the hospitality organization's products and services. By having this knowledge and setting targets for acquiring new prospects, the hospitality salesperson becomes an integral part of the sales success of the hospitality organization.

TABLE 1

IMEX AMERICA 2018
Las Vegas, Nevada, USA
SHOW STATISTICS

Total participants – Including exhibitors, buyers, press, faculty, students:	Total appointments– individual, group, and booth presentations	Individual appointments and booth presentations
13,588	**74,000**	**64,500**

HOSTED BUYERS STATISTICS

3,327

Hosted Buyers from

63 countries

74.5% from USA & Canada

25.5% International

BUYER ATTENDEE STATISTICS

1,102

Buyer attendees from

37 countries

86% from USA & Canada

14% International

EXHIBITOR STATISTICS

3,500

Exhibiting Companies

From 150 Countries

PRESS STATISTICS

132

Press Attendees

From 14 Countries

Trade Show

Photo by George G. Fenich

Collecting Information during Prospecting for Access

Regardless of the techniques used for contacting prospects, there are many pieces of information that the salesperson should collect prior to and during the contact with the prospect. Information that can be collected by sources prior to contact with the prospect include: the type of business (or association), public statistics about the business (or association), the health of the business (or association), and the industry it is in (or represents). Other information about the prospect's business such as mission, vision for the future, competition, and position within the marketplace help the hospitality salesperson to understand the prospect's challenges and speak in an intelligent fashion about the company. By doing so, the salesperson creates an atmosphere that aids in developing a business relationship. Much information can be collected when meeting with the prospect. The smart hospitality salesperson ensures that he or she has the correct spelling and pronunciation of the prospect's name by checking with the administrative assistant or receptionist prior to meeting the prospect. Information that salespeople should collect during the meeting with the prospect include details related to the prospect's title, tenure, and responsibilities within their organization. Other information that salespeople can collect includes: 1) Has the prospect worked with the hospitality organization before? 2) Does the prospect have a favorable opinion of the hospitality organization? and 3) How frequently does the prospect use a hospitality organization? As the reader may notice, all the questions described so far are related to the business or association to which the prospect belongs.

In order to establish a relationship with the prospect beyond business, the hospitality salesperson can use three conversational strategies that allow the prospect to talk about themselves. First, the salesperson can bring up points of interest (hobbies, affiliations, etc.). For example, if the salesperson is meeting the prospect in their office, observing something like a diploma from a university would give the salesperson something to talk about, especially if both of them graduated from the same university. Another example might be the salesperson who says, "I notice from your office that you seem to very involved in aviation. Can you tell me a little more about it?" Another conversational strategy that can uncover information is to make observations about current events. Sports scores, local news, or weather events can be a means by which the salesperson gets to know the

THE MEEC HOTEL	
CUSTOMER PROFILE	
Customer Contact Information	
Name of Business	
Name of Primary Contact	Title
Address	
Telephone	Email
Company General Information	
What Products / Services does company produce?	
What is the history of the company?	
What is the current standing of the company within their industry?	
What hospitality facilities has this company done business with in the past?	
What are the past bookings with the MEEC hotel?	
What future meetings, travel, etc. might the MEEC hotel be able to serve?	
Primary Contact Additional Information	
Other key contacts (assistants, etc.)	
Tenure with current company (including past positions, geographic location, etc.)	
What are the hobbies and interests of each key contact? Are there personality traits to be mindful of?	
What is most important to the primary contact and team members when holding a meeting / event?	
What are the reasons you like to hold your event in our city?	
Other information that aids in developing a relationship:	
Other Information	

FIGURE 5. Customer Profile Sheet for the MEEC Hotel

prospect's communication style. Finally, complimenting the prospect, with specifics of why you are doing so (so that you ARE genuine), can be a another means by which to develop a business relationship with the prospect, and ultimately make the sale.

Planning for the initial contact with a prospect means that the hospitality salesperson must develop skills for establishing a relationship with the

What could you learn about this prospect, based on this office picture?

© fotoret/Shutterstock.com

prospect. When speaking to a customer for the first time it is important to get their permission to ask questions and take notes, so that the salesperson has all the information he or he needs. These guidelines may seem very simple and sound formal, but when you are communicating with a potential client for the first time it communicates respect. When we are talking about sales access it is assumed that the salesperson is sitting face-to-face with the individual. What the salesperson ultimately is trying to do in the first sales communication is to collect information that will help with future elements of the sales process. Clearly, the more familiar the hospitality salesperson is with the prospect, the more likely it is that a relationship will be built, and thus that a sale can be made.

Meeting the Prospect Face to Face

When calling on prospects, the hospitality salesperson must make a strong first impression. Demonstrating expertise, giving the prospect full attention, and smiling upon meeting them all help to provide a solid first impression. Hospitality salespeople know that having a positive attitude with a voice that conveys enthusiasm comes across to prospects favorably. A professional appearance through appropriate grooming and dress demonstrate respect for the prospect and communicate that the salesperson is someone who can be trusted. Little things related to the salesperson's etiquette can help in

© sunabesyou/Shutterstock.com

Presentation of a business card during a sales call

developing rapport with the customer. How do you shake hands? The V of the thumb and index finger of the salesperson meet the V of the thumb and index finger of the prospect. The salesperson looks the prospect in the eye, and they shake hands for no more than two seconds. Handshakes should neither be "limp fish" nor "death grips." If they are wearing a nametag, the salesperson should make sure it is easy to read and placed on the right side of the chest. When shaking hands, it's natural to look to the right. Etiquette dictates the use of Mr. or Ms. with the last name. If the prospect says, "That's OK, please call me by my first name," that's fine. Hospitable salespeople always want to be at the highest level of etiquette, technique, and formality. If you don't know how formal an organization or event is, it is safer to err on the side of formality; you can always adjust your attire to be more casual at the next contact. It is important that the salesperson not come across as cocky or brash. Making eye contact indicates interest and openness; raising the eyebrows slightly in an acknowledgement of the other person reinforces your openness to meeting them. While it may seem cliché, asking if the timing is right for the meeting demonstrates respect for the prospect's time. On the other hand, an effective hospitality salesperson never apologizes for taking a prospect's time; ideally the meeting will be mutually beneficial.

FIGURE 6. Behaviors Undertaken by Hospitality Salespeople that Make a Good First Impression

- Demonstrate Positive Energy
- Seek Common Insterests
- Matching and Mirroring
- Compliments and Praise
- Etiquette
- Small Acts of Kindness

Matching and mirroring is a technique that people use to relate or resonate with the individual. Matching and mirroring is speaking to people in a body language that mirrors what they're doing. If the client is sitting doing a gesture, such as holding the thumb and forefinger on their chin, and the salesperson does a similar kind of gesture. The salesperson must be careful that the behavior is not so blatantly obvious that the client is distracted.

SUMMARY

In summary, this chapter explored the process for gaining access to potential clients through prospecting. Once the hospitality salesperson has gained access and begun to learn about the prospective customer and his or her needs, a sales conversation and a stronger business relationship ensues. In the access phase of the selling process, the hospitality salesperson should be spending 75% of the time listening and 25% of the time talking to the prospective client. In other words, the potential customer should be spending 75% of their time telling the salesperson about themselves, about their business, what their needs and issues are, and where there may be opportunities for the hospitality salesperson to satisfy their needs. By listening and demonstrating respect and interest, the hospitality salesperson begins to establish value for that prospective customer. In the next chapter, we will discuss how the hospitality salesperson establishes the sales dialogue.

KEY TERMS

prospecting	profile	DMOs/CVBs
"need for approval" emotion	cold calling	trade shows
	sales blitz	hosted buyer
potential prospects	referral	matching and
qualification	networking	mirroring

REVIEW AND DISCUSSION QUESTIONS

1. What is prospecting in hospitality sales?

2. Why do hospitality sales managers prospect?

3. Explain the need for approval emotion.

4. What is qualification?

5. Explain what a profile is.

6. Explain some different sources and means by which prospecting can occur.

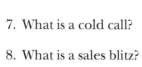

7. What is a cold call?

8. What is a sales blitz?

9. Explain the hosted buyer concept.

10. What is mirroring and matching?

CHAPTER 9

© LDprod/Shutterstock.com

LEARNING OBJECTIVES

- Outline the types of sales communications.
- Explain the use of the three sales dialogue objectives.
- Describe the four elements of the sales contact plan.

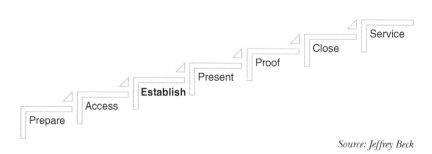

Source: Jeffrey Beck

Introduction

Over time, the hospitality salesperson *establishes* a customer's needs through a well-planned **sales dialogue** by engaging the client through different techniques to collect that information. Prospective customers do buy when they have a need or are dissatisfied, and they do buy when they have a problem or dissatisfaction they wish to resolve. Good hospitality salespeople help buyers to see the importance of resolving a need or dissatisfaction. What is most important for the hospitality salesperson to remember, then, is that people buy the hospitality product or service the salesperson offers because of what it can do for them. There are many aspects to this.

Hospitality salespeople are known for their fondness for talking to people, and this is true! But that is why there are so few great salespeople. A great hospitality salesperson listens more than they speak; they ask questions that allow the sales prospect to share about themselves, their needs, and the companies for which they work. The beauty of this strategy is that the salesperson then gains important knowledge about the prospect, and this knowledge can then be used to help the salesperson later in the selling process. Believe it or not, this is why people who are introverted tend to be great salespeople! They let the prospect do all the talking, uncover valuable information, and then use that information later to present the best options to the customer.

HELPFUL HINT

You should spend twice as much time listening as you do talking

Establishing the sales dialogue is a structured way to navigate from meeting with the prospect to convincing him or her that the hospitality organization the salesperson represents is the best option for the prospect. What great hospitality salespeople remember is that prospects don't buy when they have a problem or are dissatisfied with their current hospitality provider, they *do* buy when that problem or dissatisfaction leads them to seeking resolution. As a result, effective hospitality salespeople seek to understand how the various features or characteristics the hospitality organization offers will resolve the problems or dissatisfactions prospects have.

Types of Sales Communication

As the hospitality salesperson plans for the dialogue with the prospect, he or she must decide on the format, media, and objective for the contact. There are multiple means by which hospitality salespeople communicate with prospects. These formats include "canned" or pre-scripted presentations, written proposals, and sales dialogues with customized presentations. In the world of hospitality sales, customized sales dialogues add the greatest value for the customer/prospect.

Canned presentations consist of scripted sales calls (think of telemarketer calls), presentations that have been memorized (typically experienced at hospitality industry trade shows), and automated presentations (pre-recorded video, audio, or slide productions). Canned presentations are capable of delivering a consistent message which is logical in flow and of high production quality. Questions and concerns can be anticipated in advance, which means that the appropriate responses can be included in the presentation. Unfortunately, canned presentations do not allow for the differences in prospects; the presentation does not vary from customer to customer. This means that the needs and buying motives of the prospect are assumed to be similar to those of others, and the salesperson has little ability to adapt to the unique selling situation in front of them. On the other hand, young salespeople may gain confidence from using a canned presentation. With these types of presentations, over eighty percent of the talking is done by the salesperson. As a result, the interaction is limited, which could reduce the likelihood of a sales relationship, rather than strengthen it.

Written proposals are complete sales presentations in and of themselves. As responses to requests for proposals from meeting planners, written proposals serve to address the needs of the meeting planner and to present the hospitality organization in the best possible light. It is *very* important that the hospitality salesperson do an assessment of the meeting planner's situation before crafting their response to the request for proposal, so that the proposal addresses the buyer's requirements. There are many things the hospitality

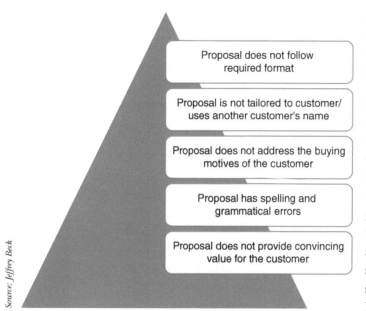

salesperson must remember when crafting a proposal. Figure 1 below lists some pitfalls to avoid if you want to write effective proposals.

Sales dialogues are generally organized with the understanding that it will take more than one contact or communication to accomplish the sale. Before the sales dialogue, the hospitality sales professional organizes a contact plan for use with the prospect. Customized sales dialogues and presentations are best suited to the process of hospitality sales. The intangible nature of the hospitality product and service, along with the varying needs of customers for those products and services, requires the hospitality sales professional to adapt to the sales situation. With customized sales dialogues, the hospitality sales professional becomes more of a *consultant*, and less of a salesperson.

Proposal does not follow required format

Proposal is not tailored to customer/ uses another customer's name

Proposal does not address the buying motives of the customer

Proposal has spelling and grammatical errors

Proposal does not provide convincing value for the customer

Source: Jeffrey Beck

FIGURE 1. Errors to Avoid when Writing Proposals

The Sales Contact Plan

What the sales professional is seeking to accomplish in any sales communication is to *collect* information and *understand* the hospitality customer's buying motives. Based on the answers to those two items, they can then *persuade* the customer that the hospitality organization that the salesperson represents offers the best solution or the best options for what the customer is looking for. That is done through a form of a **feature-and-benefit** methodology. In this sales technique the seller ties every *feature* with an advantage or *benefit* that the customer wants or thinks is desirable. At the end of any sales contact, the salesperson *confirms* the information and understanding acquired. This means that they are in quest of moving forward in the sales process. All of this becomes part of the sales contact plan.

Objectives of the Sales Dialogue

As the hospitality sales professional prepares to dialogue with the prospect, there are three objectives that must be taken into consideration. While these objectives are well known in the advertising industry, they are very important to the sales dialogue as well. Sales is a process, and these objectives arise at different times during the prospect's buying process. Like any communication, when two parties dialogue, there are objectives to be met. These objectives are to provide information, use persuasion techniques, and to remind prospects of the value of the hospitality organization's offerings. These objectives are used at various times during the sales dialogue and may be used in combination or separately.

The first objective of a sales dialogue is to *inform*. This objective is typically used when meeting with a prospect for the first time and is meant to highlight a unique element of the hospitality organization's offerings. Specifically, this is information of which the prospect may be unaware. In this age of internet search engines, prospects can gain much information on their own, so it is important that the hospitality sales professional be prepared with information that is not easily researched by the prospect. Informational sales dialogues work to create awareness about new hospitality organizations (like a newly opened hotel), new product or service offerings (a new menu), or emphasize the commitment to hospitality and service (awards, customer ratings, etc.)

The second objective of a sales dialogue is to *persuade*. A **persuasive sales dialogue** is meant to influence the prospects' opinions, point of view, and buying behaviors toward the hospitality salesperson and the organization he or she represents. With persuasion as the main objective of the sales dialogue, the hospitality salesperson is focused on asking questions to gain understanding, looking for agreement on buying objectives, and with that agreement, asking for the sale. In persuasive sales dialogues, the message of the sales professional is designed to differentiate the represented hospitality product and service from those of the competition. Again, this is done by emphasizing how the prospect will benefit from the offering of the hospitality organization.

The third objective of a sales dialogue is to *remind*. **Reminder sales dialogues** typically come later in the sales process; prospects may have met with salespeople from multiple hospitality organizations. Then, the hospitality sales professional must remind the prospect of the benefits that will be derived from the products and services offered by the organization he or she represents. The sales professional works as a consultant to remind the prospect of the most important buying objectives, or how experience with the hospitality organization led to satisfaction. Reminder messages reinforce earlier sales dialogues and experiences. These messages help to retain customers, which can increase profits to the hospitality organization.

Techniques for Beginning the Sales Dialogue

In the last chapter, we discussed the actions to be taken as the hospitality salesperson gains access to the prospect. In establishing the sales dialogue, hospitality salespeople work to develop a relationship first through social interchange before transitioning into a business discussion. The social discussion is a means by which the hospitality salesperson establishes a **rapport** with the prospect. Rapport is built when mutual trust, a business friendship, and like-mindedness are developed. This is especially true at the beginning of the sales dialogue. The most effective methods for developing rapport are: seeking to uncover common interests or acquaintances, discussing current events or other observations pertinent to the prospect, and recognizing the prospect through compliments for achievements or other areas of realization. It is very important for hospitality salespeople to use **direct eye contact**, smile, and use the prospect's name. This social interchange is many times called **small talk**. It is an important part of the sales dialogue process. The hospitality sales professional should also be mindful of the communication style of the prospect. While some customers like to spend quite of bit of their time making social contact, others wish to "get down to business." In either case, the hospitality sales professional must remember that they are representing both themselves and the hospitality organization they work for. The credibility of the hospitality sales professional is increased through behaviors such as arriving on time for appointments, not wasting the prospect's time, and following up on promises and commitments. It is *very* important that cordiality and kindness are demonstrated by the hospitality sales professional because they emphasize the essence of the hospitality industry.

Once the social interchange has run its course according to cues from the prospect, the hospitality sales professional moves into the **business discussion**. Here, the sales dialogue is intended to transition to the sales contact objectives by capturing the interest of the prospect. The methods for achieving the interest of the prospect vary depending on the sales situation, meeting location, and the number of times the salesperson and the prospect have met. There are five methods by which the salesperson gains the interest of the prospect, as seen in Table 1.

TABLE 1. FIVE METHODS FOR ATTRACTING THE INTEREST OF THE PROSPECT

1) Using an outline
2) Providing a property demonstration
3) Referring to a third party
4) Demonstrating a benefit to the prospect
5) Offering a reward or gift to the prospect at the beginning of the presentation.

Using an outline shifts the conversation from a social visit to the business purpose for the sales contact. The dialogue may go something like this:

Hospitality Salesperson: I am impressed by the number of awards you have won as an outstanding meeting planner. You must be very proud. (social contact/ recognition/compliment).	**Prospect:** Thank you.
Hospitality Salesperson: (pause with a smile) The purpose of my visit today is to take no more than 30 minutes of your time to describe our convention center and the value it provides to meeting planners. Does that agree with your schedule?	**Prospect:** Yes, it does.

The outline method is straightforward, gives the prospect a timeframe, and demonstrates that the hospitality salesperson respects the value and importance of the prospect's time. When the hospitality salesperson must meet with the prospect more than once over a given time, this technique helps the prospect to stay focused.

The **property demonstration** is used later in the sales process; typically, the hospitality salesperson has met with the prospect at least once, and the property demonstration is used as part of a persuasive sales dialogue. In this technique, the hospitality salesperson provides the prospect with a tour of the property, highlighting how features of the property will benefit the event planner and his or her attendees:

Hospitality Salesperson: Our indoor pool and spacious workout facility are perfect for the health-conscious attendees in your group. Will this meet your needs?	**Prospect:** Yes, it will, thank you.

The property demonstration can also be done with pictures and/or video, which adds realism to the demonstration. The beauty of the property demonstration, whether in person or through pictures, is that it gives the prospect a view of the hospitality property that words don't always convey.

Referring to a **third party** is probably one of the strongest methods for capturing the prospect's attention and gives the hospitality salesperson an instant credibility. One of the reasons internet retailers are successful is because of the rating systems that are provided. These ratings are a form of referral, as they come from people similar to the buyer. Further, they offer a trustworthiness that words from a salesperson do not always provide. Referrals are especially powerful when that referral comes from someone whom the prospect knows. Great hospitality salespeople always ask for referrals when working with prospects, whether they close the sale or not:

Hospitality Salesperson: I was speaking with Janet Skowhegan recently, who suggested that I speak with you as someone who plans events for this company.

Prospect: Yes, I do. How do you know Janet?

Hospitality Salesperson: Janet and I went to State College, and were members of the same sorority.

Prospect: I see, yes, I plan meetings for the company. How can your organization help me?

Demonstrating a benefit can gain the interest of the prospect, particularly if the hospitality salesperson is aware of the needs and buying motives of the prospect.

Offering a reward or gift can be the perfect way to capture attention and start a sales conversation. It is important however, that the gift be not perceived as a bribe. Many hospitality salespeople will offer coffee cups filled with candy, or similar types of offerings that are a great way to start off the encounter.

Determining Customer Needs

The effective use of questions to identify customer needs is the single greatest challenge most hospitality salespeople face. The type of questions that the hospitality salesperson asks, the timing of those questions, and how they are posed has an impact on the value the salesperson provides to the prospect.

FIGURE 2. The Sales Dialogue: Time

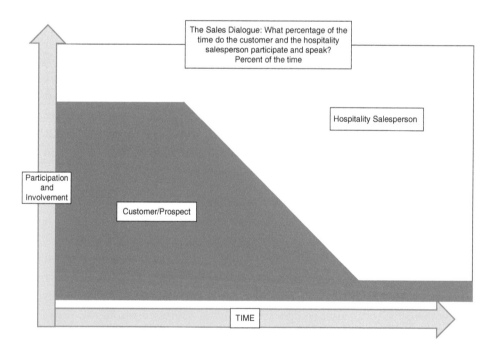

The reason that this is such a challenge is that it is easier to talk than to listen. So, the process for understanding customer needs is to ask a question, demonstrate active listening, and take notes of the prospect's answer. Taking notes allows the hospitality salesperson to record the items that are most important to the prospect and that can be used later when developing the sales presentation. When good notes are taken and the information is used in follow-up dialogue, the prospect learns to trust that the hospitality salesperson listens and understands their needs.

Hospitality Sales Questioning Process

Successful hospitality salespeople must plan in advance of the sales dialogue so that they know what they need to know and the questions they need to ask. A strategy for what type of questions need be asked and how to ask them should be formed prior to the sales contact. While the hospitality salesperson should be in control of the sales contact, this process of asking questions should be done in a manner that allows the prospect to be at ease. This activity should not make the prospect feel as if they are in a courtroom hearing! While asking questions during the sales dialogue, the hospitality salesperson should ask permission to take notes. As the prospect is offering information, the hospitality salesperson should acknowledge and validate the information. This acknowledgment can be a nodding of the head, with a "yes" or "I see." Validation also comes when the hospitality salesperson restates the information that he or she heard and confirms that this information is important.

Well-constructed questions can elicit thoughtful responses from the prospect, and actually help them to think about things that were not considered prior to the sales dialogue. This is what helps make the hospitality salesperson a trusted consultant to the prospective client. By asking questions, the hospitality salesperson takes the prospect through the buying process – the logical steps from the need, to product and service offerings, to options, to agreeing to purchase. Questions are developed based on the outcomes they are meant to achieve. Questions can be created based on the amount of information that is required, or for a specific purpose related to uncovering information from the Beck-Farrar hospitality question model to be discussed later in this chapter.

Questions relating to the amount of information required can be closed-ended, open-ended, or option questions. **Closed-ended questions** help the hospitality salesperson collect specific information and facts. The answers to closed-ended questions are simple and direct. The answers are typically yes or no; the answers are condensed to only a couple of words. These types of questions can be used to confirm the prospect's or the salesperson's understanding of information that was gathered from open-ended questions. It is risky for the hospitality salesperson to rely on closed-ended questions; it stifles the free flow of conversation.

Open-ended questions allow prospects to answer as they wish and give the hospitality salesperson deeper meaning form the prospect's perspective. Open-ended questions allow the hospitality salesperson to probe deeper into understanding the needs of the prospect. Open-ended questions can help the hospitality salesperson control the sales dialogue; when the questions are started with the words "what, where, when, why, and how," the salesperson helps the prospect to concentrate on the deeper information needed to deliver an effective presentation. **Option questions** are used later in the sales dialogue, when the hospitality salesperson is working to uncover the prospect's tastes for various options.

Questions that are of the three types above can also be classified by their use in the sales dialogue. Questions can be used to discover, probe, confirm, and satisfy objectives. **Discovery questions** are used to the uncover the facts surrounding the prospect's needs for the hospitality product. There are general discovery questions, which collect the basic information, and then specific discovery questions, which follow up the general discovery questions to acquire more detail regarding the information provided by the prospect. **Probing questions** are used to collect more detail on a particular issue. While discovery questions collect information, probing questions are used by the hospitality salesperson to uncover the root of a problem (need identification) or clarify a point made earlier by the prospect. **Confirmation questions** are used in the sales process to test the understanding of the prospect of what the hospitality

FIGURE 3. Examples of Types of Questions

Discovery Questions	Probing Questions	Confirmation Questions	Objective Fulfillment Questions
• Where do you hold your meetings? • For what purpose do you hold your meetings?	• What is your experience with the competition? • What is the biggest challenge you face when holding thsi type of meeting	• So you will be having 50 people for your training meeting next month? • Let me summarize the information I have for our last meeting..... Is this correct?	• Do you see how our spacious meeting rooms will meet your needs? • Would be helpful if we were able to have a complimentary reception prior to your meeting?

salesperson said or demonstrated. A specific type of confirmation question, known as the summary confirmation question, is used to verify that the hospitality organization's products and services will satisfy the prospect's needs. **Summary confirmation questions** are best used in multiple-sales-call situations. This type of question is used by the hospitality salesperson to outline previous dialogues and understanding on various points in the sales process. The final type of question, the **objective fulfillment question**, seeks agreement on the part of the prospect that the product and services of the hospitality organization will satisfy his or her buying objectives. When used effectively, this type of question helps to minimize concerns later in the sales and delivery processes.

The Beck-Farrar Hospitality Question Model

There are specific question types hospitality salespeople ask in order to understand the prospect's needs. These questions can be broken down into three categories: 1) technical requirements, 2) buying process requirements, and 3) client motivations. These questions are part of the Beck-Farrar hospitality question model, which seeks to uncover the customer's objectives in purchasing the hospitality product. This model is designed like a spiral staircase; the analogy of going to a higher level of relationship and understanding with the client is achieved when the customer's objectives are uncovered. Those objectives fall into the three categories stated earlier.

Technical requirement questions are the basic information related to the exact date(s) the prospect is looking for; what room, space, and menu prices the prospect is willing to spend; and how much event space, rooms, and seating the meeting planner is looking for. The technical requirement questions are the easiest to ask, because they uncover the essentials of the event or the requirements of the prospect. It is important that the hospitality salesperson doesn't play a game of "Twenty questions" where the prospect feels that he or she is being interrogated. Many of these questions will be answered via email prior to direct contact, or are on a pre-printed form, making it easy for the salesperson to collect the necessary information.

FIGURE 4. Three Categories of Questions

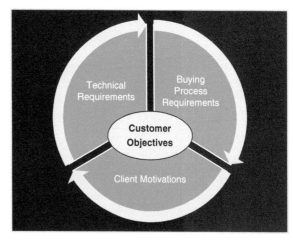

Buying process requirements are any resources that the client uses to make the buying

FIGURE 5. Four Types of Questions

Technical Need Discovery	Question to Ask	Uncovered Objective	Future Benefit *Present* Point
Ask Survey Questions (open and closed-ended)	"How many guest rooms do you need for your meeting? What dates? How many nights?"	Number of sleeping rooms	Convert attributes of requirement to benefit for prospect. (e.g., new bedding)
Listen and Acknowledge Client Response	"So you need 50 guest rooms on October 15th for three nights, with no date flexibility, correct?"	N/A	N/A

decision. These resources can be time, manpower, budget, and past data. The type of information the hospitality salesperson strives find out includes budget, number of decision makers, final decision date, past event locations (if applicable), and what competition is being considered. The information collected here also tells the hospitality salesperson a lot about the client's tastes and true budget. Hospitality salespeople sometimes rush through the buying process questions, when in fact they can acquire information that will help them make a winning presentation.

FIGURE 6. Types of Questions to Ask

Buying Process Discovery	Question to Ask	Uncovered Objective	Future Benefit *Present* Point
Ask Probing Questions	"Tell me about the meeting attendees."	The profile of the attendee, including demographic, organizational status, travel experience	"Our property is perfect for the midlevel accountants, who may be price/value sensitive"
Listen and Acknowledge Client Response	"So, it sounds like the meeting's attendees are accountants, who have been in their jobs 5 years, and whose boss is price sensitive. Is that correct?"	N/A	N/A

Client Motivation Discovery	Question to Ask	Uncovered Objective	Future Benefit *Present* Point
Ask Probing Questions (open-ended questions)	"What business objective(s) does upper management hope to accomplish with this event?"	The underlying/ implicit reason the event is being held.	"The vast amenities at our property will leave your attendees rejuvenated to face tough times ahead."
Listen and Acknowledge Client Response	"It appears that your team wants to ensure attendees walk away motivated and energized for a tough second half of the year. Is that true?"	N/A	N/A

FIGURE 7. Ask and Listen

Client motivations are the meeting objectives and business outcomes that paramount to the success of the event. These motivations are subjective in nature, and 110% client focused. When asking questions related to the client's motivations, the hospitality salesperson is asking what the prospect is trying to accomplish or solve. Information that is collected at this stage covers elements such as the purpose of the event, the status of the attendees, what the implications are for the prospect's organization, and what kind of environment or feeling the client would like attendees to experience during the event. Hospitality salespeople can set themselves apart from their competition when they ask questions related to this information; it shows the prospect that they really care. When the hospitality salesperson asks these types of questions, it sets the hospitality organization up to be a partner with the prospect and his or her organization!

Being a Trusted Consultant: Listening

There are many types of questions that can be asked to help the hospitality salesperson understand the needs and buying objectives of the prospect. But without effective listening, the hospitality salesperson will not achieve any success. **Effective listening** is one of the hospitality salesperson's most critical skills. Effective listening is listening for deep understanding of all of the information that the prospect is imparting, both with their words and with their body language.

The hospitality salesperson must concentrate, take notice of nonverbal behaviors, and acknowledge and confirm understanding of the words and meaning the prospect provides. This technique is what is known as **active listening**. When paying attention, the goal is to listen for understanding. Rather than focusing on the prospect's words and meaning, many hospitality salespeople struggle to not reply to every statement the prospect makes. When a hospitality salesperson is actively listening, eye contact and nodding of the head for acknowledgment are important. When confirming understanding, paraphrasing the prospect's statement in other words helps to verify that what was heard was what was said. Finally, notes should be taken to prevent forgetting important information that will be useful later. Prior to taking notes, the hospitality salesperson asks permission to take notes, or advises the prospect that he or she will be taking notes. Taking careful notes conveys the message that the information the prospect is providing is valuable; asking permission first helps build confidence in the prospect that the hospitality salesperson has their best interest in mind.

Establishing Buying Objectives from the Sales Dialogue

The process we have described in the chapter is sometimes called **need discovery**. The objective of the sales dialogue, as we have stated, is to uncover the needs of the prospect. These needs can then be converted into what is known as the buying objectives of the prospect. These buying objectives are the three-to-five objectives the prospect must achieve in order to complete the sale. Buying objectives can be broken down into three categories: 1) Must-have objectives, 2) Like-to-have objectives, and 3) Nice-to-have objectives. For example, a meeting planner must have a hotel close to the city's airport. So, proximity to the airport would be one of the three-to-five things the hospitality salesperson and their hotel must offer as a solution. The meeting planner might like to have a separate check-in desk for the group they represent. Like-to-have items in certain circumstances can be as important as must-have buying objectives. Like-to-have buying objectives help to separate competitors, when all other items are equal. Nice-to-have buying objectives are desirable but not necessary. An example of a nice-to-have objective might be an indoor waterpark.

In hospitality sales, small meetings that are not very complex are quite common. As a result, the person planning that meeting is more of a **transactional buyer**. This means that they are strictly focused on the technical requirement buying objectives discussed in the Beck-Farrar model. Transactional buyers do not require a consultative approach to the sales dialogue; much of the information the hospitality salesperson could offer the prospect has already been collected through internet resources. Most of the time, dates and rates are the most important pieces of information the salesperson can provide.

Once the most important buying objectives have been uncovered, the sales dialogue moves from need to discovery to presentation. This is impacted by the complexity of the product and service solutions the hospitality salesperson has to offer. With transactional or not very complex buyers, the hospitality salesperson offers suggestions that can lead to immediate purchase. With more complex requirements, the hospitality salesperson becomes more of a consultant and delivers a presentation which addresses the buying objectives of the prospect. In the next chapter, we will cover the hospitality sales presentation.

SUMMARY

The focus of this chapter is on establishing the sales dialogue. It began with a discussion of the sales dialogue. It then moved to types of sales communications, the sales contact plan, and objectives of the sales dialogue. The different techniques for beginning the sales dialogue were shared. Determining customer needs was discussed along with the sales questioning process. The chapter concluded with a discussion of a transactional buyer.

KEY TERMS

sales dialogue	small talk	confirmation questions
canned presentations	business discussion	summary confirmation
feature-and-benefit	property	questions
sales technique	demonstration	objective fulfillment
persuasive sales	third party	questions
dialogue	closed-ended questions	effective listening
reminder sales	open-ended questions	active listening
dialogues=	option questions	need discovery
rapport	discovery questions	transactional buyer
direct eye contact	probing questions	

REVIEW AND DISCUSSION QUESTIONS

1. Outline the types of sales communication.

2. Explain the use of the three sales dialogue objectives.

3. Describe the four elements of the sales contact plan.

4. Describe the feature-and-benefit sales technique.

5. What is the difference between a persuasive sales dialogue and a reminder sales dialogue?

6. What is the difference between closed-ended questions and open-ended questions?

7. Explain the differences among discovery questions, probing questions, and confirmation questions.

8. What is the difference between confirmation questions and objective fulfillment questions?

9. Explain effective listening as compared to active listening.

10. What is a transactional buyer?

CHAPTER 10

© LDprod/Shutterstock.com

LEARNING OBJECTIVES

- Define features, benefits, and linking statements.
- Explain the link between establishing the sales dialogue and presenting the product.
- Create benefit statements as a result of need discovery.
- Explain the use of each presentation technique.

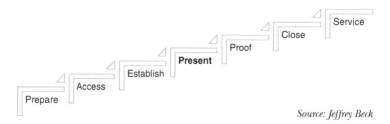

Source: Jeffrey Beck

Introduction – The Importance of the Hospitality Sales Presentation

This is where the sales dialogue moves to the "main stage," and the hospitality salesperson begins to show how the hospitality products and services they represent will benefit the potential customer (**prospect**). The hospitality sales presentation requires preparation, knowledge, and skill. Without the information collected in the sales dialogue, it is impossible for the hospitality salesperson to make a presentation that offers a solution that is specific and customized to the prospect's needs. Presentations can be very simple for the transactional buyer; we provide an informational sheet, ask technical questions, and ask for the sale (See Figure 1). In this chapter, the elements of a presentation for the complex hospitality sale will be the basis for the discussion.

In the last chapter, the process in Figure 1 was used to illustrate how the hospitality salesperson works to uncover the must-have buying objectives of the prospect. Uncovering these buying objectives helps the salesperson construct the foundation of their sales presentation. It cannot be emphasized enough that the hospitality salesperson must completely understand the prospect's needs and buying objectives before making the presentation. During the presentation, the hospitality salesperson then confirms that the buying objectives and needs that they have identified are truly the most important for the client. These buying objectives are typically five percent technical requirements, ten percent buying process, and eighty-five percent client motivations. Knowing this ratio helps the hospitality salesperson present solutions that characterize benefits that the prospect will receive or experience. It is important that interaction between the prospect and the hospitality salesperson is a dialogue.

FIGURE 1. Steps for the Transactional Buyer

The salesperson should be asking questions of agreement so that he or she stays on track with the customer. No presentation can be effective without materials or **props** that help support the solutions offered and the benefits stated. However, sales aids, technology, and other materials should never overpower the

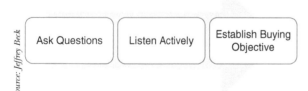

Source: Jeffrey Beck

presentation. The presentation should always focus on how the prospect will benefit from the products and services the hospitality organization has to offer.

Prospects buy for multiple reasons; they seek satisfaction for any number of challenges they face. What is most important for the hospitality salesperson is to prioritize these buying objectives to the three-topfive objectives that can be best solved by the hospitality product or service. A hospitality product and service can have many excellent characteristics – what are known in the sales vocabulary as **features**. It is important that those features be aligned with what the prospect is looking for. What the prospect is looking for is how he, she, the attendee, or the organization will **benefit** from what the hospitality organization's features have to offer. By linking features and benefits through carefully crafted statements, the hospitality salesperson helps the prospect to realize the incentives to buying from the hospitality organization the salesperson represents.

Describing Features

Features are the underlying attribute or characteristic that addresses the prospect's buying objective. Features are the facts behind the product or service; the objective qualities of the hospitality product and the tangible aspects of the service provided. It could be said that features are boring because they don't bring life to the product or tell a story. Features are the measurable and verifiable pieces of information that assist the prospect in making an objective decision. Features are the elements of the product that can be seen, heard, felt, touched, and thus measured. As a result, once the hospitality salesperson establishes what is important to the prospect (buying objectives), he or she can then identify the features that best satisfy those objectives (See Figure 2).

Offering Benefits

Benefit statements describe how the features selected by the hospitality salesperson achieve the prospect's buying objectives. Benefit statements can be defined as what the prospect will gain or will receive or will experience from using the product or service. Benefits tell the story of how the feature will satisfy the prospect's need (i.e., "blow life" into fulfilling the desires of the prospect). There

FIGURE 2. Products vs. Services

Products
- Rooms
- Meeting Spaces
- Food and Beverage Outlets
- Recreation Facilities
- Loading Docks

Services
- Concierge Service
- Self Service Beverage Stations
- Check In Kiosks
- Late Housekeeping Services
- Technology Services

Source: Jeffrey Beck

is a cliché that is worth mentioning here: "Features tell, benefits sell." Most importantly, benefits statements provide value and a context to the hospitality product and service offering. Benefit statements enhance the ability of the hospitality salesperson to close the sale. Think of benefits and their link this way: people don't buy a red (feature) convertible (feature) car for the color and soft top. They buy the red convertible car so that when they drive down the highway, the feel special and are noticed. So, the features of the car benefit the ego of the driver. One must recognize that the needs that benefits satisfy fall into a variety of categories. They can be related to the safety and security of the prospect and his or her attendees and their belongings. They may appeal to the social needs of the prospect; social catering is the perfect example of how hospitality salespeople interest prospects who are planning weddings, family gatherings, and other types of social events. Like the example of the car above, benefit statements can appeal to the ego or add to the reputation of the prospect. As you may have noticed, these are three of the five needs identified by A.H. Maslow in his famous book *A Theory of Human Motivation* (1943). Using benefit statements is at the core of hospitality sales.

It is important that the hospitality sales professional understands the buying objectives the prospect is seeking. The reason for this is that the focus should always be on specific benefits the prospect is seeking. Common benefits applied to the features of the hospitality product and service do not add value and context to the particular benefits linked to the buying objectives of the individual prospect. Hospitality salespeople who are successful link the specific benefits of the product or service that the prospect has stated as a need. Again, this is the foundation of hospitality sales; the case for buying from the hospitality organization is built by focusing on specific benefits.

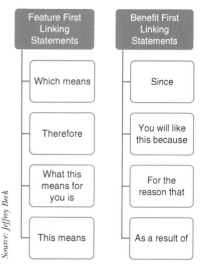

FIGURE 3. Feature Statement vs. Benefit Statements

Source: Jeffrey Beck

Linking Features and Benefits

Effective hospitality salespeople link the specific benefits sought by the prospect with the feature the hospitality product or service has to offer. These linking statements or words help to guide the prospect to a logical and beneficial conclusion. Another way of thinking of linking statements or words is that they convert hospitality organization attributes into a value context for the potential buyer. By using these linking statements, the hospitality salesperson guides the prospect to the conclusion that he or she will benefit in a way that the prospect seeks. When the benefit is presented before the feature, words that demonstrate the reason for the benefit are used in the linking statement (See Figure 3).

Prevent Feature Overload

Young hospitality salespeople, or those who are not confident in their abilities to ask questions and establish a sales dialogue, have the need to demonstrate their knowledge of the hospitality product and services they represent. As a result, they tend to "**feature spit**" everything they know about the product and services, without considering specific benefits or linking general benefits to the features they "spit" on the client. This type of behavior can be common during a property tour. The salesperson is proud of what they have to offer in the property and its services. As a result, they want to show everything rather than considering the prospect's needs. When a hospitality salesperson behaves in this fashion, they waste both the prospect's and their own time. Three-to-five well-selected features linked to benefits the prospect is seeking are far better than a dozen features and or benefits rolling off the tongue.

ACTIVITY: Identifying Benefits Based on a Feature

Using Table 1 below as a worksheet, create linking and benefit statements for the uncovered objective and features listed.

TABLE 1. LINKING FEATURES AND BENEFITS WORKSHEET

Linking Features and Benefits			
Uncovered Objective	Feature	Linking Statement	Benefit Statement
Efficient Dinner Service	One-to-Fifteen Service Ratio	which means	Your guests will receive a lovely and professional dining experience
Convenient Airport Location	Hotel is Six Blocks from the Airport		
Spacious Conference Facilities	Meeting Rooms can Accommodate from 10 to 1000 people		
Comfortable Guest Rooms	Rooms Have Recently Been Renovated		

The Presentation Process

Based on where the prospect is in the buying process, there are different techniques and formats that can be used to communicate features and benefits. Each technique has specific goals and objectives as part of the sales contact. The contact with the prospect can follow many formats. What separates

FIGURE 4. The
Presentation Process

Identify Needs
• Ask Questions
• Use Active Listening Techniques
• Confirm Buying Objective

Select Feature
• Match Buying Objective and Benefit Derived
• Verify Comprehension
• Deliver Benefit Statement

Presentation Technique
• Informational
• Persuasive
• Reminder

Source: Jeffrey Beck

the successful hospitality salesperson from his or her competitors is the quality of the benefit statements presented. The presentation method used is the result of the activities discussed in Chapter Nine and this chapter. The hospitality salesperson asks questions to identify needs, uses active listening to confirm comprehension of the prospect's needs, and confirms the most important buying objectives. Once the buying objectives have been confirmed, the hospitality salesperson selects the characteristics of the hospitality facility and services that best match the buying objectives. Once defined, these features are then translated into benefit statements that satisfy the prospect's buying objectives. The final component of the presentation process, then, is the technique with its accompanying objective: to inform, persuade, or remind.

EXHIBIT 5. PRESENTATION COMPONENTS

Enhancements	Techniques	Outcomes
Two-Way Communication	Property Tours	Realized Benefits
Trust	Interactive Portfolios	Preempt Concerns
Confidence in the Hospitality Salesperson	Strategic Selling Materials	Make the Sale
	Testimonials	Encourage Action from the Prospect

Source: Jeffrey Beck

Hospitality sales presentations should be conducted in such a way that action by the prospect is required as a result of the presentation. In order for the prospect to act, the presentation should be assembled in a distinct, easy-to-follow plan. By creating such a presentation structure, the hospitality salesperson makes it easy for the prospect to make the right decision. Need-satisfaction presentations are the approach where the hospitality salesperson and the prospect develop a win-win relationship because the hospitality salesperson is demonstrating how the prospect's needs can be satisfied (See Figures 4 and Exhibit 5).

Presentation Formats

Presentation formats are dependent upon how the prospect has contacted the hospitality salesperson. The written word through a letter, email, or **request for proposal (RFP)** is defined as an **asynchronous presentation** format. Asynchronous presentations can be the first communication between the prospect and the salesperson. This format, when initiated by the prospect, may indicate a **transactional buying process**. It can be difficult with asynchronous communication, and particularly with an RFP, to infer how the hospitality salesperson's communication will be interpreted. Further, with written communication, there is no guarantee that the receiver/prospect will read it completely or understand the meaning of the communication. On the other hand, written letters can be an attention getter, since fewer sales communications come in the form of a letter. The asynchronous presentation format is characterized by the fact that there is no immediate feedback; a delay can occur that prevents the development of a business relationship. If communication is initiated by the prospect, the prospect has complete control of how the communication takes place, and influence on the part of the hospitality salesperson is limited. On the other hand, asynchronous presentations provide an easy way to deliver information in a low-cost manner. Because of the speed with which asynchronous presentations are delivered, they can be an effective use of time by the hospitality salesperson. It is important that the hospitality salesperson is technically adept at using email and/or social media for the presentation. Most importantly, the hospitality salesperson must pay attention to the details by checking spelling and grammar, including requested information, and using quality pictures and graphics to convey the information. Using a template, rather than customizing the communication to the receiver, is a common mistake by less successful hospitality salespeople. Failure to follow these guidelines can result in the prospect disregarding the hospitality salesperson's asynchronous presentation.

FIGURE 5.
Asynchronous vs.
Synchronous
Presentations

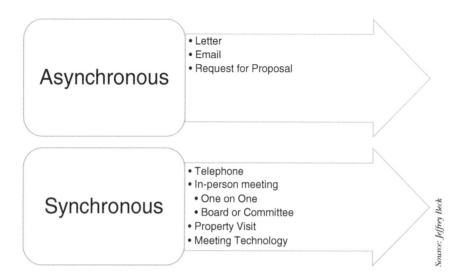

Source: Jeffrey Beck

Synchronous presentations in hospitality sales are face-to-face real-time presentations by hospitality sales professionals. With a synchronous presentation, there is an element of control on the part of the hospitality salesperson. Because there is real-time feedback through questions, body language, and other clues, the hospitality salesperson can respond appropriately. Synchronous presentations are often more influential and persuasive for both parties, since both the hospitality salesperson and the prospect are communicating in real time. Clearly, the best type of synchronous presentation is the property visit, where the hospitality salesperson takes the prospect on a tour of the facility. The use of technology, such as Zoom, Skype, GoToMeeting, or BlueJeans, is becoming more popular, and the hospitality salesperson should not underestimate their use. These types of presentations foster a relationship, help to create ownership on the part of the prospect, and enhance the opportunity for negotiation. Face-to-face presentations can be a powerful tool in getting the prospect to act. There is another old adage: hospitality salespeople don't get that many at-bats in the game, so it is important to maximize the swings given. Synchronous presentations are most powerful in getting the prospect to consider purchasing from the hospitality organization (See Figure 5).

Presentation Techniques

There are three different presentation techniques that are used at different times during the customer's buying process. These techniques are **informative presentations**, **persuasive presentations**, and **reminder presentations**.

All three techniques are based on the prospect's buying objectives which have been uncovered through questions and investigation. A prospect's needs can be stated as a response to questions, or through tacit information collected prior to, during, or after the need-discovery process.

Informative presentations put an emphasis on facts. In the hospitality industry, this presentation technique is best used for a new or newly renovated property. It can also be used with newly enhanced hospitality services. If a hotel has been rebranded, the informational presentation technique is best used to enlighten prospects about new developments. Informational presentations must be tempered with simplicity and intelligibility. It is very easy for hospitality salespeople to share too much information, thereby missing the opportunity to directly inform the prospect based on their buying objectives. Prospects may give the hospitality salesperson clues, such as "we are looking to make a change," or "we are looking to upgrade." These types of clues indicate that the prospect is looking for additional information to compare their current hospitality solution with the other options in the marketplace. With this information, it is best if the hospitality salesperson presents precisely to the buying objectives the prospect is seeking to compare.

Persuasive presentations seek to influence the prospect to act – to buy the hospitality salesperson's product and services! Influencing a prospect's attitudes about the hospitality product and services is not something that happens in one presentation. In addition, this type of presentation should be delivered using evidence that helps to change or solidify the prospect's beliefs toward the hospitality product and services. Persuasive presentations in hospitality rely on an emotional appeal. Weddings, anniversaries, and gala recognition dinners inherently have an emotional component that the hospitality salesperson can target. In addition, the intangible nature of hospitality services requires that the hospitality salesperson "tell the story" in a persuasive manner. The adage in hospitality sales is: "You aren't selling the steak; you are selling the sizzle." Successful hospitality salespeople know that the strongest appeals in the persuasive presentation can be either at the beginning or the end of the presentation: it depends on the prospect. If the appeal is in the beginning, the hospitality salesperson is seeking to get the prospect in the mood, to capture their attention. If it is at the end, it leaves the prospect with a terrific and memorable impression. Of course, hospitality salespeople should always consider the type of communication style the prospect demonstrates. Some prospects will respond better to facts and logic, while others will respond most to metaphors and testimonials (See Figure 6).

Source: Jeffrey Beck

FIGURE 6. Evidence

Reminder presentations are also known as check backs. These types of presentations work well with known or repeat clients, since there is an effort to continue the partnership or relationship and keep clients from switching to the competition. Many times, reminder presentations add service after a sale has been completed. The implicit message of the reminder presentation is that the relationship with the client or prospect is not taken for granted. In addition, reminder presentations can be used to upsell after the initial sale has been made. Upselling is a sales technique where a seller induces the customer to purchase more expensive items, upgrades, or other add-ons in an attempt to make a more profitable sale. In the hospitality industry of catering and social events, the person who makes these presentations is sometimes called a **detailer**. Reminder presentations are also used when a previous sales call failed. Although many event planners are loyal to their usual hospitality product suppliers, reminder presentations can be a means by which the hospitality salesperson influences the event planner to consider making a move to the hospitality organization they represent.

Making Effective Presentations

Making effective presentations requires three actions on the part of the hospitality salesperson. First, they should be excited and show passion for the hospitality organization they represent. Next, the hospitality salesperson must be a great listener, seeking feedback both explicit and implicit as they make their presentation. Finally, they should focus on the benefits and value that they and their organization offer. It is always important to remember that the time a hospitality salesperson spends with a prospect is valuable. Advance planning, having a sales call objective (inform, persuade, or remind), and having materials that help demonstrate value are the beginning steps to making an effective presentation.

Effective presentations follow the well-known **AIDA principle**. This model seeks first to gain the *attention* of the prospect. The techniques discussed in the previous chapter for establishing the sales dialogue come to mind. Next, a well-planned presentation stimulates *interest*. The hospitality product and service are recognized as intangible. Hospitality salespeople understand this and seek to add sensory appeal to add a tangibility to the products and services they offer. By emphasizing specific benefits that are derived from buying objectives stated by the prospect, the hospitality salesperson adds value for the prospect, which creates *desire*. When the hospitality salesperson verifies comprehension and interest, asking for the sale completes the effective presentation. In summary, the successful hospitality salesperson guides the prospect through this process, asking questions and seeking feedback along the way to arrive at a successful result, or a "win-win" for both the hospitality salesperson and the prospect.

Planning the Effective Presentation

By planning in advance what will be included in the presentation, the hospitality salesperson not only develops a smooth presentation, but also instills self-confidence because they know they are prepared. As the adage goes, "proper planning prevents poor performance." The first step in planning the presentation is to study all the information that has been collected about the prospect and his or her company. Planning a presentation customized to the prospect and the company they represent helps to develop the trust necessary to make the sale. It cannot be stated enough that the hospitality salesperson must thoroughly understand the three-to-five most important buying objectives of the prospect. These buying objectives must be at the center of the hospitality presentation and are the guide for the hospitality products and services the salesperson selects as solutions to the buying objectives of the prospect. Once the product and service solutions have been identified, the presentation technique is chosen as the objective for the sales dialogue. Earlier in the buying process, the informational technique is picked; later in the buying process a persuasive technique is more appropriate. Finally, there are materials and sales aids that help the hospitality salesperson make an effective presentation. These materials are known as strategic selling materials.

Strategic Selling Materials

Strategic selling materials (SSMs) are tangible representations of the hospitality product and services. It helps to establish a connection between the buying objectives of the prospect and the features of the hospitality organization. When these connections are demonstrated effectively by the hospitality salesperson, the benefits to the prospect are validated. This validation confirms value to the prospect. Strategic selling materials are best used to reinforce a prospect's needs wants, desires, and buying objectives. When using SSMs, hospitality salespeople state the buying objective, demonstrate the strategic selling material, and explain the SSM in terms of the benefit experienced.

Strategic selling materials are used for a variety of reasons. Most importantly, they capture the prospect's attention. Further, they generate interest, which helps the hospitality salesperson work through the AIDA process discussed earlier. Persuasive presentations become clearer with the use of SSMs. Strategic selling materials help the prospect to become involved in the presentation, which helps to stimulate a sense of purchase. Strategic selling materials, through the clarity they provide, improve the prospect's understanding of the hospitality product and service solutions being presented. When well-designed and fabricated, SSMs add to the image of the hospitality salesperson and the organization that he or she represents.

Types of SSMs

Strategic selling materials can be clustered into three categories: visual aids, electronic media, and evidence or sources of proof. When using SSMs, the materials should be placed in front of the prospect, subsequently the hospitality salesperson will "Show and Tell" how the SSM supports the point being made. It is important that an element of showmanship be used when presenting or demonstrating the SSM. **Showmanship** can be defined as the ability to do things in a lively and enthusiastic way that commands attention. By using such techniques, the hospitality salesperson conveys the essential message of information, persuasion, or reminder. It is imperative that no trickery, insincerity, or gaudiness be used as part of the presentation of SSMs (See Figure 7).

Visual aids provide clarification and both emotional and rational appeal to the presentation, which results in moving the buying process closer to

FIGURE 7. Strategic Selling Materials (SSMs)

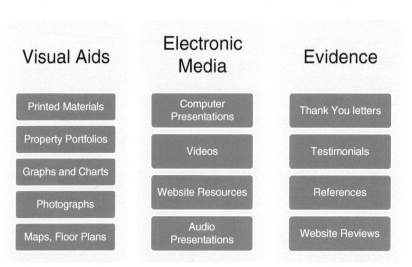

Source: Jeffrey Beck

a purchase commitment. Printed materials can include brochures, articles, reprints of news articles, and guarantees. Property portfolios are a combination of many different materials. They are best used when customized for the prospect's buying objectives, organizational needs, and personal tastes. Graphs and charts are best used for event-space capacity. Photographs provide a realistic portrayal of the hospitality property and services. Maps and floor plans, when combined with photographs, are essential to the presentation of the hospitality facility.

Electronic media can be useful when the sales dialogue takes place away from the hospitality property, or when the presentation occurs in front of a group or committee responsible for making the purchase decision. By using electronic presentation techniques, the hospitality salesperson can avoid a "canned presentation." When using presentation software, one should avoid reading the slides; instead, let the slides provide the information while adding stories, analogies, and other information. When using electronic media, hospitality salespeople should summarize the key points of the presentation or video and ask if there are any questions to be addressed.

Evidence, or forms of proof, are the most powerful of all SSMs. They build trust and confidence because they are coming from third parties. They answer the very important question, "Who says so?" In today's internet world of e-commerce, buyers rely heavily on the recommendations of others. To maximize effectiveness, testimonials and thank you letters should be used when the topic within the letter or testimonial is relevant to the prospect. For example, a thank you letter which references the food quality of an event would be appropriate to present to an event planner asking for a customized menu. References that are appropriate to a particular industry or social group are beneficial in making the prospect feel comfortable that the hospitality organization has expertise with the unique needs of similar groups.

Making the Presentation

There are very specific behaviors that should occur when making the presentation. The hospitality salesperson should always seek to strengthen the association with the prospect. This is done through the techniques described in Chapter Nine; this is the small talk before beginning the presentation. The next behavior that makes for a winning sales presentation is as simple as telling the prospect what you wish to cover by addressing their buying objectives. By confirming the buying objectives, the hospitality salesperson verifies that the buying information is still correct, and demonstrates that the hospitality salesperson has developed solutions based on that information. Next, the hospitality salesperson uses features and benefit statements to add value to the hospitality product and service answers being presented. Along with the presentation of benefits, the appropriate SSMs are used. As stated earlier, no presentation should be information overload. Hospitality salespeople always pause to gain feedback, both verbal and nonverbal. This feedback helps to verify understanding and address any concerns that the prospect may have.

Before making the presentation, the hospitality salesperson must consider a number of factors. The location for the sales presentation can have either a positive or a negative impact on success. It is important that interruptions and distractions be kept to a minimum. The prospect must be at ease, open to ideas, and willing to listen. If the prospect's office does not allow for such an environment, an off-site location can be more productive. "Meeting for coffee" or a meal may be suitable, as the salesperson becomes the host, which is the perfect scenario for capturing the prospect's attention. Of course, the ideal location is the hospitality facility. Regardless of the location, it is best to take the nonverbal cues of the prospect for where to sit or stand. When conducting property tours, standing two to four feet at an angle from the prospect is usually best. In seating arrangements, being at an angle, rather than straight across from the prospect, seems to work best.

Practice before Presentation

The successful hospitality sales professional knows that sales presentations must be planned for, sometimes weeks in advance. Speech tone, body language, hand gestures, and how SSMs are used all become part of the practice. If possible, having the sales presentation video recorded can be instructive and helpful in improving sales presentation skills. Fear of failure comes from a lack of practice; confidence is undermined. Many sales trainers suggest that word pacing, movement, and timing are the vital skills a salesperson must acquire. These only come with practice. Finally, the specific words used can have a positive or a negative impact on the overall success of the sales presentation. Words such as "pitch" or "spiel" have a negative connotation that the sales presentation is canned. Hospitality salespeople should avoid the use of slang, or industry words that the prospect would not be familiar with. Words that imply negativity, such as "don't," "obviously," and "can't" must be avoided. Common words that foster a negative image are "discount" and "cheap" or "cheaper." Words such as these present an image of an inferior product or service; making it harder for the prospect to make the value proposition.

SUMMARY

Hospitality salespeople must use a variety of skills to make effective presentations to prospects. They must be able to use questions to obtain feedback and verify that both parties understand each other. It is essential that the hospitality salesperson matches the features and benefits of the hospitality products and services with the three-to-five buying objectives of the prospect. When this connection is made, the prospect becomes more interested in the hospitality offering, leading to the action of making the sale.

KEY TERMS

prospect

props

features

benefit

benefit statements

feature spit

request for proposal (RFP)

asynchronous
   presentation

synchronous
   presentations

transactional buying
   process

informative presentations

persuasive
   presentations

reminder presentations

detailer

AIDA principle

strategic selling materials (SSMs)

REVIEW AND DISCUSSION QUESTIONS

1. What percentage of buying objectives do the following represent: technical requirements, buying process, and client motivations?

2. Explain the steps in planning an effective presentation.

3. What behaviors should occur when making the presentation?

4. Define features, benefits, and linking statements.

5. Explain the link between establishing the sales dialogue and presenting the product.

6. Create benefit statements as a result of need discovery.

7. Explain the use of each presentation technique.

8. What three actions on the part of the hospitality sales professional are necessary for effective presentations?

9. Explain the AIDA principle.

10. Strategic selling materials can be clustered into what three categories?

CHAPTER 11

© Joseph Sohm/Shutterstock.com

Getting the Customer to Say Yes

LEARNING OBJECTIVES

- Explain why it is important to anticipate buyer resistance.
- Describe why clients raise objections.
- Describe the five sales "stop signs."
- Describe the relationship between hospitality salespeople and revenue managers.

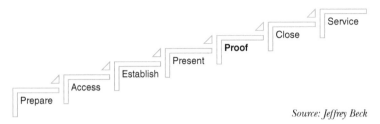

Source: Jeffrey Beck

Introduction

Thus far, the hospitality salesperson has followed the sales process by working to gain access to the prospect, qualified the prospect (the prospect is the decisionmaker, has the budget, and is looking to purchase in the near future), established a sales dialogue and made a presentation based on the buying objectives of the prospect. And now the prospect will buy, right? Wrong. It is not that simple. In fact, the successful hospitality salesperson knows that no matter how well the earlier steps in the sales process went, the prospect is likely to have areas of concern. These areas of concern are also known as **buyer resistance**. If possible, the hospitality salesperson will bring out the most important prospect concerns while asking questions and establishing the prospect's buying objectives. By knowing that the client is likely to resist, the hospitality salesperson can prepare in advance for such concerns and employ various methods to overcome any resistance. In addressing these concerns to the satisfaction of the prospect, a sincere discussion occurs. This sincere discussion helps to develop a long-term relationship and may lead to a commitment by the prospect to sign a contract for hospitality services.

People resist buying because they want additional proof that they are making the right decision. They also resist buying because they need more time to consider their possible decision. They may resist buying because the hospitality salesperson did not understand fully what buying objective the prospect considered most important. Finally, prospects may express concern during the sales presentation, and the hospitality salesperson may fail to address the concern or concerns. As a result, the prospect resists. The hospitality salesperson knows that resistance, or areas of concern, is a good thing. When prospects voice concern, they are indicating that they have been listening and may be interested. However, they have not made the link between the products and services the hospitality salesperson has to offer or they have not been convinced of the value they will receive. In short, they are not clear of *what is in it for them.* Prospects also voice objections when they are very interested; in this case, the objections are likely mild and easy to address. Assuming that the prospect has been qualified, some clients voice concerns because they are not interested at the time. When this occurs, it is likely that they have not received the necessary information to become interested in what the hospitality salesperson and his or her organization have to offer.

Reasons for Concern

There are many reasons why prospects raise concerns. It should be understood that these concerns may occur during an initial sales dialogue, or later in the sales process. First, prospects may resist because a sales dialogue takes time, and thus is hard to fit into an already busy day. It is important for the hospitality salesperson to make an appointment and to ensure that a meeting or phone call is still appropriate, given the prospect's schedule. If a prospect has not been adequately qualified, the hospitality salesperson will experience resistance. Very early in establishing the dialogue, the hospitality salesperson should confirm a **need**, **necessary budget**, and that the prospect is the decision maker or part of the decision-making committee. Many event planners represent a client which requires them to get the best possible agreement. For that reason, they are likely to resist accepting the first offering of the salesperson. Some prospects resist change. They have developed a relationship with a salesperson from another hospitality organization, they don't want to make a decision to change, or fear that changing the present circumstances will cause mistakes. This can be a challenging reason to overcome by a competing hospitality salesperson. In this case, reminder sales communications that emphasize value are the best course of action until the motivation for change arises. Sometimes, prospects will "try" the hospitality organization with smaller events, in order to give the hospitality salesperson a chance. Finally, prospects demonstrate resistance when they do not have all the information necessary to make a commitment. All resistance stems from a lack of information. It is important that the hospitality salesperson provides the right information, adequate information, and confirms that the prospect understands what is being discussed or presented.

A prospect's objections are **authentic reasons** the client believes that he or she is unable to purchase from the hospitality organization. A client's excuses are fabricated explanations why the prospect does not want to purchase the hospitality organization's product. While the two are similar, there are differences that the hospitality salesperson must uncover; failing to do so can waste time for both the prospect and the hospitality salesperson. The fundamental difference between the two is that excuses derive from a lack of motivation to consider the hospitality organization as a viable solution and the prospect is likely preoccupied with other business issues. When the response to a question of commitment from the hospitality salesperson is vague, it is likely an excuse. Additional inquiries will help to differentiate between excuses and objections. When a more specific reason is given, it is likely an **objection**.

Forms of Objections

Objections and areas of concern fall into five categories. Many clients want to have "time to think it over." After the presentation, this can be the easiest way for the prospect to alleviate the pressure of being obligated to commit to purchase immediately. Another time objection in hospitality can be related to the availability of space. Many times, based on demand, some dates are at a price that is higher than the prospect can afford. Alternative dates can be more affordable. The most common area of concern is a statement of too high a price, even when the budget has been qualified. However, if price were the sole factor, luxury hospitality products and services would not be offered in the marketplace. A lack of need for the hospitality product or service can also be an objection or type of resistance. Event planners, or the organizations they represent, may not be seeking proposals at the time. This is why many hospitality salespeople will qualify with questions such as, how often to do you plan events, when do you hold events, etc. There are two other broad forms of objections. The first is related to the product. Product objections may be related to quality, both service quality and physical product quality. Product objections can be based on the characteristics of the product. For example, the meeting space may be too small or too large, there may be too few guest rooms, or so many rooms that event attendees will feel lost. The location of the hospitality facility may be inconvenient for the type of event being held. Think back to the discussion in Chapter Six related to client motivations and the reason an event or meeting is being held. Another reason for reluctance to book is the facility, its brand, or the hospitality organization are not ones that the event planner has worked with in the past. These are known as source objections.

Resistance: The Sales Stop Signs

NEED · SOURCE · PRICE · PRODUCT · TIME

Source: Jeffrey Beck

Sales Stop Signs

The first hospitality **sales stop sign** is the lack of need for the product or services represented by the hospitality salesperson. Many prospects immediately respond to inquiry by hospitality salespeople by stating that they don't have a need. This may be for a variety of reasons; not having a need can be an excuse for other more relevant objections. **Need resistance** that is genuine is the most difficult for the hospitality salesperson to overcome. The hospitality salesperson who encounters a need objection must take the time to prove the value and resulting benefit the prospect will experience from the hospitality product and service. This is a time when positioning the product is essential. There are times when prospects don't realize that they have a need that can be satisfied by the hospitality salesperson's product and service. Sincere need objections are an opportunity for hospitality salespeople to sell themselves and encourage need satisfaction through the benefits provided.

The second hospitality stop sign is concern about the hospitality product and service. Product and service areas of concern are typically related to features the prospect is looking for that the hospitality salesperson cannot provide. For example, there are only a handful of hotels in Michigan with more than 500 guest rooms; event planners from Michigan-based associations with large memberships have a built-in product objection for their annual conferences. Product objections can also be a result of a lack of knowledge on the part of the prospect. It may be that the hospitality facility is new, has undergone expansion, or has been renovated. Product and service objections can be either rational or emotional. Specifications, like the number of hotel rooms described earlier, are examples of rational objections. Appearance, décor, menu style, and other subjective elements describe emotional areas of concern. Hospitality salespeople must be clear that they understand the buying objectives that are most important to the prospect, then bundle those in a manner that emphasizes the benefits the prospect will receive from those bundled features.

The destination/brand/source hospitality stop sign can be a difficult one to overcome, especially if an alliance has been built with another hospitality organization. Devotion to a hospitality organization is hard to shake, especially with the loyalty programs that are offered by many hospitality organizations. In these cases, the hospitality salesperson works vigorously to identify how the organization he or she represents may provide a greater benefit. Relationships are important with source objections. The use of referrals, having many contacts within the prospect's organization, and using reminder presentations help to address source objections.

The time hospitality stop sign can be a stalling tactic or can be based on the desired dates for an event not being available. If the time objection is used as a stalling tactic, the hospitality salesperson knows to explore further by asking questions about what is causing the stall. It could be that the stall is a means to reject the hospitality salesperson's offer without actually saying so. For complex hospitality sales, such as multiple-day events, high-profile events, or events that involve a committee of decision makers, a request for time to review is certainly warranted. If the dates that the prospect is seeking to reserve are a challenge, this can also be a time objection. In this case, it may be that the dates desired are completely booked. It could also be that the dates desired are being quoted at a price that is higher than the prospect is willing to pay. In these circumstances, the hospitality salesperson seeks to determine priorities, and offer options where possible.

The last, and probably most common, hospitality stop sign is related to price. Budget constraints must be clearly understood by the hospitality salesperson before a price offering is made, avoiding the time objection described above. Further, **transactional buyers** seek the lowest possible price with little regard to value. As a result, transactional buyers who state that the price is too high haven't been persuaded that the hospitality salesperson's offering is the best alternative. Event planners want to believe that they have received a "deal" and typically are skilled in negotiation. Therefore, negotiation techniques that will be described later in this chapter become valuable, but, importantly, the prospect who perceives value is more likely to buy. One away to address price concerns is to avoid discussing price during the presentation; when the client asks, "How much is this going to cost me" the hospitality salesperson postpones the price discussion until the point that a contract or summary of charges is presented. Hospitality salespeople also know that if they have worked hard to develop a relationship with the prospect, minor resistance to price is less likely.

The Plan for Addressing Concerns

Hospitality salespeople must have an approach for addressing the various concerns that may arise prior to, during the presentation, and when asking for a signed contract. Prior to making a presentation to the client, the hospitality salesperson expects to be challenged with objections. For this reason, he or she will evaluate the presentation against the types of objections likely to arise. Once the likely objections have been uncovered, a game plan for addressing those objections will be developed. Like a sports coach, it can be a good idea for the hospitality salesperson to develop notes as a reminder of what the best possible responses should be for the concern raised.

Prospects will raise objections, but if the hospitality salesperson did a good job qualifying the buyer, the resistance shouldn't be insurmountable.

Perhaps the most essential component of handling buyer resistance is listening. Prospects want to perceive a net gain in value from the exchange (purchase) before committing to it. Making a purchase is inherently risky; finding ways to reduce perceived risk will increase the probability of the client committing to the purchase. The purchase decision is a true test of the extent to which the buyer trusts the hospitality salesperson.

During the sales call the hospitality salesperson, having planned in advance, should be prepared for concerns to arise. When the objection does arise, the hospitality salesperson remembers not to express any anger. Instead the hospitality salesperson listens actively to what the client is thinking and feeling. Next, he or she acknowledges the concern without offering any judgment on the client's position. Once the acknowledgement has taken place, the hospitality salesperson assesses the degree of the concern by asking questions of clarification. After confirming a complete understanding of the concerns, the hospitality salesperson presents possible options and solutions to address the concerns. Finally, the hospitality salesperson asks for a commitment to move forward.

Traffic light © Sebastian Kaulitzki/Shutterstock.com

Techniques for Overcoming Objections

The **direct denial technique** is a straightforward response to an inaccurate opinion or belief of the prospect. This technique is considered risky, as people do not like to be told that they are incorrect in their opinion or belief. The attitude of the hospitality salesperson when using this technique is not to come off as a know-it-all. In all cases, the attitude should be one of patience and authenticity. This technique is best used with clients the hospitality salesperson has worked with before.

Demonstrations are effective when the client is skeptical about the products and services the hospitality salesperson represents. Demonstrations are best used when the prospect is in the process of comparing hospitality facilities.

As such, strategic selling materials that provide factual comparisons with the hospitality organization's competitors are a means by which the hospitality salesperson can discuss the competitive advantage of the products and services they represent. Demonstrations, as defined here, are typically conducted in the prospect's office, or in another location other than the hospitality facility. Needless to say, hospitality salespeople must come prepared with demonstration materials that address the prospect's areas of concern.

Property tours are a form of demonstration that allow the hospitality salesperson to offer tangible proof that refutes a client's area of concern. As stated in an earlier chapter, property tours must not turn into an overload of information and features without addressing the prospect's areas of concern and emphasizing their buying objectives. During property tours, hospitality salespeople know to be flexible in the agenda, since every event is different in design. Many hospitality salespeople provide three-dimensional diagrams of how the space will look when set up for the event. The more tangible the hospitality product and services can become for the prospect, the more likely skepticism can be countered.

Trial offers are a form of resistance buster where the prospect tries the hospitality product or service without making a purchase commitment. A complimentary dinner or lodging stay would be an example of a trial offer. Familiarization trips are provided as a means for the prospect to understand the benefits of the various hospitality organizations and destinations. By providing such trips these organizations circumvent the possible resistance a prospect might demonstrate.

Third-party referrals are one of the most powerful hospitality resistance busters; an authentic statement of support from a neutral third party can be the strongest means to negate a prospect's areas of concern. People who buy products online, when unsure if a product will satisfy a buying need, look at reviews and ratings. Hospitality salespeople provide similar assistance when they present third-party endorsements. Hospitality sales "brag books" are portfolios that include thank you letters, letters of endorsement, and other third-party communications that help to support the salesperson's claims. Third-party endorsements rarely prompt resistance from the client.

The **indirect denial technique** for addressing resistance is less direct; the technique refutes the opinion by stating that other prospects and clients have had similar concerns. By doing so, the hospitality salesperson acknowledges the concern is partially valid but provides additional information that overcomes the objection. The indirect denial technique verbiage is summarized in what is commonly known as "feel-felt-found." Using this technique, the hospitality salesperson conveys that other prospects have had similar concerns, but those concerns were unfounded. For example:

> **Prospect:** "I am concerned that the number of loading dock bays will not be sufficient for the move in and out of our event."

> **Hospitality salesperson:** "I understand how you feel. The event planner from the XYZ association felt the same way; but upon arrival, there were an adequate number of bays to accommodate their move in and move out."

This technique is widely taught to salespeople in all industries, but nowhere does it work as effectively as in hospitality sales because of the intangible nature of the hospitality product and service offering and the perceived risk associated with such products.

Exceptional benefit resistance busters emphasize the value received. Also known as a **compensation technique**, this resistance buster is most commonly used with price concerns. The hospitality salesperson acknowledges that there is a valid concern, then spotlights the incomparable benefit that the prospect found to be most important. For example, "Our price differential maybe higher, but our conference center is exactly what you are looking for in a location." This is another technique, when the appropriate feature/benefit is used, that typically avoids argument from clients. It is important that the offsetting benefit is of the highest value to the prospect.

Using questions that link the buying objectives to the area of concern is a resistance buster that can be used at any time during the sales process. For example, "Wouldn't it interest you to provide your guests a newly renovated, first-class lodging facility at a minor price differential to the XYZ hotel?" Notice that questions of this type suggest possession or ownership; the question, then, implies a resolution to the problem exposed. Questions can also be used to better assess what problem the prospect has identified, if the communication is unclear.

Revenue Management and Sales

Revenue management is commonly defined as selling the right *product* at the right *price* to the right *market segment* at the right *time*, through the right *distribution channel* in order to maximize revenue. In a hospitality establishment, the hotel rooms, meeting space, and restaurant seats are "perishable" products; there is only one opportunity to sell each product each day. Because these items are perishable, hospitality organizations develop strategies to sell rooms, space, and seats at prices that optimize revenues; this is why revenue management exists in the hospitality industry today.

The second component of the revenue management definition is price; hospitality organizations have different prices to offer clients based on who the guest is, when they want to stay, how much revenue they might bring to the hotel, and internal factors that play a role in pricing. Marketing objectives of the hospitality organization, such as product quality leadership, market share leadership, and profit maximization, affect pricing. Pricing depends greatly on past history and current market conditions, information that hospitality revenue managers have at their fingertips. This data guides selling strategies by helping hospitality salespeople offer appropriate prices based on demand.

The next component of the revenue management function is the market segment. Different sales approaches are used with different market segments (refer to Chapter Six). These selling strategies ideally save the most popular dates and best products for the best market segments. Revenue managers and hospitality salespeople work together to determine what clients are best served with the space available. The fourth component of revenue management is time. Revenue optimization relies on the dates and the amount of space a client is seeking. Needless to say, the relationship developed by the hospitality salesperson plays a role in what business should be booked. Distribution channel also has an impact on what percentage of business comes from various market segments, which has an impact on selling strategy.

The final component of revenue management is maximizing revenue. Hospitality revenue managers and salespeople work in partnership to set rates, accept group business, and forecast future business. Given the different roles and objectives of hospitality revenue managers and salespeople, a better understanding of each position responsibility is necessary. As the technical issues related to dates, rates, and space become more under the control of the revenue manager, the hospitality salesperson must be aware of what prices to quote. This can be a double-edged sword; trying to get the best possible rates for the hotel may jeopardize the relationships that the hospitality salesperson is seeking to develop. As a result, areas of concern related to dates, rates, and space are not always discussed in real time.

Negotiation Techniques

Negotiation is defined as working to reach an agreement that is mutually satisfactory to both the buyer and the seller. It is a process that is used when the hospitality salesperson cannot justify or outweigh the client's objection to price or other areas of concern. The task for the hospitality salesperson is to avoid making price the central issue in the negotiation and emphasizing value. Successful hospitality salespeople know that selling hospitality and the negotiation that results are not a "we versus they" process. If the trust is strong, negotiation becomes a partnership to work toward an equitable agreement. If an attitude of cooperative communication takes place, both the client and the hospitality salesperson and the organizations they represent are successful. When the participants do not embrace a cooperative attitude, negotiations become contentious. By demonstrating integrity, competency, and frankness, the hospitality salesperson develops trust and maintains long-term relationships.

Negotiation contains three elements: time, knowledge, and power. There is no clear start or end time to negotiations; it is a function of the deadlines set by each party. The knowledge the hospitality salesperson possesses related to the client's needs must be extensive. The power in negotiation is defined as the ability to influence the other party and the situation. In negotiation, the earlier deadline is the weakest position; the closer the deadline, the more concessions take place. Like the Pareto principle, 80 percent of the negotiations take place in the last 20 percent of the time available. As part of the buying process questions discussed in Chapter 9, the hospitality salesperson should ask for the deadline for deciding. Hospitality salespeople seek never to say "no" in negotiations, that behavior only stalls communication. Instead, hospitality salespeople understand the value of consideration and work to offer alternatives versus discounting prices or saying "no."

Understanding the prospect's most important buying objective is the key knowledge a hospitality salesperson must retain in negotiations. This is why the use of questioning techniques are so important earlier in the sales process. It is very tough to gather information during the negotiating process. It is also important that the client have all the information necessary to make an informed decision. The hospitality sales professional understands the difference between wanting a low price or "deal" and the true give and take that results in a win-win outcome.

Negotiation is persuading, based on each party's needs; the persuasion is the result of the influence skills held by the client and the hospitality salesperson. Ideally, the power in negotiation is equal for the client and the hospitality salesperson. The focus should be on the client's needs and their level of understanding of the benefits the hospitality organization provides. This information is dependent upon the amount of time and knowledge the client possesses, and the availability and the perceived value of the client's business the hospitality salesperson retains. Good hospitality sales negotiators don't indicate early that they will negotiate, but they don't have a "take it or leave it" attitude either. At this point, true give and take is the best possible outcome, and should never be a function of price.

When price *is* part of the negotiation, discounting the price too soon devalues the process followed and the hospitality offering. The hospitality salesperson seeks to learn the total number of items to be negotiated. For example, "So, if we are able to solve your rate concerns, and address the key executive's VIP check-in, there are no other issues standing in the way of a commitment with us today?" Successful hospitality salespeople seek to add value rather than discounting room rate. For example, instead of lowering the room rate by ten dollars, a welcome fruit basket or other added service may make the difference.

When negotiating, hospitality salespeople know that not all of the competition is cheaper. They make sure they have all the information they need as early as possible. They remain objective in negotiations, and do not allow ego or emotions to get the better of them. Hospitality salespeople know when to walk away from a negotiation (i.e., the rates and prices a prospect seeks are far out of line with the hospitality organization's offering). Hospitality salespeople do not speak much during the negotiation process; it gives the client time to think and can become an effective strategy. Hospitality salespeople never fear losing a sale, especially if the alternative is one side wins and the other side doesn't.

SUMMARY

A major element of the sales process is the likely buyer resistance that the hospitality salesperson will encounter. Most prospects are not ready to buy immediately after the sales presentation. Even though the prospect has been qualified for need, budget, and authority to purchase, concerns may arise. These concerns include price, source, product, time and need for the specific offering. Hospitality salespeople use various techniques to overcome these concerns through the use of techniques that address the concerns in a fashion that respects the prospect's concerns. Revenue managers in hospitality organizations play a role in the negotiation process, and hospitality salespeople must work with both the client and the revenue manager to arrive at a win-win situation.

KEY TERMS

buyer resistance	need resistance	indirect denial
need	transactional buyers	technique
necessary budget	direct denial technique	compensation
authentic reasons	demonstrations	technique
objection	trial offers	revenue management
sales stop sign	third-party referrals	negotiation

REVIEW AND DISCUSSION QUESTIONS

1. Discuss the reasons why prospects raise concerns.

2. Explain the five categories of objections and areas of concern.

3. Explain the various sales stop signs.

4. Explain the direct denial technique.

5. Explain the difference between the direct denial technique and the indirect denial technique.

6. Discuss revenue management.

7. Explain why it is important to anticipate buyer resistance.

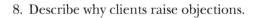

8. Describe why clients raise objections.

9. Discuss negotiation.

10. Describe the relationship between hospitality salespeople and revenue managers.

CHAPTER 12

Asking for the Sale

© fizkes/Shutterstock.com

LEARNING OBJECTIVES

- Describe the elements of the closing process.
- Outline the plan for closing the sale.
- List the common elements of a hotel contract.
- List the common elements of an event contract.

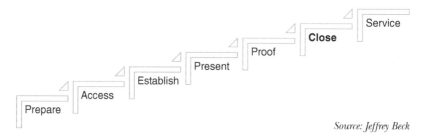

Source: Jeffrey Beck

Introduction

When the hospitality salesperson seeks a commitment to purchase from the prospect, closing or achieving a sales agreement occurs. It is thought that closing the sale is the most difficult step in the process; some hospitality salespeople are hesitant to ask because they fear being told "no." This fear of rejection results in a lack of action; if they are not rejected, they won't be humiliated or let down. Young hospitality salespeople are afraid of being viewed as too aggressive, so they may avoid **capping** all of their efforts into a request for commitment. Ultimately, closing the sale is necessary for those who wish to be successful in hospitality sales. Asking for the commitment should come naturally after all the other steps in the process have been accomplished. In fact, many prospects expect the hospitality salesperson to make the first move by asking for the sale.

Some hospitality salespeople consider the **closing process** and asking for the sale as the fun part of being in sales. Why? For some, it is the "thrill of the hunt." This is what is known in the sales industry as a **hunter** mentality. Hunters are great at solving clients' problems, cold-calling, and handle rejection easily. Hunters have short memories; they forget the last "no" because they are on to the next opportunity. The opposite of the hunter, the **gatherer**, sees the sales close and commitment as an affirmation that they have created a relationship with the prospect, and the client has found the hospitality salesperson's organization, attitude, and presentation compelling. Both hunters and gatherers can be successful in the hospitality sales process; they go about gaining commitment in different ways based on their personalities.

Closing the sale by asking for a commitment is only viewed as aggressive when the prospect isn't ready to buy. Successful hospitality salespeople sense through the closing cues provided by the client when it is the appropriate time to ask for the sale. It is widely believed that the hospitality salesperson must ask for the sale at least five times before they gain commitment from the prospect. That means, then, that the prospect has said "no" at least four times. When a prospect says no, it can be simply a form of resistance as described in the previous chapter; successful hospitality salespeople welcome a

PROFESSIONAL SALES AND SELLING

"no" response because it means that there is more information to be shared. This sharing of information and an ultimate agreement means that both the client and the hospitality salesperson have entered into a win-win relationship; it is the beginning of a long-term partnership.

The Plan to Close the Sale

Hospitality salespeople must have a plan for closing the sale when the opportunity presents itself in the form of client cues. Prior to asking for commitment from the client, the hospitality salesperson should address objections, resolve concerns, then ask for the sale. For that reason, prior to the sales call where he or she will ask for the sale, the hospitality salesperson evaluates the hurdles that may arise while attempting to gain commitment. Once the likely hurdles have been uncovered, a game plan for gaining commitment should be developed. A review of the prospect's buying objectives should be undertaken by the hospitality salesperson so that a "closing script" can be created. Knowing that asking for the sale is a dynamic process, there are various techniques that should be considered for use. Those closing techniques should also be a function of the signals that the prospect transmits to the hospitality salesperson.

Prospects offer cues as to when they are ready to close the sale; hospitality salespeople must be alert to the verbal and nonverbal cues that indicate a readiness to commit. Nonverbal cues, such as looking the hospitality salesperson in the eye or showing a positive mood, facial expressions such as nodding and friendliness, and a body angle that is leaning toward the hospitality salesperson ("open") are just some of the cues that a prospect who is ready to make the commitment may display. Verbal cues will include questions, statements that acknowledge the value of the offering, and statements that detail conditions that must be addressed before the commitment can be made. When the prospect exhibits these nonverbal cues, followed by the verbal cues described, a "shift" toward commitment and purchase is transpiring.

During the presentation sales call the hospitality salesperson, having planned in advance, should be prepared to ask for the sale. After recognizing the nonverbal and verbal cues, the hospitality salesperson should focus on the client's buying objectives. These motives should be clear to the hospitality salesperson and restated to verify that they are still accurate, and no other key objectives have been missed or changed. Once the buying objectives have been verified, the hospitality salesperson should focus on the one or two most important buying objectives; this will help the prospect make the shift to being a buyer. During this sales call, the hospitality salesperson must display confidence that the solutions presented are the best answer to the prospect's buying objectives. Many times, there are concerns (addressed in the last chapter) that must be reexamined; confirming that these concerns have been addressed helps the closing process proceed more smoothly. While the sales call is taking place, the hospitality salesperson asks questions to gauge interest that validates the nonverbal and verbal cues described earlier. These questions are designed to move the prospect toward action; they are intended to "**trial close**" the sale with the prospect. Hospitality salespeople could ask questions like:

- Is this what you had in mind?

- What would be the next step in the process?

- Does this solution make sense to you?

- What do you think of this proposal?

- What do you think of the (product feature/benefit)?

If a prospect offers a positive answer to a question of this type, the hospitality salesperson can proceed toward closing the sale using techniques that will be discussed later in this chapter. If the answer is not positive, or the prospect does not seem to be ready to make a commitment, the hospitality salesperson should ask a question such as "is there anything that you are uncertain about, or that doesn't address your buying motives?" Trial closes are not the same as asking for the sale; the hospitality salesperson is assessing interest on a particular feature, the proposal, or some other element of the hospitality organization's product and service.

Between the trial close questions and the actual close techniques, the hospitality salesperson must be prepared to ask more than once for the sale. There are several techniques that can be used; successful hospitality salespeople are *comfortable* with using any of the techniques discussed in the next section of this chapter. As a reminder, if the prospect says no approximately five times, the hospitality salesperson should be able to employ at least five different closing techniques.

Techniques for Closing the Sale

There are many different techniques for closing the sale; any popular how-to sales book will describe at least eight methods. Some of them are consistent across all authors, with different names to them, others are particular favorites. The key to each closing technique is the situation in which the hospitality salesperson finds themselves. Successful hospitality salespeople discover the techniques that work best for them through experience but know that they must be comfortable with multiple techniques, since the communication style of the prospect will influence the closing interchange.

The **direct request** is a simple statement asking for the sale. It is also called the basic close, or direct appeal close. As the name implies, it is a direct request for the sale. Many young hospitality salespeople have difficulty with this technique, because they do not want to appear to be overly aggressive. However, it has been estimated that in 70 percent of all sales presentations, a request for the sale is never made. Closing the sale is all about timing; using the direct request too early can backfire. When using the basic close technique, the hospitality salesperson must remember to be silent and patient after the request. A big mistake with the direct request method is to continue selling after the "ask." When hospitality salespeople continue to talk after asking for the sale, it may betray a lack of confidence with the response they receive from the prospect.

The **assumptive close** is a common technique that minimizes the amount of pressure on the client to buy. The hospitality salesperson embraces an attitude that assumes that the prospect is going to buy the product and services from the hospitality organization. It is important for the hospitality salesperson to have a confident attitude and display that attitude without appearing to be overly cocky. Trial close questions during the presentation are required, especially with the assumptive close technique. The assumptive close technique employs statements that address one or multiple minor points. For example, the hospitality salesperson might state, "When you have your meeting in our Forest Room, your attendees will experience as atmosphere of solitude, much like a forest." The assumptive close helps to "transfer ownership," helping the prospect to feel as if they have purchased the hospitality product or service. An example of an assumptive close question the hospitality salesperson might utilize would be, "What email address will I send a confirmation of the contract to?" Assumptive close techniques work very well when a solid relationship has formed between the prospect and the hospitality salesperson.

The **alternatives close** offers product and service options to the prospect. The hospitality salesperson selects the options in advance. Care must be taken that a limited number of options (typically two) are offered, so that confusion on the part of the prospect does not occur. In this technique it can also appear that the hospitality salesperson is not being thoughtful about what will be best for the prospect, since multiple options are presented. Care must be taken to demonstrate that the hospitality salesperson has taken buying objectives into account when presenting choices. Alternative close techniques work

Closing Techniques

- Direct Request
- Assumptive
- Alternatives
- Completed Contract
- Objectives Summary
- Balance Sheet
- Non-Price Consideration
- Now or Never

best with transactional buyers, where price is a concern. For example, the hospitality salesperson might state, "We can do your meeting on February 3rd through the 5th for $125 per person, or we can host your meeting on April 25th through the 27th for $145 per person." Note that the language used may help to steer the prospect; in the example, the hotel can either "do" the meeting or "host" it. With this technique, the prospect has little opportunity to say no, and the sale is likely to move forward.

The completed contract close is also known as the written close. Hospitality contracts will be discussed later in this chapter; using a completed contract ensures a customized solution. The completed contract technique requires the hospitality salesperson to have listened carefully and taken good notes when asking technical, buying process, and client motivation questions. Because the completed contract technique compels the prospect to apply their signature, there is a strong probability of a positive outcome. Needless to say, advance preparation is required, but the planning is worth it since a sale results a large percentage of the time. Another benefit of the completed contract approach is that it stimulates conversation for real-time modifications. The completed contract can be combined with other techniques, such as the assumptive approach.

The objectives summary close emphasizes benefits important to the prospect. This technique is also called the summary close or the summary of benefits close. This method is very popular; it provides a review of the recognized benefits and proposes a course of action for the prospect that leads to commitment. Note that this technique is designed as a restatement of the buying objectives and of how the hospitality organization will satisfy those buying needs through the features presented by the hospitality salesperson. For example, the hospitality salesperson might state, "So you are looking for a hotel on the water, a ballroom with a 20-foot ceiling, and a competitive room rate. We are able to provide all of these requirements, which means your attendees will have a successful event. May I make this a definite booking for you?" By presenting the buying objectives in such a way, the logical next step is to ask for the commitment.

The balance sheet closing or t-account closing method outlines reasons to book now, versus reasons to wait. If the prospect is deciding between two different hospitality organizations, this technique, while risky, can be used for comparison. When it is used for comparison, the hospitality salesperson must display supreme confidence. Whether it is used as a "buy now versus later" or comparison closing technique, the balance sheet approach engages the prospect in the process. With this technique, the prospect must do most of the talking, so that they convince themselves of the reason to buy, or the reason for choosing the hospitality organization the salesperson represents. Many times, hospitality salespeople have strategic selling materials that compare the organization's products and services to competitors; if you go this route, be mindful not to ridicule competitors, just provide facts.

The non-price consideration close offers an incentive to act immediately. It can be a compromise in the price or in other contract terms. Many times, the hospitality salesperson will make a consideration, such as a special add-on, rather than lowering the price. These add-ons will many times preserve the profitability of the contracted terms versus reducing the menu price or room rate. Special add-ons can include welcome receptions, morning or afternoon breaks, no-charge meeting room rentals, or a VIP gift for the executive in charge. This closing method must be used with care so that the prospect equates added value with the concession. The hospitality salesperson must feel confident that the concessions made will be met with approval by his or her superior. Further, negotiation becomes central to the effective use of this technique; the hospitality salesperson must be adept at finding the middle ground.

The now-or-never close creates a sense of urgency with the prospect, especially when the hospitality salesperson has a limited amount of space for a particular date or dates. When prospects are unsure of whether to decide, *and price is not a concern,* this technique can use the emotion of fear in a positive way to encourage the prospect to act. For example, the hospitality salesperson might say, "We have had some inquiries for the Forest meeting room you are interested in on the date you are interested in. If you do not book now, I cannot guarantee it will be available later." The Christmas and New Year's holidays are very popular for catered events in hospitality; the now-or-never technique is commonly used when prospects are considering their options during that time span. The same holds true for weddings.

The complexity of the hospitality sale based on the prospect's buying objectives can also have an influence on the closing technique employed. Intricate or unusual event requirements, the long-term potential of the prospect, along with their importance to the community, can all play a role in the closing scenario. When the client's buying objectives are not complex, less consultation and fewer sales contacts are likely necessary to close the sale. The sophistication of the prospect, their knowledge of the event industry, the

Position with Client	Closing Technique	Closing Phrases
Repeat business: Past Client looking for dates, rates, and space.	Assumptive	I have those dates and space. I will send you a contract to sign today.
New Client: Cues from client indicate strong interest compared to competitors.	Balance Sheet	Compared to your other choices, our location and service quality are superior. While we don't have your first choice of dates, don't you agree we are your best choice?

Position with Client	Closing Technique	Closing Phrases
Price Sensitive Client: Cues from client indicate need for flexibility and budget consideration	Alternatives	We have March 15th at $149, or I can offer you March 19th at $179. Which is more favorable to your committee and you?
Potential Long-Term Client: Cues from Client indicate the need for a discount or other consideration	Non-Price Consideration	Although we cannot meet your guest room price requirement, we would like to offer you a complimentary wine and cheese reception for your attendees during your stay with us.

market segment they belong to, and their status in their company and community can also have an impact on closing techniques. For that reason, the hospitality salesperson should practice using closing worksheets such as those below.

Some prospects want to evaluate competing hospitality products and services. A consultative hospitality salesperson will do everything possible to help the prospect make an intelligent comparison. It is important for the hospitality salesperson to emphasize where the features of the organization he or she represents are stronger. By taking on this type of attitude, the hospitality salesperson is almost taking on another type of closing technique by "waiting in the wings." There is no push for a decision, but rather a desire to "stay in the game" as a resource when the prospect comes closer to deciding to purchase. The contacts with the prospect have the objective to remind the client; tenacity is the key. In fact, demonstrating patience with a resolve to help the prospect can lead to the sale.

Hospitality Contracts

The common elements of a **hospitality contract** are generally the "who, what, where, and when" of the event in legal terms. The important elements of sleeping rooms, space, and event provisions give a detailed analysis of the event in economic terms. The clauses required in a hospitality contract help to protect both the hospitality organization and the client. An effective hospitality contract shields both the organization and the client; contracts are written with the idea that all parties are optimistic but know that sometimes things happen. Contracts help to make clear the expectations of both the hospitality organization and the client. By putting the terms of the agreement in writing, both parties are specific as to what they will do in terms of performance.

A contract should include the parties in the agreement, who will be doing what, when, where, and for what result. Contracts should have dates, deadlines, and timelines for completion of responsibilities. Billing arrangements, deposit policies, and payment schedules are common elements to a contract. The legal authority of the signatories, which means who is explicitly responsible for signing a contract, must be identified. Obviously, signatures are required for agreement. When an event is to be held, or hospitality products and services provided more than a year from the sale closing, a written agreement must be drafted.

Event planners requiring guest rooms for their attendees' reserve what is known as a block of rooms. Room block contract items include the arrival and departure patterns, check in and out times, deadlines for additions and changes, room rates and services included, and reservation guarantee and payment policies. Besides the rates being charged for attendees, descriptions of the various types of rooms, and whether complimentary rooms will be offered based on the number of rooms sold are written into a guest room contract. In addition, any fees related to early departures and failure to fill the room block are specified.

Space contract items can be broken into meeting space and exhibit space. Meeting space items include specific rooms or spaces (e.g., around the outdoor swimming pool), dates and times of use, specific room set-ups, audiovisual service requirements, set up and teardown times, convention service and staffing requirements, and meeting room rental fees, if applicable. Recently, guest room to space ratios have become part of the contract terms and are influenced by revenue management principles. Exclusive providers may be listed as part of the contract. For example, hospitality organizations may require that the event planner hire the organization's staff for cleaning, security, paramedic, and décor services, to name a few, *or* that they must use a specified audiovisual provider. On occasion, other public areas may be made available for the event planner. Lobbies, balconies, foyers, garages, and even helicopter pads may be used for special, but restricted, event space. These restrictions must be spelled out in the contract.

Exhibit space contracts address items that are similar to the items specified in meeting space contracts, but exhibit space contracts also include storage arrangements, hall capacities, fire marshal/other code approvals, assignment of responsibility for security, and exhibitor and other contractor liability assignments. Factors such as utilities (heating and A/C during exhibit hours), office space, internet service, and housekeeping services specific to the event space are typically included in the contract provisions.

Event contract items, which focus on occasions that include food and beverage, describe what food and beverage items can and cannot be purchased from outside the hospitality facility. Staffing levels for food service, based on the service style, will be documented. If alcoholic beverages requiring bartenders or servers is required, such ratios and fees will be stated. Because of the perishability of food, and the requirements for ordering both food and beverage, guarantees will be outlined. Tax and gratuities, along with any other service charges or fees must be explicitly stated.

There are other clauses that apply to the hospitality contract, regardless of rooms, exhibits, space, or events. Depending on the space needs, clauses that describe potential sound conflicts, or understandings that companies that are competitors of the company the event planner represents will not hold meetings simultaneously will be included in the contract. If a guest room block is part of the contract, provisions for the possibility of guests being "walked" due to overbooking (alternative accommodations) will be included. The format of the report that the hospitality facility will generate is part of the contract. Any maintenance or renovation taking place (or planned for) will be addressed. Cancellation schedules are part of any contract; typically, a graduated scale is included that indicates higher penalties for cancellations closer to the contracted date.

Other clauses include **force majeure** or act of god, which protects both parties from unforeseen uncontrollable circumstances. Liability insurance, liquor liability, deterioration of the facility, and both parties' adherence to local and national codes, laws, and regulations are included in contracts. While many hospitality companies have standard contracts, hospitality salespeople must be sure that the contract presented protects both the hospitality organization and the client, is simple enough to read that someone not part of the negotiations would understand the terms, and that both parties are fairly compensated for items that are not acted upon per the contract.

Common Contract Items
❏ Purpose of the function
❏ Contracting parties, including appointed agents
❏ Contract option and agreement dates

- ❏ Billing arrangement and payment schedule
- ❏ Contract review and revision, change dates
- ❏ Deposit policy (individual)
- ❏ Deposit policy (master account)
- ❏ Event contracted for
- ❏ Legal authority of signatories
- ❏ Signatures of authorized parties

Sleeping Rooms
- ❏ Arrival *I* departure pattern of individual guest rooms
- ❏ Arrival/departure pattern of suites by type/date
- ❏ Check-in and check-out times
- ❏ Complimentary accommodations and other rooms
- ❏ Concessions
- ❏ Control of group room/suite blocks
- ❏ Cut-off date for additions, changes, replacements
- ❏ Procedure for handling requests received after the cut-off

Reservation Guarantee and Payment Policies: Group
- ❏ Reservations procedure
- ❏ Room rate (net commissionable) + services included over meeting dates, pre & post rates, family rates
- ❏ Early departure fee
- ❏ Site visits

Function Space Utilization: Meetings
- ❏ Audiovisual services provided complimentary or at cost
- ❏ Cut-off date of space control by group
- ❏ Exclusive provider list, if any
- ❏ Final program due date
- ❏ Meeting space rental
- ❏ Specific days/times of space reserved
- ❏ Special room set-up charges

Other
- ❏ Other amenities and concessions, VIP services
- ❏ Special attendee services required

Function Space Utilization: Exhibit
- ❏ Schedule: move-in, open, and move-out by day/date/hour
- ❏ Space rental rates, including move-in and move-out days
- ❏ Exclusive provider list, if any

- ❑ Storage arrangements
- ❑ Hall capacity: booths, floor load, utilities
- ❑ Assignment of responsibility for security
- ❑ Fire marshal code approval procedures
- ❑ Exhibitor and contracting parties' liability assignment

Catering
- ❑ Allowability of items purchased outside the hotel
- ❑ Bartender *I* waiter minimum charges and staffing levels
- ❑ Deadline for final guarantees plus overage allowance
- ❑ Menu price finalization date
- ❑ Tax and gratuities requirements
- ❑ Attrition

Contract Management Issues: *Protection for all parties*
- ❑ Agreement to use CLC post-convention report format
- ❑ Alternative accommodations (''walk clause")
- ❑ Americans with Disabilities Act compliance
- ❑ Auxiliary group room *I* space usage control
- ❑ Cancellation by any party
- ❑ Change of management obligation
- ❑ Notification of competing groups
- ❑ Dispute resolution method and jurisdiction
- ❑ Attrition
- ❑ Force majeure allowance
- ❑ Liability insurance *I* indemnification provision
- ❑ Liquidated damages (breach of contract)
- ❑ Liquor liability
- ❑ Property compliance with federal *I* local labor, safety, etc. laws and regulations, fire codes
- ❑ Program interference
- ❑ Deterioration of property
- ❑ Property construction/renovation notification

The Start of the Relationship

When the customer agrees to sign the proposal, the relationship begins! The first thing the hospitality salesperson should do is to thank the client for the business. Next, a review of the details is performed to ensure all information is correct. During the review, and at other appropriate times, the hospitality salesperson reassures the client that they have made the right decision to select the hospitality salesperson's organization. **Buyer's remorse** is the feeling of remorse or guilt that arises after making an expensive and/or difficult decision. It is important that hospitality salespeople and the hospitality staff who provide service up through the post-event continue to confirm that the client made the correct decision through their actions.

Once the review of details has been completed, the hospitality salesperson **ASKS FOR REFERRALS.** There is no time better than after the proposal (or contract) has been signed to ask for other contacts or potential customers. The hospitality salesperson might say, "We are really excited to have you as a client at the Forest Hotel. Do you know anyone else in your company or industry that might have a need for our services?" Gaining a referral is the best form of prospecting, and a technique that successful hospitality salespeople use regularly. A written (or email) note of follow up is also an important gesture on the part of the hospitality salesperson. It is also important that the director of sales and marketing, general manager, or other senior managers of the hospitality facility follow up as well. Again, such gestures are important to strengthen the relationship and minimize second thoughts on the part of the client.

There are times when the customer says no, and there is no resistance busting or negotiation that can occur at that time. The hospitality salesperson must confirm that no further actions on his or her part will make a difference; a review of where the hospitality salesperson is in the sales process is important. A reconsideration of the resistance busters may be appropriate for use in the future. Whatever the case, the hospitality salesperson does nothing to jeopardize the relationship. If the prospect is considering other hospitality facilities, the hospitality salesperson works as a consultant to prepare the prospect for comparisons and questions to ask when evaluating the competition. Hospitality salespeople who are successful recognize that their "time is money" and do not spend too much time brooding over a lost sale.

Sometimes prospects, especially those with which the hospitality salesperson has done business in the past, may say no openly and sincerely. Again, the hospitality salesperson should do nothing to jeopardize the relationship. A thank you note as follow up is a great way to maintain connection. In this situation, it is always a good idea to ask for referrals as well. Although some hospitality salespeople believe that to ask is awkward, prospects sometimes feel bad that they must say no and will offer other contacts. The hospitality salesperson continues with reminder sales contacts, hoping for another chance to bid for business. Finally, the most successful hospitality salespeople analyze the sales process that was followed to identify strengths in their performance, and areas in which they can improve.

SUMMARY

This chapter focuses on the topic of *asking for the sale*. It begins by describing the elements of the closing process. That is followed by a discussion of developing and implementing a plan for closing the sale. Then comes a review of hotel contracts and what is in them. The chapter closes with a review of the common elements of an events contract.

KEY TERMS

capping	assumptive close	the non-price consideration close
closing process	alternatives close	
hunter	the completed contract	the now-or-never close
gatherer	objective summary close	hospitality contract
plan to close the sale		force majeure
trial close	balance sheet closing	buyer's remorse
direct request		

REVIEW AND DISCUSSION QUESTIONS

1. Discuss the differences between hospitality sales professionals who are hunters vs. gatherers.

2. Discuss the plan to close the sale.

3. Describe the different techniques for closing the sale.

4. Explain hospitality sales contracts.

5. Describe the elements of the closing process.

6. Outline the plan for closing the sale.

7. List the common elements of a hotel contract.

8. List the common elements of an event contract.

9. What is force majeure?

10. Explain buyer's remorse.

CHAPTER 13

Service after the Sale

AFTER SALES SERVICES

After Sales Service is the Last Piece of the Sales Process Puzzle
© Tuan_Azizi/Shutterstock.com

LEARNING OBJECTIVES

- Outline the steps for follow-up after an event.
- Explain the technique for upselling.
- List the five elements of problem resolution (LEARN).

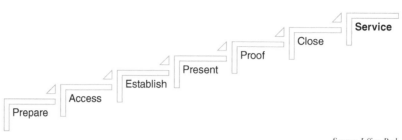

Source: Jeffrey Beck

Introduction

Successful hospitality salespeople, once the contract has been signed, look for ways to maximize revenue, while providing suggestions to enhance the client's program. Hospitality salespeople follow up before, during, and after the event to ensure that the client and attendees have a positive experience. Picking up where Chapter 12 left off, the hospitality salesperson must communicate regularly with the client; not only to assure the client that they have made the right decision, but also to organize the service process prior to the actual event. Hospitality salespeople conduct a **post-event meeting** that includes feedback and invoice review with the event planner and hospitality organization staff.

Hospitality salespeople know that the sales process is ongoing; the development of a solid business relationship is continual. That relationship can be jeopardized if promises made are not kept. Clients of hospitality organizations have expectations that increase with the promise of added value and benefit. If those promises do not materialize, hospitality salespeople must be skilled at handling customer complaints. To minimize customer complaints, solid communication, well-trained staff, attention to detail, and a **can-do attitude** are required. The hospitality salesperson must do everything they can to enrich the business relationship.

Providing Service that Strengthens the Relationship

Upselling, **follow-up**, and **on-property service coordination** are the three service strategies used to provide outstanding customer service to recently engaged clients. Upselling in the hospitality environment is very common; restaurant servers always ask if appetizers, premium drinks, or dessert are of interest to the diner. The hospitality salesperson knows that the key to successful upselling is to do so only after the initial sale is assured. Attempting to upsell while seeking to close the sale makes the hospitality salesperson look pushy, and not maintaining the best interest of the client. Hospitality salespeople make sure that the upsell is logical for the client; offering a signature calorie-rich dessert to a health-conscious group would be an obvious example of an upsell that is not logical. Next, when it comes to upselling, the hospitality salesperson works to make the offer attractive. For example, with the same health-conscious group, a traditional continental breakfast for a group is loaded with sugary cereals and pastries. Adding steel-cut oats or other healthy breakfast bowls at a minimal additional charge is a more thoughtful food offering. Such an offering is typically made at a time when menus are reviewed, but it could be done at any time that helps the client to perceive added value. Upselling, as mentioned earlier, should be done at logical times in the after-the-sale service process; it should not be last minute. Attempting to upsell at the last minute is perceived as an afterthought, which then implies that the hospitality salesperson does not have the best interest of the client in mind. The hospitality salesperson may attempt to upsell in the follow-up call, and if it is not to be, an upselling effort can occur while on-property service coordination takes place.

Follow up by the hospitality salesperson must be consistent and continuous; a methodical and logical approach to follow up after the contract is signed is a hallmark of successful sales in hospitality. Follow up is part of a consistent routine in the sales process for hospitality professionals. Practicing and experimenting with various follow-up methods is the way successful hospitality salespeople become effective at follow up. Follow up should be set up in such a way that all clients receive a communication from the hospitality salesperson, not just after a contract signing. The use of follow up is not only for reminder purposes, but also for educating clients through trade articles, new product and service offerings, and other materials that help them make informed purchase decisions. Clients should be aware of when it is best to contact the hospitality salesperson. If there are standard office hours, those hours should be communicated, and the hospitality salesperson should be accessible during those times. Hospitality salespeople run the risk of being an annoyance during these very busy times. There is a balance between being a supportive business partner and a nuisance. Successful hospitality salespeople know that every client is different and finding that balance is essential. Follow up that is short and at times that are convenient for the client makes it much more likely that the communication will be well received. Whatever the case, the hospitality salesperson should seek permission to call the client again (good manners) and ask for referrals (good business). It is recommended that follow up should be memorable, so that the hospitality salesperson and the organization he or she represents is at the top of mind the next time the client needs hospitality services.

Portable Computer Hard Drive with Midway Museum Logo

Hospitality salespeople can follow up via telephone, regular mail, email, text, or other electronic means. Telephone is the easiest and quickest, yet it is the most difficult way to impress the client with a top-of-mind experience. Having something to sell, or another attention-grabbing message, is a better way to make the message memorable. The hospitality salesperson knows that ignored phone calls that go to voicemail are also a perfect vehicle for leaving a prepared message. Using the techniques described in Chapter Four, hospitality salespeople know how to generate interest in the message they leave. Another means for communication follow up is traditional mail. With traditional mail, giveaways (coupons, pens, or key rings) that have contact information about the hospitality organization can be a notable means of communication, especially with a theme linked to the letter. For obvious reasons, email follow-up messages have become the most common form of communication. Again, follow-up messages do not need to be after sales closings; these messages can be after meeting at a networking event, a voicemail left in the prospect's voice mailbox, or an email referral. No matter the occasion, email messages must have subject lines that grab attention, be personalized to the receiver, have a theme of how the receiver of the email will encounter value, and be to the point.

While the importance of referrals was discussed in Chapter Twelve, the techniques for acquiring referrals will be further discussed as "follow up" in this section. Hospitality salespeople know that their best opportunity for new business comes from referrals from existing clients. The fact that clients are recommending the hospitality organization offers the most solid form of proof that the prospect should consider the hospitality salesperson's offerings because someone they know and trust is promoting that organization. There are many different times that the hospitality salesperson can ask for a referral. Most evident is after the hospitality salesperson has closed the sale; however, after the event has occurred (but before the bill or invoice has been presented) can also be an opportune time. There are some basic steps to acquiring referrals. First, the hospitality salesperson helps the client recall the names of potential prospects. If there is an occasion to qualify these prospects, the hospitality salesperson should do so. Most importantly, the hospitality salesperson should ask permission to contact these prospects. When they do, the hospitality salesperson asks for names and contact information, especially the office phone and email address. A very effective technique after asking for contact information is for the hospitality salesperson to ask the client to call the referral prospect and explain why a conversation would benefit the prospect. It is best that the hospitality salesperson confirms that the client has made the call to the prospect, via an email carbon copy "CC" or through a follow up from the hospitality salesperson. The hospitality salesperson remembers that although they have a solid sales lead, they must still use effective sales techniques to move through the sales process and lead to another sale. It takes a positive attitude on the part of the hospitality salesperson with both the client and the referred lead that the hospitality organization is the best solution. Just because the hospitality salesperson has a solid lead does not mean that the deal is confirmed. By using this technique regularly, hospitality salespeople can become well known through outstanding service.

On-Property Service

There are three different approaches to serving the client and his or her event at the facility. The first approach excludes the hospitality salesperson in the process. Responsibility for service before, during, and after the client's event is the responsibility of **on-site event managers**. The hospitality salesperson in this case focuses on bringing in new business and is not involved with on-site service. This is typical, especially when the hospitality organization uses a third-party sales representation service, or the organization "clusters" its sales team; in a clustered organization, hospitality salespeople represent multiple facilities and service of the client and actual events are separate from the sales function.

The second, and most common, approach joins the hospitality salesperson with an **on-property event manager** who services the client's event. This is different than the example in the first approach, because the hospitality salesperson directly represents the hospitality facility, and not multiple facilities. Think of the staff organization at a car dealership; there is a salesperson who sells the car, a contract manager or finance manager who creates the contract and financing plan, then a service coordinator who services the car and upsells services and products when the customer brings the car in for regular servicing. This sales and service method is most typically used in large convention hotels and convention centers. In fact, selling to the client may be a team approach where the event services manager and the hospitality salesperson work together to persuade a prospect to "buy" the facility they represent. There are variations of this model; in some, the hospitality salesperson is involved at the beginning of the event and at the end, and the event services manager is the point of contact while the client is on property. In other scenarios, the hospitality salesperson is the point of contact for the client while the event services manager works behind the scenes.

The final approach requires that the hospitality salesperson sells and services the event. In this approach, the hospitality facility may be smaller, which makes this approach best suited for the complexity of the facility. Meeting space and guest room requirements are smaller and easily served by the person who also sells the event. The other philosophy behind this approach is that the hospitality salesperson who sells and services the event has more "**skin in the game**"; they have more involvement in providing high-quality service to the client. In larger facilities, where small events can be less of a priority, a sales position known as the **executive meeting manager** or the event sales manager position is used to sell and service smaller, less complex groups and the events they require.

Catering/Convention/Event Services

In hospitality facilities where an on-site staff services the event sold by the hospitality salesperson, the title of the individual responsible for on-site service is the **convention service manager** or event service manager. At smaller facilities, the title may be catering manager, event manager, or event coordinator. Regardless of title, this position is responsible for all of the details for the event or events: menus, room set-ups, reservations, logistics, and billing. This makes the individual in this position the key contact for the event planner when challenges arise or needs change.

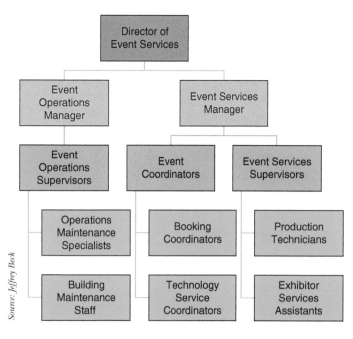

Source: Jeffrey Beck

For the purposes of this section, the term event services manager will be used to describe the position and the role played in on-site services. Event services managers provide professional client services support in planning, organizing, and management of the events within the hospitality facility. Further, the **event services manager** coordinates all activities from when the contract has been signed through the conclusion of the event, including move out and billing. Event services managers are responsible for communicating event details to all internal and external contacts to ensure events are effectively coordinated to meet client expectations; they are the communication link between the hospitality facility and the client. In larger facilities, there will be a director of event (or convention) services who oversees all events taking place, with event services managers assigned to individual events.

The event services department and its staff can be structured in a variety of ways depending on the hospitality facility. The organization chart shown above is for a middle-tier city convention center. Hotels have similar organizational charts, where building maintenance is be the responsibility of the engineering and housekeeping departments. The event services department is responsible for production, set-up, event coordination, and other client needs. The *director of event services* reports to the general manager of the facility, the executive director of the convention center, or the director of sales and marketing, depending on the size and type of hospitality facility. This position is responsible for administration of the event services department, which includes human resources functions related to staff, assisting event service managers and coordinators with providing quality service to clients, and addressing complaints or problems experienced by clients prior, during, and after events. *Event services managers* service the events assigned by the director of event services; they become the primary contact for the client for the hospitality facility. Event services managers meet with representatives of groups and organizations to plan their meeting or special event. They also meet with the heads of other departments in the hospitality facility to coordinate any planned events. Event services managers monitor events and address unexpected problems as they arise to make sure that the event operates as planned. *Event coordinators* are typically entry-level positions that assist event services managers. *Event services supervisors* are sometimes known as convention floor managers or banquet floor managers, depending on the facility. They are responsible for move in and out of a convention, set-up of meeting, event, and exhibit spaces, and assisting third-party event vendors and exhibitors. For catered functions, this position is responsible for acting as a contact person for the client during the event and for supervising banquet staff and set-up staff, ensuring the function is set correctly. This position works with kitchen staff for speed of service, special requests, and number of attendees. *Booking coordinators* manage the reservations, space allocations, and calendar of the hospitality facility. This position may be a single person, or a very small group depending on the size of the facility. This position works closely with sales, event services, and catering staff members. *Technology service coordinators* work as their titles describe; they focus on audiovisual, internet, and other event technologies. In some hospitality organizations technology services are provided by third-party vendors; in the majority of hotels, audiovisual services are provided exclusively by third-party companies such as PSAV and LMG.

Production technicians and exhibitor services assistants work with events that have trade show and/or theatrical/entertainment components. Both positions are front line, working with the client, third-party exhibit service companies, and entertainment production companies. Large facilities have dedicated staff, smaller facilities authorize third-party companies to coordinate such efforts.

The On-Site Service Process

There is an evolution that occurs from sales to service; when that shift takes place is dependent upon the client and the structure of the hospitality organization. As previously mentioned, the event services manager can be intimately involved in the sales process, so the transition to on-site service is seamless. In other circumstances, the facility or the event planner may wish to have the event services manager be a part of the site inspection process. This allows both parties to to get to know each other, and allows the event planner to evaluate the person who will be most important to the servicing of the event, prior to the booking. In this regard, the event services manager becomes both a feature and a benefit to be considered by the event planner.

Some event planners wish to meet the event services manager at the time of contract signing or immediately after; this is a natural move from "outside" to "inside" and begins the service after the sale. For those hospitality organizations seeking to develop strong relationships with their clients, this is probably the best way to transition.

It is important, however, that the hospitality salesperson still be in the communication loop, so that future bookings are possible. Finally, some event planners, especially if the contracted event is not for some years out, do not begin communicating with the event services manager and staff until one year ahead of the event. Whatever the method, the process of shifting from sales to service should be performed smoothly, so that the client does not believe they have been abandoned. In some cases, the selling process may have taken multiple years with communications solely with the hospitality salesperson; there must be an element of reassurance when the transition occurs. Hospitality salespeople best serve as hosts when the event is actually on-site; greeting the client at the beginning, checking attitude during, and wishing farewell with a possible future booking at the end is the best possible behavior for the hospitality salesperson.

The next step occurs when "the time has come" and the event planner is on the hospitality property getting ready for the event that is about to occur. Event planners, once on site, hold a pre-convention (also called the **pre-con**) meeting with the event services manager at the hospitality facility. It is essentially the "pre-game" meeting before the event. If the event is very large, the planner may be a professional event planner representing a major association, or an executive event planner of the corporation. In this case, the director of event services and/or a senior event services manager will represent the hospitality facility. For smaller events, or at smaller facilities, the catering or banquet manager will represent the facility. The pre-con meeting is designed to give the event planner the opportunity to walk through the schedule and double-check the logistics of the event. It also allows the event services manager and his or her staff to address any changes and problems that may have arisen.

Depending on the size and complexity of the event, the attendees for this meeting may be just the event planner and the event services manager, or for large events, representatives from many departments. This meeting is the perfect time for the event planner to establish an understanding with the departments or areas most critical to the success of the event. The pre-con meeting is a review of all of the planning that has already taken place. The document used for this purpose is known as the event specification guide (**ESG**). The ESG has become the standard set forth by the Events Industry Council. Formerly known as the event résumé or specification sheet, the ESG provides all relevant information about the event.

This information includes food and beverage requirements (attendance guarantees, etc.) guest rooming lists (room types, billing policies, and VIP requirements), space requirements (meetings, exhibitions, and

Pre-Convention Meeting Attendees

- Event Planner and Staff
- Facility Director of Event Services
- Outside Vendors (as necessary)
- Hospitality Salesperson
- Facility Director of Sales and Marketing
- Facility General Manager
- Event Coordinators
- Food and Beverage Managers
- Rooms Division Managers (if in a hotel)
- Facility Director of Finance

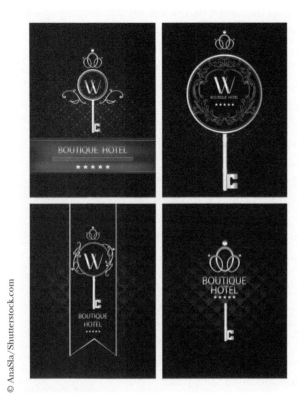

Hotel Lapel Pins

events) and floor plan set-ups, technical requirements (electrical and telecommunications), and other details such as signage placement and exhibit hall security. Many event planners will request a guide to key staff members of each major area; while these people might be in attendance during the pre-con meeting, the event services manager should have this list available for the event planner's reference. Once the ESG has been covered and all details and changes have been addressed, a brief statement of welcome from the director of event services will take place, along with the presentation of lapel pins to the event planner and his or her key staff members that identify them as very important people to the hotel, and signal to facility staff that these individuals are authorized to make changes or special requests. These unique pins are coveted by event planners; the convention hotel that the first author worked at in San Francisco provided one-of-a-kind miniature cable cars in pewter as the lapel pin for event planners.

Resolving Issues

It is common for clients not to initiate verbal or written complaints until after the event is over, if ever. It is common knowledge, however, that dissatisfied clients will tell others about their experience, especially on the internet and other public forums. The result of such behavior is the loss of business from the client and wariness from others regarding the hospitality organization. Problems that occur prior to, during, and after an event is completed must be addressed by both the hospitality salesperson and the event services manager. These complaints and problems should be looked upon as an opportunity to strengthen the business relationship by demonstrating responsiveness and empathy to the client's concerns. As was stated earlier, hospitality salespeople should "check the temperature" of their clients to give them the opportunity to divulge any problems or complaints that they have.

Marriott International has coined the term **LEARN** as an acronym to help facility staff address client complaints:

- **L**istening to the client and allowing them to speak—many times that is all they are looking for: someone to listen to them. Asking questions, taking notes, and being polite are important to resolving issues.

- **E**mpathy requires the hospitality salesperson to put themselves in the shoes of the client. Demonstrating an understanding of the client's concern helps the hospitality salesperson see the problem from the client's point of view.

- Hospitality salespeople and event services managers know to **A**pologize; they understand that the complaint is not personal. Sincerity is critical with the apology. This is not the time to offer a reason or alibi. The hospitality salesperson knows that if they blame someone or something, they are ridiculing their own hospitality organization.

- Hospitality salespeople know that it does not matter whether the problem is real or perceived; **R**eacting to issues quickly is imperative. Keeping promises made, offering solutions, and keeping the client updated as to how the problem is being resolved are important to service recovery.

- **N**otification of the concerns of the event planner with the department or area concerned is a must, especially if the hospitality salesperson of event services manager cannot resolve the problem. The notes taken by the hospitality salesperson or event services manager should be documented for the post-event report and to avoid the problem from occurring in the future.

Successful hospitality salespeople respond to issues either face to face with the client, or by telephone. Never should a client's concerns be addressed by email. Minor grievances can be handled by telephone, but major complaints must be handled face to face.

Post-Event Follow Up

Post-convention meetings (**post-con**), like their pre-con counterparts, are an important part of the sales and services process for the hospitality facility. Typically, the attendees of the pre-convention meeting will attend the post-convention meeting. The purpose of the post-convention meeting is to address the performance of the group, such as room nights (if applicable), banquet checks for review, and other miscellaneous charges that were incurred. Reviewing these documents ensures billing accuracy. Many hospitality facilities take pride in being accurate in their billing; they know that accurate bills mean less time before payment. In addition, accurate billing makes the event planner's life easier as well.

Another reason for the post-convention meeting is to address the performance of the hospitality facility. By conducting this review immediately after the event concludes (many times before the planner leaves the facility), the pluses and minuses of the facilities performance will be fresh in everyone's mind. Many event planners are ready to head home after a major event, so facility performance may not be fully reviewed. In this case, detailed notes and items of greatest importance to the planner should be shared with the hospitality facility as soon as practicable. The Events Industry Council (**EIC**) has developed a **post-event report (PER)** template that is used for collecting, storing, and sharing data on events of all types.

The PER is essential to planning the event planner's next event for the group they represent. It allows the event planner and the hospitality salesperson and event services manager to evaluate the fit between the facility and the group. Many event planners, as part of the contract, stipulate that the final bill will not be paid until a complete and accurate PER has been returned. Service after the sale starts after the contract is signed but does not end until the Post Event Report has been delivered to the client.

SUMMARY

The focus of this chapter is on the last step in the hospitality sales process: service after the sale. The chapter began with a discussion of providing service that strengthens the relationship between the sales professional and the clients. It discussed three service strategies used to accomplish that: upselling, follow-up, and on-property service coordination. That was followed by delving into catering, convention services, and event services. Then came a review of the on-site service process followed by a process for resolving issues, including LEARN. The chapter closed with a discussion of post-event follow up.

KEY TERMS

can-do attitude	on-property event	production technicians
post-event meeting	manager	pre-con
upselling	skin in the game	post-con
follow up	executive meeting	ESG
on-property service	manager	LEARN
coordination	convention service	EIC
referrals	manager	Post-event report
on-site event managers	event services manager	(PER)

REVIEW AND DISCUSSION QUESTIONS

1. Explain three service strategies used to provide outstanding customer service to recently engaged clients.

2. Discuss the three different approaches to servicing the client and his or her event at the facility.

3. Explain how the event services department and its staff can be structured.

4. Outline the steps for follow up after an event.

5. Explain the technique for upselling.

6. List the five elements of problem resolution (LEARN).

7. Explain follow up in hospitality sales.

8. Describe different techniques for getting referrals.

9. Describe the on-site services process

10. What is a post-con and what transpires at one?

CHAPTER 14

Management of the Sales Force and Practical Applications (Part 1)

© f11photo/Shutterstock.com

LEARNING OBJECTIVES

- Describe the sales force organization that is typically "above the property."
- List the typical responsibilities of a global sales manager.
- Explain how professional services differ from selling the hospitality product.
- List the ways third-party service providers can be effective partners.
- Explain the three types of experiences destinations use to showcase their geographic locations.
- Describe the three reasons associations meet.
- Compare and contrast the three types of sales organizations used by destination management companies (DMCs).
- Clarify the sources of lead generation for DMCs.

Introduction

The central premise of this book has been to describe the process for conducting sales in the hospitality industry. Many hospitality salespeople have been trained following a process similar to the one described in this book. In this chapter and the one that follows, five hospitality sales professionals describe their "corners" of the very large world of sales in the meetings, events, exhibitions, and convention industry. The major themes of the guest authors are varied, and yet very important to hospitality sales success. Gus Vonderheide, Vice President of Global Sales for Hyatt, describes the organization of the sales force beyond the local hotel sales staff. Terri Woodin, Vice President of Marketing & Global Meeting Services for Meeting Sites Resource, started her career in hotel sales. In her current position, she helps meeting planners locate sites and facilities for meetings and events. Her company works as an intermediary; selling the value of the location and facility to the planner and selling the planner's meeting value to the location and facility. Jim LaBadie, National Account Executive for Visit Houston, also started in hotel sales. Jim is responsible for selling Houston as a convention location. Jim has the unique opportunity of selling experiences and the city of Houston as a member of the Houston Convention and Visitors Bureau, known as Visit Houston. David E. Rome is Director of Sales for BBC Destination Management Company, New Orleans premier destination management company (DMC). In this role, David sells the expertise of BBC on local knowledge, resources, and all the other aspects of event production in the city of New Orleans. In a way, David and his company sell a vision to those planners bringing their clients to New Orleans. The founder, Bonnie Boyd, says on their website, "We know every bougainvillea plant and banquet hall in the city, allowing us to match your vision with New Orleans' finest people, places, and experiences." John Flood, Founder and Managing Director of elevate, writes about selling food, beverage, equipment, and supplies to support hospitality. John has been engaged in the hospitality business for 39 years, working on the affiliated, supply side of the industry. This chapter will help the reader interested in hospitality sales learn that there are many opportunities for a successful career in hospitality sales. Research conducted with hospitality sales professionals indicates that those truly interested in sales will do whatever they can to improve in their craft. There is little chance that they will move into management; they want to become the best at what they do. Elaine Williams is the Director of Sales for the Ernest Morial Convention Center in New Orleans, Louisiana. It has about 1.1 million square feet (102,000 m²) of exhibit space, covering almost 11 blocks, and over 3 million square feet (280,000 m²) of total space. The front of the main building is 1 kilometer long. Elaine books events that will take place far into the future, some over 20 years from when they are booked. After you read their sections, you will see why they are leaders in the world of hospitality sales.

Management of the Sales Force and Practical Applications in Hotels and Hotel Chains*

By
Gus Vonderheide
VP Global Sales
Hyatt Sales Force

On-Property Sales

The opportunity to sell a major hotel brand came to me 13 years after I began my hotel career. A chance to lead a sales team for Hyatt Hotel & Resorts first took me to Louisville, Kentucky. That property would be the first of three Hyatts over the next four years – Dearborn, Michigan followed by Washington, DC all gave me the first glance into a major brand. Hyatt has years of successful ownership and management in hundreds of hotels globally. Having the culture, resources, reputation, and customer loyalty opens doors and exposes a young sales person to a family-like structure that is fascinating. That, aligned with an honest and strong work ethic, set my career on a path that has strung almost 40 years. Still with Hyatt and as Vice President of Global Sales, I have had the opportunity to see all aspects of selling in a hotel environment.

All hotel companies rely heavily on their sales teams to generate new business, their revenue managers to price the hotel properly, and their event team to service the event so well that the customer returns. These three departments have very different job descriptions, yet must work hand in hand and be in step throughout the process. Selling a hotel to a perfect sell-out might not be rocket science but it's truly a science.

On-property sales teams vary in size depending on several factors, such as amount of guest rooms or total square footage of function space. A team can be as small as two and can reach numbers of greater than twenty. Type of property can also play into this. A full-service convention or resort hotel typically requires more sellers specializing in specific market segments. A select or limited service property will be handled by fewer people. A director of

---

*Contributed by Gus Vonderheide. © Kendall Hunt Publishing Company.

sales (DOS) or in some cases a director of sales and marketing will lead the sales efforts on the property. He or she will report to the general manager and be part of the hotel's senior leadership team. They have the responsibility of hiring, coaching, and managing the day-to-day activities in the sales office. They set expectations for sales calls, outside appointments, site inspections, and revenue quotas. A daily Definite Business Review meeting is typically run by the DOS. At this meeting, sellers come prepared to "pitch" and justify booking a piece of business.

Typically, sellers' quotas are set monthly, but they can, although rarely, be set quarterly or even annually. An associate director of sales (ADOS) is second in command, and is responsible for managing sales activities in the absence of the DOS. In most cases they manage the entry-level sales managers and administrative assistants in the office. They may also be responsible for handling citywide business and other repeat accounts. A senior sales manager, major market manager, and small meetings managers also have group sales responsibility and typically are assigned to a specific type of business. A business travel manager rounds out a common "on-property" sales force.

As group sellers, managers are assigned a market segment, a geographical territory, a specific size account, or perhaps a vertical market to solicit, find business, and secure group business. Market segments include corporate, association or specialty (aka SMERF, a collection of hobby and non-professional groups; i.e., social, military, education, religious and fraternal). A geographical territory can be a territory within the country or even a section of the local city or state. Depending on global interest, other countries could be assigned as well. Vertical sales deployment assigns a specific industry to the seller. Their focus is on all organizations recognized as financial, high-tech, pharmaceuticals, etc. As a transient seller the responsibility is to build relationships with local and national corporate accounts and have your hotel included in their travel programs as a "preferred hotel." This ensures that a corporate traveler has the approval from their company to use your hotel when traveling to your city or destination.

Position	Avg. Salary Range	Bonus potential	Reports to:
Director of Sales	$150 - $170	Y	GM
Associate Director	$100 - $125	Y	DOS
Senior Sales Manager	$85 - $100	Y	DOS
Major Market Manager	$75 - $90	Y	DOS
Small Business Manager	$40- $60	Y	ADOS
Business Travel Manager	$85 - $100	Y	ADOS

Above Property Sales

A hotel owner or developer chooses a large brand to manage their asset for several reasons. The benefits derived from assets such as marketing, technology, and of course the "above property" or chain sales team can be a decision maker. Where the "on property" sales team sells just the hotel they work for, the primary responsibility of a brand's sales force is to represent the entire portfolio. We win if we secure business into a Hyatt-branded property before our competition attempts to do the same. In many cases we are chasing the same customer with the same business.

The Hyatt Sales Force (HSF) consists of nearly 200 sellers located in major locations around the globe. These sellers typically are seasoned in their career, have on property sales experience, and are more strategic than transactional in their sales approach. Let me explain. At this level, a seller is asked to build collaboration opportunities between our company and theirs. Finding touch points and synergies within our goals and priorities will often drive business into our properties. Often members of this team will be defined as either **hunters** or **farmers**. Where a hunter will be challenged to find and develop new business, a farmer is expected to grow additional business by further penetrating their assigned accounts and looking for new business opportunities. Peeling back the onion exposes additional departments, contacts, and fresh revenue-generating options. At this level, the sales force must be deployed against a variety of business segments.

Hyatt's above property sales force is divided into five specific teams:

- Global Enterprise (GE): This team manages a small but mighty list of 55 corporate accounts. We work these accounts with a "total account management" model, meaning that one seller and their team is responsible for all revenue opportunities from that organization – MICE (meetings, conferences, incentives, expositions), transient, and catering business are all tracked and used to assign quotas. To be considered a GE account, we require them to generate a minimum of $5M annually, do business on at least two continents, and be willing and able to work in a strategic partnership. This is not a transactional sell.

- Vertical Sales Team: This team focused solely on MICE business is deployed against a specific industry. Focusing a seller or team on high tech, pharmaceutical, financial, etc., allows them to truly become an expert in their assigned vertical. Knowledge of government regulations and general industry buying behaviors gives these sellers a great advantage to share best practices and repurpose successful tactics.

- Regional Sales Team: It's also extremely important to place sellers where the customers live/work. A Regional Team are typically "hunters," looking for new business. They are based and deployed in regional pockets of the country, state, etc.

- Transient/Travel Management Company (TMC) Sales Team: This team is quite unique from the others – completely focused on the corporate travel buyer versus the meeting planner. Like their on-property counterpart, these sellers attempt to add their branded properties to a preferred list of hotels that a corporation will endorse as approved for their travelers. Every major brand and independents are hoping to have their hotels included, therefore creating a competitive opportunity. Most accounts limit the number of preferred properties that are allowed to be marketed.

- Leisure, Luxury, and Lifestyle Sales Team: For as long as there has been money, there has been those with more of it. Satisfying the wealthiest of our customers takes a special team of sellers with a much different approach. These travelers have high expectations and have seen and experienced more than most. They require unique and special accommodations, destinations, and experiences. Luxury travel agencies such as Virtuoso, Ensemble, and Signature service these customers. Our sellers manage those relationships and provide the agencies with choices within our brands.

Clearly there are many sales opportunities both on and above property for an individual to grow within the industry. A career path is easy to define as one moves through a chain or chains and steps up in responsibility and leadership opportunities.

The job description below is for a global manager within the global enterprise team. Although somewhat specific to this position, there are many requirements and expectations that are shared throughout our division.

Position	Avg. Salary Range	Bonus potential	Reports to:
VP Global Sales	$250 – $300	Y	SVP Sales
RVP Global Sales	$175 - $225	Y	VP Sales
Director Global Sales	$100 - $150	Y	RVP Sales
Manager Global Sales	$80 - $95	Y	Director Global Sales

Global Sales Manager

We're in search of a hotel sales professional with a dynamic, cross-functional background in group and transient sales. The all-star Global Enterprise Team is a division within the Hyatt Sales Force that comprises 50 of Hyatt Hotels' key revenue producing corporate accounts globally. The corporate accounts are typically deployed to teams of three (Global Director, Global Manager, and Global Coordinator). The exceptionally passionate Global Sales Manager will align and strategize daily with the Global Director to achieve semiannual financial production goals across all segments, group, transient, and events. The manager will engage with our on property sellers while consistently digging deeper to uncover new decision makers and new businesses opportunities within their assigned account list. The manager and team will have the exciting responsibility of creating, growing, and developing innovative tactics with their elite customers which increase transient and group revenue while shifting share and loyalty to the Hyatt family of hotels around the world. Hyatt's purpose is to care for people so they can be their best, our purpose extends to our customers and successful team members develop and maintain strong relationships with defined customers by being the trusted liaison between the account and our 800+ Hyatt Hotels. Engaging with our customers through creative, memorable strategic planning that embodies the Hyatt Sales Force spirit of being the most interesting team in the world is a top priority. If you're someone who thrives on having fun, working hard, and utilizing all of your hotel background into one role, this is the opportunity for you!

Typical Responsibilities but we always welcome new paths to success:

- Total Account Management of assigned customers – (managing group business, leisure, corporate travel program and events)

- Manage every field question, customer question, and outside question as it relates to your account base

- Manage Envision database with contacts for both transient and group

- Develop and Implement Strategic Action plans in collaboration with the Hyatt sales vision

- RFP distribution, follow up, and support through Envision for all accounts group, events, and transient needs

- Negotiate and facilitate customers' contract needs, questions, and concerns in partnership with hotel sellers

- Collaborate with team members on memorable marketing tactics which drive awareness of global team and resources available to account base

- Create and maintain a "who's who" when determining end users on group contracts and decision makers who drive revenue

- Research leads booking at our competitive hotels and uncover ways to shift share

- Will be well versed in Hyatt's Loyalty program

- Demonstrate a commitment to Hyatt core values

- The position responsibilities outlined above are in no way to be construed as all-encompassing. Other duties, responsibilities, and qualifications may be required and/or assigned as necessary

Experience

- Previous Hotel/Travel sales experience - 5 years minimum

Education

- 4-year degree preferred

A Day in the Life of a Global Sales Director

This question was asked of my team with the assumption that I would receive back a wide variety of responses. I was not disappointed. I've decided to summarize these positions and "a day in the life" with the following thoughts:

- I'm a coach, a cheerleader, a negotiator, and a referee.

- Our hotels expect me to be the expert on my accounts while my accounts expect me to be the expert on all 800 of our hotels - "Big Responsibility."

- I work strategically to find common touch points between Hyatt and my accounts. The more I find, the more connections are made and business opportunities come from those connections.

- I am asked to be the middle person between my accounts and our hotels. It's important that I wear both hats; representing and protecting our assets while being the voice of my customer.

- I must have a global mindset in everything I do – whether it's culture, currency, time zones, or just business behaviors, I have to stay engaged at all times.

- My specific job is penetrating my account base and finding new ways to generate revenue opportunities. This takes creativity, passion for my product, and the ability to connect those dots.

- Remembering that I am in the hospitality business, everything I do must be centered around making lives better. "Finding solutions is the best part of my job."

- Finding a Hyatt hotel to accommodate every piece of my business is my top goal. We have serious competition trying to do the same. I am always finding the differentials that will win us the business.

Management of the Sales Force and Practical Applications in Convention Centers*

BY

Elaine Williams, CMP, CEM

Director of Sales

Ernest N. Morial Convention Center

New Orleans, LA/USA

ewilliams@mccno.com

About Me

Just like a large part of the hospitality industry, this career path is not the one I intended for myself when I was in college. My plan was to earn a graduate degree or head to medical school with the goal of working with children. I was well on my way to that goal when I took a part-time job at a family-owned wedding/special events facility. It did not take long to become hooked! By simply passing a tray of overstuffed sandwiches, I discovered serving others was more gratifying than I could ever imagine. Though I did stick with psychology long enough to get a degree, the hospitality industry kept calling. After a short period of work at a hotel, my true career began. I took a job with the Food and Beverage Company in the New Orleans Ernest N. Morial Convention Center (ENMCC) in 1996 and have never looked back.

After spending 10 years working in food and beverage holding titles ranging from sales manager to general manager with several others in between, i took a role as a member of the sales team for the convention center. I have now spent the last 12 years on this team and still find it fascinating each day.

About the Center

With 1.1 million square feet of prime exhibit space, in an entirely contiguous hall, the New Orleans Ernest N. Morial Convention Center (ENMCC) in New Orleans Louisiana, USA provides the largest single (contiguous) exhibit space in the country. The New Orleans Ernest N. Morial Convention Center features an award-winning staff and first-class amenities and is the sixth-largest convention center in the nation. A consistent Top 10 host of the largest conventions and trade shows in the nation annually, the Convention Center has also been named one of the city's "Top Workplaces." A leading contributor to the city's robust tourism economy, the Convention Center's event activity has produced $85.7 billion in economic impact since its 1985 opening, including $5.4 billion in new tax revenue for state and local governments. The New Orleans Ernest N. Morial Convention Center is a subsidiary of the state of Louisiana and has a governing board referred to as the Ernest N. Morial New Orleans Exhibition Hall Authority. The Authority is composed of a 12-member board of commissioners, nine appointed by the Governor of Louisiana, and three appointed by the Mayor of New Orleans. The gubernatorial appointees serve at the pleasure of the governor, while the mayor's appointees serve four-year terms. The Convention Center has a president/ general manager who leads the team of over 300 full-time employees.

The mission of the Center is to deliver unrivaled results for our internal and external customers in safe, hospitable, exceptionally well-maintained facilities through innovative and collaborative efforts that contribute significant benefits to the New Orleans and Louisiana economy. We derive our revenue from two main streams: the services we provide to the events we host, including facility rental, technology, production, food and beverage, etc., and the taxes paid by patrons of the local hotels and restaurants we support.

It is an exciting time at the Center with the creation of a new Pedestrian Park, a headquarter hotel slated for development on the south end of the Center and the commitment to invest nearly $400,000,000 in the interior of the Center to include renovations of: meeting rooms, vertical transportation, bathrooms, lobbies, meeting room corridors, etc.

About Our Team

Convention centers can be governed in several different ways, involving city ownership, state ownership, and even a combination of the two. This crucial difference in management can affect how the sales process is handled from convention center to convention center. However, fundamental similarities exist regardless of the overall governance structure. The most common goal is to generate business in the destination to support the economy of a city, state, and even the region.

Because of this unique, universal goal, selling a convention center differs greatly from traditional "sales" roles. There is no exchange of goods or set price tag per se. The sale is more about how an event can work logistically in your center while offering a unique attendee experience, rather than selling a physical product. There is never a mantra of "sell it and forget it."

With a small team of five, our sales department is responsible for over $9,000,000 in facility rental and over $20,000,000 in ancillary revenue. Although not every sales team works in the same way, we divide the country geographically to determine which sales manager will be assigned to an account. Our four geographic regions are the Northeast from New York to Washington DC, the Southeast from Florida up to Washington DC, the Midwest, and the West Coast. As the director of sales, I maintain key accounts in all regions for a variety of reasons, with a large concentration in the Washington DC and Chicago areas. There is heavy concentration in these two cities simply due to the large number of associations and corporations headquartered in those areas. We also retain some vertical markets as well, including sports, technology, and pharmaceutical; but the true assignments are geographical.

Marketing/Communications

Selling a center actually starts with effective marketing to potential customers. It is critical for a center to have a strong marketing/communications team working side by side with the sales managers. Whether it is developing marketing materials for trade shows, creating an informative website, or producing an easily legible floorplan, a clear consistent message is needed.

As part of marketing the convention center, the sales team members actively participate in a large array of industry organizations, including the International Association of Venue Managers (IAVM), the Professional Convention

Management Association (PCMA), Meeting Professionals International (MPI), the American Society of Association Executives (ASAE), the International Association of Exhibitions and Events (IAEE), and the Society of Independent Show Organizers (SISO). All of these groups hold at least one annual trade show or meeting that the sales team attends in order to promote the destination and network with clients, as well as to gain industry knowledge by attending education sessions. These education sessions allow our sales team to attain industry designations such as Certified Meeting Professional (CMP) and Certified Event Manager (CEM) in order to further convey our understanding of the industry to our clients.

Type of Events

The ENMCC plays host to several types of events, including conventions, trade shows, corporate meetings, public events, concerts, sporting events, and competitions. To further understand our business, we also classify each event into a market segment, such as agricultural, athletic, educational, governmental, medical, military, pharmaceutical, social, and technological. Most centers host similar events but differ in their total mix of each type and market segment. For example, some destinations, like New York City, host one consumer show after another, where in destinations like New Orleans, consumer shows make up less than 5% of the business base. The vastly different demographics of these two cities help to explain these large variances. The city of New Orleans proper is only made up of 400,000 people and even with our outlying suburbs the number only approaches 1 million. Compared to the 4 million people in New York City, you realize that New Orleans is a very small "big" city. Successful consumer shows in New Orleans are those that attract attendees from not only Louisiana, but from the surrounding states, including Mississippi, Alabama, Texas, and Florida. Multiple consumer shows focusing on the same subject matter within the same year can be challenging in a city of this size due to market saturation.

How We Book Events

Every event starts with a lead, which can come from a number of sources. The most common source is the destination marketing organization (DMO) or convention and visitors bureau (CVB) in the destination. Other sources of leads are through an event sourcing website, a local hotel, or even a simple phone call or email to the sales department. New Orleans & Company

(NO&C) functions as our CVB with the goal of cultivating and maintaining what we call a "virtuous cycle" between the businesses and attractions that make up the tourism industry, the visitors who patronize those businesses and attractions, and the local residents who benefit from the tax revenues collected from tourism activities. As New Orleans' promotion and offerings evolve, New Orleans & Company will continue to support the New Orleans local economy by providing more career opportunities and generating revenues to fuel a vibrant economy in which all of the residents can find a path to prosperity.

The cultivation of leads is a true team effort with the New Orleans & Company team of over twenty sales managers and the convention center sales team of five. The partnership between these two entities is critical for any destination. Some destinations combine both sales teams into one in an attempt to create one source of communication. In New Orleans, we are two separate entities working very closely together. Certain destinations divide leads and events between the two sales teams depending on the timeframe of the event. In such a case, the CVB sales team may handle all business that will occur more than two years in the future and the center sales team would handle any event within two years. In New Orleans, we truly partner on *all* business. Since our CVB relies mainly on a hotel tax for every room night sold in the city, their focus is not on our annual local groups. The center sales manager will lead the process for these events. However, both parties fully understand the value of all business in the destination. Annual local groups help fill holes in the calendar that are typically driven by the time of year they occur.

Regardless of their source, most leads are accompanied by a document containing event details. Typically, those leads originating with the CVB have a more robust form than a "call in" lead would have. The CVB leads are typically accompanied by a full RFP (request for proposal) filled with information like: organization details, event description, attendee demographics, preferred dates, alternate dates, history of the event, room flow, space needs, decision time frame, etc.

Once we collectively decide to bid on a certain lead, the assigned CVB sales team member will work on gathering the hotel and off-site venue information while the center sales team member works on appropriate placement of the event within the center.

How a center captures the information about the account, contact, and event is critical. Every center utilizes facility management software that has integrated customer relationship management (CRM), event management, and financial/accounting platforms. At the Convention Center in New Orleans we utilize Ungerboeck Software (USI) which we use for all aspects of an event. Ungerboeck has been a global leader in flexible, comprehensive event and venue management software for over 25 years.

Several factors are considered when placing events in the Convention Center, including overall space needs, attendance, peak room nights, total rooms nights, event history, and our competition. Placing an event in the facility is similar to completing a large very complicated puzzle. The difference is that you need to move the puzzle pieces around freely when placing an event. In the center world, it is often said that it is not about what you book, but about what you can strategically move. At the scale of the ENMCC, the puzzle can be exhilarating! If the event comes from a source other than the CVB, the same process ensues. Once the event is placed on the calendar the real behind-the-scenes work begins.

Determining Rental

The center sales manager will spend quite a bit of time gathering information about the event in order to determine a pricing structure that makes sense. As most centers, we have our rack rates (standard rates); however, these are just a starting point and guide. We use a cost model to help capture those services that would be included in the rental. Additionally, we consider what other revenue this event will bring into the center.

It is critical to keep in mind what an event generates for the destination. However, the ENMCC is not a not-for-profit entity and is aiming to generate revenue whenever possible.

Variables that affect pricing include:

- Seasonality (off-season or peak season)

- Attendance

- Number of peak rooms

- Total number of room nights

- Public relations opportunities (Super Bowl, Final Four, political debates, etc.)

- Competition for the event (knowing your competitor is critical)

- Food and beverage generated from the event

- Ancillary revenue of the event (utilities, technology, production)

Determining a rental rate for a group is never an exact science. The total amount spent in ancillary services, especially in food and beverage, is weighed heavily. In New Orleans, like in quite a few other destinations, the food and beverage is contracted out to an exclusive provider. In New Orleans the current provider is Centerplate (now owned by Sodexho). The exact agreement between exclusive providers and centers differ from center to center. Some centers are based on a profit and loss model and others are composed of a fee that the center pays the provider annually. Either way it represents a large revenue source for the center, often the number one source of revenue. The more food and beverage revenue an event can bring to the table (no pun intended), the more the space rental fee may be decreased.

Another key ancillary revenue source to consider is the revenue generated by exhibitors. A large exhibit floor with several booths will generate internet and electrical revenue that a corporate meeting or educational meeting may not. In turn, that corporate meeting will generally feed most of the attendees' breakfast and lunch each day, generating food and beverage dollars. Pricing can be looked at as a delicate dance, one step forward for one revenue source and two steps back for another.

All pricing is reviewed by the director of sales to ensure the big picture is considered. You can look at the pricing of the center as being similar to that of hotel rooms. The rate for the same space over the same dates can differ for several reasons. One example would be when an event is booked for the center/destination, short term versus far out into the future.

Generating a Proposal

Each sales proposal should include general information about the convention center, the details of the space, dates and rates offered, and most importantly the concessions offered to the client. Some centers include brief information about future upgrades to the center, accolades won by the center and information about the destination.

Space, dates, and rates used to be the most significant section in a proposal. With the increase in supply of convention center space, several destinations will be able to bid, which puts pressure on the rates. The CVB will also need to determine if city concessions can be provided to help the destination stand out. Several destinations will have the hotel room package and a convention center with the appropriate space, but they may not have a center/destination concession package that merits a closer look from the client. In New

Orleans we aim to add *lagniappe* (a little something extra) to help make our destination stand out. When you consider the client's review process, which is often putting each city onto a spreadsheet and comparing the pros and cons of each, you realize how important it is to stand out. Too often, the fluff of the proposal is impossible to include on a spreadsheet so that information is just tossed aside.

Once completed, the proposal will be sent to the client if the lead does not come from the CVB. Otherwise it is typically sent to the CVB team to be included in the overall city proposal or city bid. The follow up process now begins, which is a critical time. Traces (reminders to check in) should be developed by the center sales manager (along with the CVB sales partner when applicable) to determine how the bid looks compared to others, if there any questions about the space, have all questions been answered, etc.

The proposal review process consists of considerable back and forth between the sales manager and client. Clients compare one city to another and may ask one city to match the deal points of another. This frequently includes negotiating hotel rates, center rental, or even the overall deal of the city. At this point, the CVB, hotel community, and center sales team need to come together to make a decision. Does this event represent a value (financial or otherwise) that makes it worth revising the overall deal points? This decision takes thorough analysis and looks at what the overall value is to the destination as well as to the hospitality community. Most of the players involved are "for-profit" organizations and must consider the bottom line for their own business/organization. If there is an agreement by all parties, revisions are made to the proposal.

Site Visits

A client will most often conduct a site visit in those destinations that are considered to be finalists. This visit is a chance for each partner to stand out and show their best. The client will typically visit the airport, the center, the hotels, venues, and restaurants to get an overall feel of how the event will work. It is critical to have coordination between all hospitality parties in a destination. Without sharing too many secrets, there are several out-of-the-box ideas that have been executed in New Orleans. Having all staff (300 team members) welcoming the client as a group, a second line parade in the street, and providing a helicopter ride to transport the show manager from the center to the airport are just a few of the creative tactics that have been employed in

New Orleans. A "wow" factor is often critical. Of course, New Orleans can also speak for itself with over 1,500 restaurants, countless museums, live music venues, festivals, etc.!

New Orleans is Selected to Host the Meeting, What's Next

Once a city is verbally selected, the process of confirming the event begins. Our CVB develops a letter of intent (LOI) that includes the hotel information, the Convention Center information, and the city concessions. The letter of intent is shared with the center for review and is sent to the client for signature. Once this letter is signed, the event is considered confirmed at the convention center. In this document, dates of when the center contracts are required to be signed are detailed along with the signature dates for the headquarter hotel. The center team will follow up with a Convention Center Letter of Agreement if the event will occur five years or more in the future and a Convention Center Facility Use Agreement if the event is within three years. Hotels begin following up according to their guidelines as well. Not every city utilizes a city LOI. Unfortunately, the cities that do use a LOI have very little or no cancellation penalties included in the LOI, which makes the time between this document's signature and that of the center or headquarter hotel nerve wracking. Both the hotel and the center documents detail a cancellation policy that enforces a significant penalty to cancel. Those cities that do not use a LOI make the client either sign a center agreement or headquarter hotel contract, or sometimes both, to confirm an event. This can be time consuming; however, it does help prevent cancellations.

Just as in most centers, the cancellation penalty for the ENMCC does not kick in until 5 years prior to the start of an event. This, again, causes vulnerability between the signing of the LOI and five years before the event.

The Convention Center Letter of Agreement (LOA) details the *space, dates* and *rates* of the event as well as the cancellation policy. Included with this document is the Facility Use Agreement (FUA) detailing the terms. When a client signs a LOA, they are also agreeing to the terms of the FUA, which they will sign approximately three years out. The FUA has several terms that clients look to negotiate, like: indemnity, insurance, cancellation, and default. At the ENMCC, we work closely with each client to come to an agreement, bringing in our legal department when needed. These negotiations often take quite a bit of time.

Once the contract is negotiated, the sales manager takes a small step back and introduces the event manager. A large step back is not an option as the sales manager should always remain present. The sales relationship is critical and must be maintained long before and long after an event occurs.

It is also very important to note that as an event approaches, *everyone* is in sales. In order to ensure a client's return to New Orleans, everyone needs to participate. From the facility services team to the food and beverage team, to the technology team, all must be on their game with the goal of not only producing a successful meeting but also ensuring the consideration of a future meeting.

In Conclusion

A center sales manager does not just need to know how to sell. They need to be experts on how to market, how to negotiate, how to value an event, how to service an event in-house, how to "talk like a lawyer," and how to explain a final invoice, not to mention the most important piece: how to develop and maintain relationships. A sales manager is re-selling as often as they are selling.

From puzzle making to delicate dancing, a sales manager has to carry a brief-case over-stuffed with skills. That is what is most attractive about selling in this particular industry. No two days are the same. When a new challenge arises the sales team member steps to the plate ready to "swing away."

NOTE: Since this chapter contains case studies of practical applications of sales there is not a concluding summary of the chapter, nor key terms or discussion questions.

CHAPTER 15

Management of the Sales Force and Practical Applications (Part 2)

© Simone Hogan/Shutterstock.com

LEARNING OBJECTIVES

- Describe the sales force organization that is typically "above the property."
- List the typical responsibilities of a global sales manager.
- Explain how professional services differ from selling the hospitality product.
- List the ways third-party service providers can be effective partners.
- Explain the three types of experiences destinations use to showcase their geographic locations.
- Describe the three reasons associations meet.
- Compare and contrast the three types of sales organizations used by destination management companies (DMCs).
- Clarify the sources of lead generation for DMCs.

Management of the Sales Force and Practical Applications in Third Parties
Terri Woodin, CMP
Vice President of Marketing & Global Meeting Services
Meeting Sites Resource

Since 1993, Meeting Sites Resource has been the leading global strategic meeting management solutions organization delivering meeting excellence. This includes global hotel sourcing, custom contract negotiations, professional meeting support services, and strategic meeting management consulting.

How prospects buy consulting and professional services like a third-party outsource partner such as Meeting Sites Resource, HelmsBriscoe, Experient, McVeigh Associates, Conference Direct, and others as compared to buying a product/hotel is very different. In professional services, you must determine how to build a bridge from your expertise to those that you can help. Selling professional services is sold on relationships, referrals, and reputation. In contrast, selling a product/hotel is based on features or attributes like physical building style, number of rooms, square feet of meeting space, etc. It is the difference between an intangible and tangible sale.

Much of what we know about selling in the "sales funnel" process to generate X number of leads, qualify them, sell to the prospect, and close does not apply to consulting and professional services companies. Business development in professional services is not selling, you are helping others succeed. Connecting and building relationships and nurturing those relationships over time helps you stand out among other expert services providers.

How Do Prospects Buy Professional Services?

First, they must be aware of your company and understand what you do and then they must understand how your solutions will be helpful to them in achieving their goals. Respect for you personally and your company's reputation are on the line, and, as your reputation precedes you, it provides credibility for them to trust you. Lastly, the prospect must have the ability to hire you and the timing must be right for them to be able to do so.

Your expertise and knowledge create value and you need to discover, understand, and solve the prospect's problems to obtain them as a client. The goal is not to sell what you do but to be invited by prospects into their projects as a trusted advisor/partner.

Let's look more closely at what we can do to move a prospect to a client. It takes an average of eight contacts or interactions to show a prospect you are serious in developing the relationship beyond an acquaintance to a quality relationship. Stay positive and persistent. Solve their problem, do not sell.

The market is flooded with third parties that service organizations in sourcing and contracting their meetings and events. How do you stand out? In this global economy it is also harder for buyers and sellers to find each other. Identifying a community and positioning the third party to serve it over time and focusing on it helps achieve the company's revenue goals. For example, focusing on a vertical market segment like medical or financial or perhaps drilling down even further and working with organizations of a certain size or revenue producing within a vertical market segment…just own it.

First, do the prospects know who you are, and do they know the name of your company? To buy from you, they need to know you and recognize your organization's name. You want to create awareness so they think of you or your company when they have a problem that you can solve. A great way to do this is to introduce yourself to the community you wish to serve as noted above by asking for their help instead of contacting them and stating that you are with your company and you are available to do work for them. This is sort of like interviewing for information. Ask for advice…get their perspective on where the industry is headed. Ask if there are others with whom you should be talking and if the person minds if you use their name when reaching out to others. Make your highest priority to serve and when you introduce yourself always be learning. Determine who you should be speaking to and find the time to introduce yourself to all within this targeted community.

Prospects buy based on who they know (relationships), who they trust (referral), and track record (reputation). So, stand out by adding value. Invest in the relationship.

Tips for being a successful third-party outsource partner:

- Ask for advice.

- Send links to articles you know they would be interested in.

- Introduce them to people who would be helpful to them.

- Speak at industry conferences and webinars to your target audience.

- Publish your point of view in a particular segment and stay focused to it to be known as a dominant and consistent voice in the industry.

- Host or sponsor industry roundtables with meeting planners to discuss best practices.

- Share your recognition and awards.

- Network at industry events: host a lunch, dinner, or a coffee around the event to meet the 15 people you do not know.

- Write newsletters and send to an email list.

- Mail a copy of your latest article with a handwritten note and follow up with a call a week later inviting them to a roundtable discussion on the topic to discuss their thoughts.

Do great work, make new friends, build your network, and believe that organizations have a desire for the true value you bring with your expertise and experience. Build rapport with those you wish to serve and stay focused on the community you wish to serve of your top 200 contacts. Select two or three of the above that best suit your style and stick with it for the long haul to be positioned to be of help.

Second, do the prospects understand what you do? Prospective clients may have heard of you, but they may not understand what you do, who you serve, and how your organization is unique. Your prospect is someone who would benefit from your expertise and not realize that you and your organization is their problem solver. This is where specializing in a specific community you wish to serve creates awareness within that niche and communicating to this target audience what you do, who you serve, and how you are unique will help them remember you. Create a clear connection between you that they can trust and the problem you can solve. Create your differentiation in the marketplace of what are you are a subject matter expert of and the best at and then define and communicate it consistently.

Thirdly, in order for prospects to continue the conversation with you, they need to believe what you do is relevant to their goals and believe your services must have a significant positive impact on those goals. How does what you do make a difference to a prospect's success with what value you bring to the table? The goal is to be a problem solver and create solutions for them. This requires a lot of listening to learn about their problems and asking questions to understand their perspective in order to help them reach their goals.

People do not like being sold to so it is important not to talk to prospects about how you can help them but instead listen to how they want to be helped. We can't rush to demonstrate our expertise and miss the opportunity to provide value. A good practice is to share your knowledge about the meeting planning industry, and their industry.

Lastly, when a prospect respects your experience, background, and track record, they will be confident you will get the job done for them. They want to know that you have done similar work for other clients in the same niche successfully. Tell your story to share these successes. Have a prepared follow-up piece you can send to them after the introductory conversation. Be sure to clearly explain what you do, support your track record with case studies, include logos of past and current clients to create credibility, include your bio because clients like to know who they will be working with, and then your contact information.

So never say sell! Commit yourself to identifying your community within your specialty niche that you would like to be of service to and then do everything you can to help connect those with introductions, meetings, and articles, etc. to grow your connections and provide value to turn them into clients.

Management of the Sales Force and Practical Applications in Destination Marketing Organizations (DMOs)
BY
Jim LaBadie
National Account Executive
Visit Houston
jlabadie@visithouston.com

Over the four and half decades that I have been in the hospitality industry, we have witnessed nearly constant change in our industry. Back in the 1970s and 1980s, hotels were primarily divided into the categories of limited-service and full-service properties. Limited service is a fairly clear description in that the hotel rooms were basic in design and in amenities. And the building that contained the rooms offered no other services than the front desk. Occasionally one might uncover one of these types of hotels with a swimming pool. However, very few offered any food service and at that time none of them had event space.

Full-service hotels offered the traveler a more complete package. The properties were larger, the rooms had more guest amenities, the guest probably had access to a pool and a choice of restaurants, and they were usually designed with meeting and event space.

While these choices may seem to be rather limited, they were driven by the customer's needs. And if the room rate was an important consideration for the guest, they had a choice to pay less and relinquish access to the additional perks full-service hotels could offer.

As a sales professional "back in the day," the mantra we marched to was "space, dates and rates." And we always said that the customer could have two of the three. If they name the dates and the space they want, we would set the rates. If they had specific space requirements and rate parameters, then we would pick the dates. And whether you were a salesperson with a specific hotel or with the convention and visitors bureau for a specific city, your chief concern was to package it all properly, so the customer became a buyer.

Clearly that has all changed…on both sides of the equation. Sales professionals working for a single hotel or with a convention bureau representing a city, state, or region now must have a full databank of knowledge in order to get the buyer to "Yes"! Let's focus on the bureau aspect of our business.

For nearly a century, cities, regions, and states have maintained an agency whose function was to create the demand for travel to their specific area of influence. Those agencies were referred to as convention and visitors bureaus. However, not every entity that employed an organization to promote travel to its destination had a convention center or other urban elements that would support convention business. And, as is mentioned in the mission statement above, the economic impact derived from travel, whether it be individual or group travel, is important. And so, in 2005, a new term was born – destination marketing organizations.

Destinations International is a trade association representing the interests of destination marketing organizations (DMOs) from around the world. And from their mission statement comes a very tidy summary of what their members do. That is "…to drive destination economic impact, job creation, community sustainability and quality of life through travel."

First and foremost, travelers to a destination create jobs. Those jobs exist in restaurants, hotels, convention centers, taxi and shared-ride companies, airports, etc. And while many of those jobs exist to serve the local community, in most cases the ability of a destination to bring visitors into the area is the additional revenue needed to create steady, year-round employment.

DMOs of every size are focused on bringing visitors to their city, town, community, or region. And those visitors create estimated economic impact or EEI. That is the common measurement tool we use to understand the financial boost the destination receives from every visitor – whether they are a single traveler, married on a honeymoon, summer vacation with family or friends, or coming to a city to attend a meeting or convention. While the metric for each of these distinct traveler categories is different, the impact on the community is important.

The travel market is segmented in many ways – far beyond whether or not the person is alone, with their family or a few friends, or part of a large group. And because that is the nature of the market, every DMO must have resources that are dedicated to those markets they believe they can succeed in attracting to their area. Firstt-ier cities like New York, Chicago, Los Angeles, and others have demand generators in every category. They have created a brand that appeals to individuals who travel for myriad reasons. Visitors may want the museum experience. They may be the culinary crowd looking for the hottest new restaurants and craft breweries. Or maybe sports drives their choice of a city for travel.

And in the group market, cities like these have large investments in the infrastructure required to attract large national and international conventions. And this is where we have seen tremendous growth. DMOs around the world have become very focused on ensuring that they are into group marketing at some level and have hired the sales and marketing professionals to reach their goals. And we have moved past "space, dates, and rates!"

Life is now about the experience. Personal experiences. Social experiences. Professional experiences. I would like to concentrate on the professional experience. The ones we derive from our chosen profession. And how DMOs have adapted their products and their marketing practices to showcase their destination.

Let's use an example from my own work – Houston's growth in the global meetings and convention market.

National associations offer a large pool of business for cities in this market. Nearly every association stages meetings at a variety of levels, from local one-day workshops on their industry to an annual meeting that may draw a global audience both in-person and online. And while every association is concerned about the space they need to conduct their business, the available dates and room rates, those are many times the secondary considerations when selecting a site for their next annual meeting.

Association meetings are all held for three primary reasons. The first is networking. By their very nature, successful associations have a healthy membership that is growing and looks forward to the opportunity to attend the meeting offered by the organization. It is still today one of the most important elements – the ability to meet new people who share your passion or profession and learn from them at a convention or conference.

The second reason is content or education. Whether we are talking about trade associations (where the memberships are purchased by corporations or other entities) or professional associations (where the membership is a personal investment), when a member makes the decision to attend it is to learn.

And the third reason is financial management. Practically every association uses the annual meeting platform to generate operating revenue. In fact, the average association generates over 35% of their annual operating budget from the annual meeting. As a DMO sales professional, we must showcase our city in such a way as to show our customer how they are able to reach these goals if they choose our destination.

Now let's take a more specific example and illustrate how the process works.

The first step is to do your homework – on both sides of the equation. We must build a deep knowledge base of the assets of our city. Also, understand how to present those assets to our client as features with very specific benefits to the customer's organization and their meeting delegates. On the other side is knowing your customer. Not just the name of the group or their mission statement. We need to have total knowledge of the business of the group. What are their burning issues? What are the hot topics that their members are discussing? Because until we have that kind of deep, beyond-the-cover-page insight, we would not be in a position to discuss appropriate features and benefits that will truly make a difference. And that is the essence of what we are trying to do – differentiate ourselves from our competitors.

A great case in point is the medical association market. Because Houston is home to the Texas Medical Center, by far the largest medical center in the world, we focus a lot of our resources on connecting with and selling to medical association executives.

So, let's start with networking – the first element we cited earlier in the reason the meeting is held. Healthcare professionals enjoy the networking element of meeting attendance more than any other market segment with which I have worked. Outside of the plenary session and breakouts, physicians will gather together to discuss and learn from each other at every junction. Thus, when we present our product, we are always ensuring that our clients are aware of what our city can do to enhance this important need. We'll showcase the abundance of flexible space that can be used for informal conversation during the morning coffee break or after the final gavel right at the convention center. There are a large number of restaurants in the central business district for lunch away from the center or an evening with friends and colleagues. And, of course, they are close so no time is lost in long transports to or from suburban eateries.

The hotels also play into this element. Houston is fortunate to have hotels connected to the convention center. This is another key factor that keeps the attendees close and in touch with one another.

And finally, the Texas Medical Center. We can provide access to arguably the greatest collection of medical minds located in one place. Talk about networking!

The second tenet of every meeting is content and education. This is the one area, especially when talking about medical associations, in which Houston has a distinct advantage. The close proximity of the world's most advanced medical facilities and human capital ensures that our clients in this field have ready access to limitless opportunities to enhance their programming. And, in our particular case, you can make that same point in the fields of aeronautics and aerospace, energy, and other industries.

The last element we presented was financial management. A destination's sensitivity and contribution to that aspect of meeting planning is the final consideration. The more we know about an organization's structure and goals for the event, the better position we are in to contribute to their bottom line. I actually had a client last year for whom the annual meeting had absolutely no impact on the budget of the association! Her mindset in the negotiations was obviously much different than someone who needed to support the association with greater than 30% of their operating budget. But again, it is our responsibility to know this information and then deliver the product so that the goals of the client are met.

Many refer to the times we live in as the era of big data. I could not agree more. In my 40+ years of hospitality sales and marketing, never have I had to "do my homework" more diligently that I do now! But the results have been terrific. We are not just creating sales, we are creating customers. Buyers who will be bringing a huge investment to Houston based on the knowledge that the destination will be able to provide the kind of support necessary to help them reach their goals and not just create another booking for the city.

Going forward, quite honestly, I see more of the same. The type of sales environment we are in now will continue. Whereas this kind of "connecting the

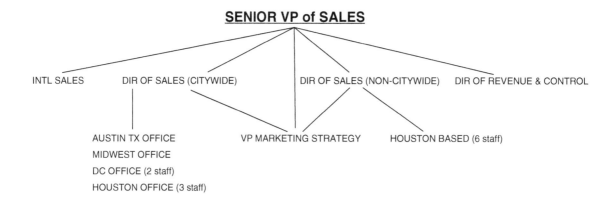

SENIOR VP of SALES

INTL SALES — DIR OF SALES (CITYWIDE) — DIR OF SALES (NON-CITYWIDE) — DIR OF REVENUE & CONTROL

AUSTIN TX OFFICE
MIDWEST OFFICE
DC OFFICE (2 staff)
HOUSTON OFFICE (3 staff)

VP MARKETING STRATEGY   HOUSTON BASED (6 staff)

dots" with customers was creative and welcome, it will become necessary and expected. Those cities that do this will compete.

I can honestly say that my 19 prior years in hotel/resort sales and marketing was a great building block for what I am doing now. However, the level of satisfaction received in the sales environment I just described is very high. Our knowledge of our client goes way beyond their value to the city. Relationships that began as business colleagues in many cases have blossomed into personal friendships that have lasted for years. And the challenge to uncover the next association with a connection to our city and find that singular advantage we may have over another city makes our sales job that much more intriguing.

Management of the Sales Force and Practical Applications in Destination Management Companies (DMCs)

BY
David E. Rome, CMP, DMCP
Director of Sales
BBC Destination Management, A Global DMC Partner
New Orleans, LA
drome@bbcdmc.com

What is a DMC? According to ADMEI (Association of Destination Management Executives International), a destination management company, or a DMC, is a professional services company located in their destination which specializes in local expertise and resources. The DMC is your strategic partner to provide creative local experiences in event management, tours/activities, transportation, entertainment, décor, and program logistics. ADMEI members must demonstrate that they provide tours/activities and transportation, and two of the following: event management, entertainment, and program logistics.

Types of Office Configuration

DMCs can set up the configuration of their offices as they see fit. There is no one right way to do this, so each DMC decides either out of necessity or habit what fits their business the best.

- Sales Department – Operations Department: In this scenario, the sales department is responsible for finding business through lead generation and working closely with clients to develop a program or itinerary (proposal) to suit their needs and/or budget. Then, typically, once a contract is signed, the file or information is shared with the operations department and turned over to them. they produce the event(s) that sales has contracted with the client.

- Sales Department – Creative Writing Department – Operations Department: This scenario is very similar to the Sales – Operations configuration but with one major change. The sales department finds the business, but then has a creative writing team produce the proposal based on the client's needs. This allows the sales team more time to research and find more business. after the client signs off on the program (signs the contract), the operations department takes over, just as in the first scenario.

- Sales Department and Operations Department; one and the same: This third scenario seems to work better for smaller DMCs with only a handful of employees. The salesperson stays as the only contact throughout the entire process. They sell the ideas, contract with the client, and service them through the end of the event(s). Essentially, they are sales and operations, one contact for the client.

There are pros and cons to each of these configurations. The type of set-up is sometimes based on the size of the company. A smaller company works well with the sales/operations being one and the same. For example, in a third-tier city, a two-person DMC will work as the sales person and the operations person, giving them the capability of running two programs (at least) at the same time. This seems to be harder to do when you have a DMC in a first-tier city with a large staff. The Sales-Operations configuration can be somewhat more efficient as the sales team can be securing the business while the operations team is producing events. Time management can get muddled if one person is doing both duties at the same time and could make for long wait times for proposals to clients.

Lead Generation

DMCs are no different than any other company that relies on sales to stay in business. And leads are the best way to find business. But, it's not as easy as you would think to find leads for decent, profitable business. There are many ways to find a lead and it's best to utilize many of the channels available to you. Here is a list of common lead-generating avenues:

- CVB/Convention Center: If you are a member of your local convention and visitors bureau, part of the membership should include getting leads on business that is coming to your town. It could be in the form of a calendar of future business or in the form of actual requests from clients that are looking for DMC services during their conference. FAM (familiarization) trips can be organized by your local CVB and are a great opportunity to get in front of many clients at the same time. FAM trips offer the DMC a chance to have potential clients visit their city/town to showcase what can be offered to their attendees, such as tours, hotels, restaurants, and venues that could accommodate their group or potential future group. This, in turn, will hopefully lead to lead generation.

- Trade Shows: Exhibiting at a trade show is normally a paid admission for suppliers like DMCs. This allows you to set an appointment with clients that are potentially looking at your city or your company for a conference or incentive trip. Trade shows can be expensive to attend, but the chance of making a connection and building a relationship with a possible client is higher than contacting the client by traditional methods of cold calling or emailing. A face-to-face meeting is one of the best ways to sell yourself and your company to potential leads/clients. An example of a well-attended show is IMEX, one of the largest exhibitions for the incentive travel market. It is held annually in Las Vegas in October and allows the DMC to have quality appointments with actual customers. DMCs can either buy into a city's convention and visitors booth or their own DMC consortium's booth, or purchase their own booth. In all three cases, appointments are scheduled for one-on-one conversations about your destination and the client's needs.

- Hotels: The first connection with a city that a client usually has is checking availability at hotels. A DMC should maintain a healthy relationship with the hotel sales team and convention services team in the hope that a referral or recommendation from them to the client will take place early in the planning process. DMCs also partner with hotels in their city on FAM trips or site inspections to get to know the client better. The site inspection is crucial to the client determining if the city is a right fit for their program and to see if the DMC is a good fit. Site visits (sites) allow DMCs to show the client firsthand how they perform regarding transportation, tours, dinners, creative ideas, and venue choices. This is usually a mutually beneficial relationship. DMCs can suggest one hotel over another to their clients and in return hotels can introduce the client staying with them.

- Consortiums: Consortiums are groups of like-minded or like-service DMCs. Examples of consortiums are Global DMC Partners, PRA, Access, the DMC Network, Host Global Alliance, etc. Some consortiums represent company DMCs, while others act more as marketing firms to independently owned DMCs. Either way, they are useful for referring business to each representative company as well as referring business between the DMC partners in the consortium. An example of a consortium that markets for independently owned DMCs is Global DMC Partners. This consortium represents independently owned DMCs that offer similarly high levels of service and are usually representative of the top DMCs in their city, state, and country. BBC Destination Management in New Orleans is part of Global DMC Partners.

- Vendors: Most DMs do not own any of the services they sell. They excel or fail by the quality of the vendors that they work with. The type of vendors that we work with are venues, restaurants, florists, entertainers, and transportation companies. When you work with vendors for an extended period of time and have a great relationship with them, you will sometimes find that they refer business back to the DMC. The old adage of treating others as you would want to be treated speaks volumes here because a good vendor could also lead to a good client.

- Social Media: it's very difficult to prove the ROI on social media, especially as a DMC representing one city or one state or one country. But a DMC lives or dies by its brand, and social media is the modern way of getting your brand out there and setting in stone what that brand represents. Through blogs, event posts, company philosophies, or company hires and announcements, your brand takes on a life of its own and hopefully clients will recognize that brand for years to come.

- Repeat: The best thank you a client can ever give you is coming back and utilizing your services again. For any DMC, the goal of having a satisfied client is being able to consider them a repeat client. It is also recommended to ask these repeat clients for referrals, which is usually highly effective in obtaining additional business.

Lead Management

Once leads are received and researched, the DMC needs to be able to keep track of that client/lead. A database of some sort is needed to take note of pertinent information like company, client, name, address, phone, and email, as well as information about the needs of the client. Keeping track of the correspondence with a client is very important as well. Listed below are several programs that are used for client data.

- CRM or customer relationship management is the use of technology and software to monitor the relationship between you and the customer. Examples would be Salesforce, Zoho, and Microsoft Dynamics. Most platforms can be used across an entire network of DMCs and allow everyone to see the status and history of every client that has been contacted/reached in some way.

- Excel/PowerPoint/Word: Many of the Microsoft Office products can keep a DMC organized. Excel is commonly used for cost sheets, finance reports, and contracts. PowerPoint and Word are commonly used for proposal writing.

- Outlook/Calendar is the key to keeping track of client interactions and when to contact a client regarding a program, contract due dates, or deposit due dates. Keeping an organized calendar with reminders and "to-do" lists allows you to stay on top of clients' needs and communication.

- Company Database/Shared Drive: It is helpful to have a shared drive utilized throughout the company that can be accessed by all employees and can keep track of all client files.

The Lukewarm Call vs. the Cold Call

If you have ever been in sales, you have heard the term, "cold call," meaning picking up the phone and calling a potential client to offer your services to them without ever having any interaction with the particular client. This is usually not very effective, especially in the DMC world, because a client may not have an interest or business to bring to your particular city. Rather than a cold call I like to use a phrase I coined called a "lukewarm call." To obtain a lukewarm call, research must be done. You need to drill down into the lead and find a common ground or a common person between you and the client that could lead to an introduction, or, at least, be that link between you and the client to open the door to know that the client may have business for your city and in turn giving you a chance to do business with them.

Do Your Research: Drilling Down into the Lead

There are several ways to turn a cold call into a lukewarm call.

- Research the client online and see where they may have met before or where they may be meeting.

- Contact any partner DMCs that may have worked with the client in another city and request an introduction.

- Research your own database to see if anyone in your company has worked with the client before; if you have worked with the company before and have a relationship with another employee, you can ask that employee for an introduction.

- Lastly, if you know the hotel that the client is looking at, you could talk to the sales person in charge of that account and see if they would mind making an introduction for you.

A DAY IN THE LIFE OF A DMC DIRECTOR OF SALES

Most of my career has been working directly with clients in creating the perfect program (event) to help accomplish their goals and objectives for their meeting. The longer you are in a career, and if you so desire, you get the honor of managing a team. This, unfortunately, gives you less contact directly with clients, but fortunately, your team becomes your top priority. So, most of my day as a director of sales involves daily direction of our company values, goals, and standards to my sales team. I support them in their daily work load from brainstorming ideas, reviewing proposals and contracts, to keeping an eye on the budgets.

One day I can be on a site inspection with one of my account executives all day touring clients through the city and trying new restaurants. Another day I can be at a trade show showcasing my amazing city and trying to get clients to add us to their city selection process.

At all other times, I am online researching possible new clients or staying in touch with past clients and hotel contacts to stay relevant and top of mind.

I find it is usually part luck and part persistence that gets you in front of the client at the right time…

David E. Rome, CMP, DMCP is Director of Sales for BBC Destination Management Company, A Global DMC Partner. BBC Destination Management is New Orleans' premier destination management company with over 26 years of experience. Led by President and CEO Bonnie Boyd, CMP, DMCP, a sixth-generation New Orleanian, the BBC team knows New Orleans. The BBC team navigates the rich cultural landscape of the city, to steer clients in the right direction for an authentic, seamless, and culturally enlightening event. From the best local restaurants and entertainment, to décor and custom tours—the BBC team has the right contacts and attention to detail to produce the perfect New Orleans meeting. BBC goes the extra mile to ensure that visions are accomplished, goals are achieved, and stress is eliminated.

Allied Industry: Selling Food, Beverage, Equipment and Supplies to Support Hospitality[*]
by John Flood

For any hospitality venue to be successful they must rely heavily on the expertise of allied suppliers to be able to offer the variety of food, beverage, and other services that are required. Allied suppliers range from food and beverage companies like PepsiCo, Smucker's, and Smithfield to service companies like Ecolab and broadline suppliers like Gordon Foodservice, Sysco, and US Foods.

Many who study and have a desire to be engaged in the hospitality industry often do not have awareness or consider the array of opportunities to be directly involved with and able to impact the direction and future of hospitality directly as a supplier. These suppliers strategize and interact every day with the hotels, catering operations, restaurants, stadiums, and event companies that make up the hospitality industry. To be able to operate any of these venues, the industry is reliant on these suppliers to source the needed ingredients, equipment, packaging, beverages, and any other supply required to run the back-of-house operations.

Every single food, beverage, ingredient, and supply is produced by a manufacturer who is expert in and focuses their energy in supplying the industry. There are thousands of companies that support the hospitality industry

Contributed by John Flood. © Kendall Hunt Publishing Company.
*Portions of this content were taken from IFMA (International Foodservice Manufacturing Association) Education Foundation – PEOPLE FUTURE 2025 research, November 2018.

Source: John Flood

that generates sales in food and beverage of $872 billion. **Food and beverage alone in hospitality is approaching ONE TRILLION dollars in revenue!**

Working for and selling on the supply side of hospitality is described as challenging, rewarding, dynamic ,and fun by those who currently work in the industry.

The purpose of this chapter is to create awareness, not to suggest that selling either on the operations or the supply side is better. We will spend very little time discussing sales on the operations side as that subject is covered in depth in the other chapters.

If you are pursuing sales on the operations side, it is important to know that **many of the best hospitality venues and those involved in sales develop and leverage the expertise of the affiliated suppliers to ensure their business and go to market approach remains on trend** and able to tap into resources that may not be available in-house. Having an understanding of these companies can help those with sales responsibility to be able to keep up with trends and use this knowledge when working with clients who may be looking for special needs. Often, the supplier companies have visibility to trends that other hospitality competitors are having success with. **Always look beyond your organization to listen, learn, and adapt to best practices.**

Occasionally, someone who loves and begins their career on the operations side of the hospitality industry will look for a change and want to make a career change for personal reasons, and, not knowing that there are opportunities on the supply side, end up in other industries where their passion and talent may not be a good fit. This is a loss for the individual and the industry that can use their talent. Fortunately, the reality is that there may be an excellent fit for both the person seeking to make a change and the companies that are supplying the industry.

Many of the most successful companies recognize, look for, and hire talent that has a passion for and understanding of the hospitality industry. They know that the ability to understand and be able to connect is much easier for someone who has experience on the operations side of hospitality. These companies have culinary, R&D, and marketing teams that work directly with the decision makers at each of the venues to make recommendations, help write menus, and create dining experiences that have the research and consumer insights behind them to make the operations most appealing.

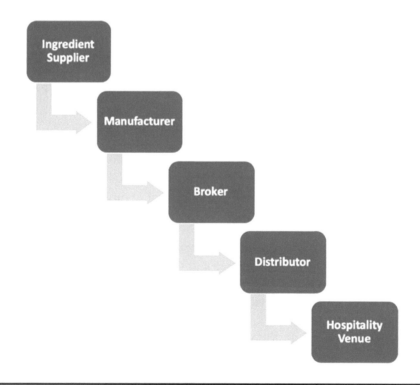

Source: John Flood

Sales opportunities in the hospitality industry start with the initial raw material (ingredient) and flow through the entire supply chain, ending up in the specific venue to be sold to the consumer. Sales opportunities to leverage hospitality understanding and expertise exist in each connected, affiliated link.

Affiliated Suppliers Can be a Great Option and Fit

- **The industry provides employees with the ability to use all the skill sets in one's toolbox, and the ability to get involved in multiple disciplines is something that is rarely found in other industries.**

- Given the lean, entrepreneurial nature of many foodservice manufacturing companies (or divisions), employees gain a more well-rounded experience than in the retail food channel (or other industries).

- There is a huge opportunity to learn and grow—something that many in the industry feel is poorly understood by those outside the industry.

Average Tenure in the Industry Is 21.5 years

- Once an employee finds a job in the industry, they tend to stay.

- **The industry breeds longevity and the pay can be lucrative for the large percentage who stay within foodservice.**

- Ninety-four percent (94%) of industry professionals indicate that in two years, they expect to still be working in the foodservice industry. Additionally, 85% expect to still be with their current company.

- **Overall, industry veterans report a high degree of satisfaction and would recommend the industry highly to young people.**

Reasons for Affiliated Industry Desirability

- Being both a stable and growing industry leads IFMA members surveyed to believe that new grads would find the foodservice industry to be an attractive place. The need for foodservice will never disappear and has many directions in which to pursue a particular passion.

- In qualitative interviews, more than one industry leader pointed out that the industry is ready for an influx of new talent.

- *"There will be lots of opportunity in the next ten years. People will be retiring and making room for young talent in a stable industry."*

- *"We need a diverse group of new talent. Diversity in gender and race but also skill sets. There are so many ways to plug yourself in to the industry. Supply chain, purchasing, sales, marketing..."*

- *"The industry is looking for talent. They don't care about your age. Just prove you can do the job."*

Very few graduates know the exact career path or trajectory they will take as they move through their working life. Success requires discipline that can help you be successful in every facet of sales (both hospitality and affiliated), and quite frankly in every facet of life, job, or task you undertake. So, consider the following tips and life lessons from an industry veteran who began in restaurant operations, moved over to the affiliated, supply side of the hospitality industry where he began in sales, moved into marketing ,and then to executive positions up to president of a Fortune 500 company able to retire before the age of 60.

- **Never, ever chase the money.** So many are looking for the highest paying job when they graduate, whether it is a good fit or not, believing that it is all about the money and that they will learn to like or "fit" with the company. Over time they typically are unhappy, leave, or get fired. It is very difficult to perform at your best when your values are not aligned with those you work with and for, or you simply do not believe in the products or services you are selling.

- **Never, ever chase the next promotion.** When you are in a job and all you think about is your next promotion it becomes easy to get distracted, not put your full energy or focus in your current job, and fail to get promoted because your job performance was not what it needed to be. Focus on your current job and excel; the promotions will follow.

- **Do your job (continuously rewrite your job description).** Understand that the job description you are given is simply a document created at a historical moment in time and reflects the proven behaviors that worked best at the time it was written. **Understand from your boss what outcomes he/she desires and then commit yourself to figuring out how**

to most efficiently accomplish and exceed them. In these rapidly changing, dynamic times you will be exposed to different approaches, technology, and techniques that may not have been available to your boss or others that they may not even be aware of. When you begin to apply these new, better practices and share them upstream with your boss **you will be recognized first for your ability to exceed your job expectations and secondly as someone who can critically think, someone able to take on greater responsibility.** Someone whom they will want to consider for a promotion!

- **Know that you are not fully qualified for any new job you go into!** The simple fact is that no one is 100% qualified for a new role simply because they have never done it, the company may be new, the customers or products may be different than what you know. **There will be something you do not know.** Understand that the person or company hiring you is not hiring you because you know everything, they are hiring you because they believe in you and in your capacity to quickly learn. **So, be a learner, ask questions, and then go do.**

- **Take on assignments no one else wants, the difficult, the ugly, the ones that, when you succeed, will set you apart.** One of the quickest ways to get noticed and move through an organization is to take on tasks that may not be fun but need to be done. Have the confidence when taking on these assignments that often all that is needed is for someone like you to care, is willing to probe and ask questions, and then to take action, which will result in a path to follow, a path to success.

- **The minute you fear failure is the minute your career progression will stop.** Know that the only way you will learn if a new approach, idea, or concept will work is to actually go try it. The only way you will move to a new, higher level of performance or promotion is to improve your skills by trying something new. **The best performers are those who are always seeking to improve, knowing that each time that they stumble, make a mistake, or fail is just a learning opportunity.** When doing this, it is critical that you fail fast, then admit you made a mistake, discuss with your boss what happened, what you learned, and how it will help you and the company going forward. You will be amazed at the appreciation and help others are willing to give you when you are honest and want to listen and learn how to improve. Companies know that the only way they will move forward is by having people who are not afraid of the failure to push them forward.

- Repeat after me; **"Never, ever chase the money!"** Focus on your relationships, treat others with respect, collaborate, and share success.

  - **Never, ever chase the next promotion**

  - **Do your job (continuously rewrite your job description)**

  - **Know that you are not fully qualified for any new job you go into!**

  - **Take on assignments no one else wants, the difficult, the ugly, the ones when you succeed will set you apart.**

  - **The minute you fear failure is the minute your career progression will stop.**

When you apply these disciplines, you don't have to chase the money. The money will follow as companies seek the best, proven talent. Go, be the best, prove yourself, and, **Let the money chase you!**

NOTE: Since this chapter contains case studies of practical applications of sales there is not a concluding summary of the chapter, nor key terms or discussion questions.

Accountability A characteristic of the hospitality sales professional. Linked to personal integrity and ethics, hospitality sales professionals hold themselves accountable when a mistake has been made.

Active listening The hospitality salesperson must concentrate, take notice of nonverbal behaviors, and acknowledge and confirm understanding of the words and meaning the prospect provides. When paying attention, the goal is to listen for understanding.

Advantage Also called general benefits. Describe what the feature does to benefit the prospective customer.

AIDA principle Guides effective presentations. Seeks to gain the *attention* of the prospect. Next, a well-planned presentation stimulates *interest*. By emphasizing specific benefits that are derived from buying objectives stated by the prospect, the hospitality salesperson adds value for the prospect which creates *desire*.

Alternatives close Offers product and service options to the prospect.

Analyzers They want the numbers more than anything. They want strictly the facts.

Artifacts The items and other things that people surround and adorn themselves with.

Association An organization of individuals who come together to expand their own knowledge of their profession or interest area and the guidelines under which they operate.

Association Management Companies Can be hired to run the association and/or its events. They offer the expertise, staffing, and resources that allow smaller professional societies, trade groups, not-for-profits, and philanthropic organizations to effectively manage day-to-day operations and advance their long-term goals.

Assumptive close A common technique that minimizes the amount of pressure on the client to buy. The hospitality salesperson embraces an attitude that assumes the prospect is going to buy the product and services from the hospitality organization.

Asynchronous presentation The written word through a letter, email, or request for proposal (RFP) is defined as an asynchronous presentation format. Asynchronous presentations can be the first communication between the prospect and the salesperson.

Augmented products Those elements that add to the atmosphere, interaction, and experience that the customer will encounter.

Authentic reasons A prospect's objections stating why the client believes that he or she is unable to purchase from the hospitality organization.

Balance sheet closing Or t-account closing method outlines reasons to book now, versus reasons to wait.

Benefit Justify why the customer should choose the products and services the hospitality salesperson represents

Benefit statements Describe how the features selected by the hospitality salesperson achieve the prospect's buying objectives. Benefit statements can be defined as how the prospect will gain or will receive or will experience from using the product or service.

Bleisure travel Combination of business and leisure travel.

Business discussion The sales dialogue is planned in such a way as to transition to the sales contact objectives by capturing the interest of the prospect.

Business etiquette The established protocol of behavior in business settings.

Business event A gathering of 10 or more participants for a minimum of four hours in a contracted venue. These business events include conventions, conferences, exhibitions, and incentive travel.

Buyer resistance A prospect's areas of concern in the sales process.

Buyer resolution theory   This theory emphasizes that a customer's purchase behavior is dependent upon the buyer's mental steps that surround five issues that must be decided to complete the purchase. Ultimately, the customer must have answers to five questions: Why should I buy? What should I buy? From whom should I buy? What is a fair price, what is the best value? Finally, when should I buy?

Buyer's remorse   The feeling of remorse or guilt that arises after making an expensive and/or difficult decision.

Buying motivations   Can be summarized as one of three general themes: fear, need, or greed.

Can-do attitude   The mentality of a hospitality salesperson in which they are willing to do everything they can to enrich the business relationship.

Canned presentations   Consist of scripted sales calls, presentations that have been memorized, and automated presentations.

Capping   When the salesperson asks for commitment to purchase from the prospect.

Casual workdays   Days when company policy allows employees to dress in more casual attire.

Closed-ended questions   Help the hospitality salesperson collect specific information and facts. The answers to closed-ended questions are simple and direct. The answers are typically yes or no; the answers are condensed to only a couple of words.

Closing process   When the hospitality salesperson seeks a commitment to purchase from the prospect. Hospitality salespeople must have a plan for closing the sale when the opportunity presents itself in the form of client cues. Prior to asking for commitment from the client, the hospitality salesperson should address objections, resolve concerns, then ask for the sale.

Cold calling   Making telephone calls to prospects without prior arrangement

Communication etiquette   Involves a complex set of unwritten rules governing speech, written correspondence, and body language that varies in different parts of the world.

Communication style   How someone likes to do something.

Compensation technique   Exceptional benefit resistance buster; this resistance buster is most commonly used with price concerns. The hospitality salesperson acknowledges that there is a valid concern, then spotlights the incomparable benefit that the prospect found to be most important.

Competition analysis worksheet   Compares the property the salesperson represents with those of the top three competitors. In rating the competition, the salesperson should identify those that are better than the property the salesperson represents, those that are the same, and those that are worse than the property the salesperson represents.

Completed Contract   Also known as the written close. Ensures a customized solution. Requires the hospitality salesperson to have listened carefully and taken good notes when asking technical, buying process, and client motivation questions.

Confirmation questions   Used in the sales process to test the understanding of the prospect of what the hospitality salesperson said or demonstrated.

Congress   The European word for a convention; attendees are referred to as delegates.

Controlled   Talking with a very determined or really specific type of style.

Convention and visitor bureaus (CVBs)   Created to promote the city as a convention destination, as well as represent the city and its many hotels to bid for that business. Have now evolved to not only market but help develop and manage tourism in their destinations. Most recently, the term "DMO" is being used in place of CVB.

Convention service manager (CSM)   Or event service manager. Provide the services that a convention sales manager contracted with the customer.

Convention   A type of event where the primary purpose is for attendees to attend educational sessions, participate in meetings and discussions, network, and attend recognition events.

Core products   The most basic level of hospitality offering.

Corporation A corporation is a firm that meets certain legal requirements to be recognized as having a legal existence, as an entity separate and distinct from its owners. Corporations are owned by their stockholders (shareholders) who share in profits and losses generated through the firm's operations. Corporations have three distinct characteristics 1) Legal existence, 2) Limited liability, 3) Continuity of existence.

Customer selling strategy Concentrates on who the hospitality organization sells to, what products and services will be offered, and what selling techniques will be used.

Customer service representative Also known as the gatherer. An inside salesperson, this role is typically the equivalent of being an order taker. In most situations, the gatherer responds to inquiries from prospective customers.

Delegation An important skill for hospitality sales managers to learn; the act of empowering to act for another.

Delivery personnel The on-site individuals who follow through with the contract created by the demand creator. Delivery personnel can be considered the service after the sale.

Demand creator Also known as the hunter. The sales professionals in this role, as the name implies, spend much of their time seeking out: 1) new business, 2) additional business from existing customers, and 3) new business from existing customers.

Demonstrations Effective when the client is skeptical about the products and services the hospitality salesperson represents. Demonstrations are best used when the prospect is in the process of comparing hospitality facilities.

Destination marketing organizations (DMO) Also called convention and visitor bureaus (CVBs). Created to promote the city as a convention destination, as well as represent the city and its many hotels to bid for that business. Have now evolved to not only market but help develop and manage tourism in their destinations.

Detailer A common name for the person who makes reminder presentations in the hospitality industry of catering and social events.

Direct competition Can have similar product offerings, ratings by third parties, pricing, and a nearby location.

Direct denial technique A straightforward response to an inaccurate opinion or belief of the prospect.

Direct eye contact Visual contact with another person's eyes.

Direct request A simple statement asking for the sale. It is also called the basic close or direct appeal close.

Discovery questions Used to the uncover the facts surrounding the prospect's needs for the hospitality product. There are general discovery questions, which collect the basic information, and then specific discovery questions, which follow up the general discovery questions to acquire more detail regarding the information provided by the prospect.

Distribution The actual delivery of the idea, good, or service.

DMC Destination management company; performs a variety of services to accommodate the MEEC planner.

Effective listening Considered to be one of the most critical skills necessary for the hospitality salesperson. Effective listening means that what was said and what was meant by the prospect incorporates all of the information that the salesperson should be taking note of.

Elevator speech It is thirty seconds in length, which is typically the amount of time an individual would have to ride from the bottom to the top of a building. The scheme behind the thirty-second commercial is that the hospitality salesperson has a message prepared that can be delivered anytime, anywhere, even on an elevator.

Emotional intelligence It is the capacity to be aware of, control, and express one's emotions, and to handle interpersonal relationships judiciously and empathetically.

Event services manager Coordinates all activities from the moment the contract is been signed to the conclusion of the event, including move out and billing. Event services managers are responsible for communicating event details to all internal and external contacts to ensure events are effectively coordinated to meet client expectations; they are the communication link between the hospitality facility and the client.

Event specification guide (ESG) A comprehensive document that provides the who, what, where, when, and how of the MEEC event. The ESG conveys information clearly and accurately to MEEC venues and suppliers regarding all requirements for an event. This guide provides all products and services required during the day or days of the event.

Events Organized occasions such as special celebrations, gala dinners, marketing events, incentive group events, and product launches. Events can be held by corporations, associations, government agencies, and individuals.

Events Industry Council (EIC) 30+ member organizations represent over 103,500 individuals and 19,500 firms and properties involved in the events industry. Four signature programs—Sustainability, Industry Insights, Knowledge, and Leadership—represent the key initiatives, assets, services, and products for the Events Industry Council. The Council works to advance the events industry and the professionals who lead the business of meetings.

Executive meeting manager Or event sales manager. In larger facilities, where small events can be less of a priority, this position is used to sell and service smaller, less complex groups and the events they require.

Exhibitions Have different meanings in different parts of the world. Exhibitions can be trade shows, expositions, fairs, or expos. Exhibitions are designed to display, and potentially sell, goods and services to customers in a particular market segment.

Facilitating products Those products or services that must be in existence for the customer to buy.

Feature spit A behavior of hospitality salespeople in which they "spit" everything they know about the product and services to the client, without considering specific benefits or linking general benefits to the features.

Feature-and-benefit sales technique Used to describe how a prospective customer will be satisfied with what the hospitality organization has to offer.

Features The characteristics or attributes of the hospitality facility and organization.

Follow up Must be consistent and continuous; a methodical and logical approach to follow up after the contract is signed is a hallmark of successful sales in hospitality.

Force majeure Or act of god; a clause which protects both parties from unforeseen uncontrollable circumstances.

Gatherer A mentality of some salespeople. Sees the sales close and commitment as an affirmation that they have created a relationship with the prospect, and that the client has found the hospitality salesperson's organization, attitude, and presentation compelling.

General benefits Easily recognized and can be of benefit to any prospective customer.

Hospitable salesperson Must be "on the same wavelength" with the people they communicate with. The analogy you want to remember is two tuning forks that are at the same frequency, so they sync with each other.

Hospitality contract Common elements of a hospitality contract are generally the "who, what, where, and when" of the event in legal terms. The clauses required in a hospitality contract help to protect both the hospitality organization and the client.

Hospitality industry In this industry, salespeople sell both to individual consumers and to organizations.

Hospitality sales process The steps a hospitality salesperson must follow to align with the customer's buying process. The hospitality sales process includes seven steps: 1) Prepare, 2) Access, 3) Establish, 4) Present, 5) Proof, 6) Close, and 7) Service.

Hosted buyer The potential buyer or prospect pre-registers for the trade show and provides documentation that they are qualified to make purchase decisions. In return they are "hosted" by the trade show and receive reimbursement of airfare and hotel costs. In return, the prospect agrees, in advance, to participate in scheduled meetings with vendors who have products that can meet their wants and needs.

Hunter A mentality of some salespeople. Hunters are great at solving clients' problems and cold calling, and handle rejection easily. Hunters have short memories; they forget the last "no" because they are on to the next opportunity.

Incentive meetings Used to reward employee achievement, effort, and contribution to the success of the organization and are typically held at ultra-luxury hotels and resorts.

Indirect competition Typically in a nearby location, but do not offer identical services.

Indirect denial technique Refutes the prospect's opinion by stating that other prospects and clients have had similar concerns which turned out to be invalid.

Informative presentations Put an emphasis on facts. In the hospitality industry, this presentation technique is best used for a new or newly renovated property. It can also be used with newly enhanced hospitality services.

Inside salesperson Also known as the gatherer. An inside salesperson is a customer service representative who is typically the equivalent of being an order taker. In most situations, the gatherer responds to inquiries from prospective customers.

LEARN Listening, Empathy, Apologize, Reacting, Notification. Marriott International has coined the term LEARN as an acronym for helping facility staff to address client complaints.

Market segmentation When we divide our current and potential customers into groups with common characteristics.

Marketing The process of planning and executing the conception, pricing, promotion, and distribution of ideas, goods, and services to create exchanges that satisfy individual and organizational objectives.

Matching and mirroring A technique that people use to relate or resonate with the individual. Matching and mirroring is to speak to people in a body language that mirrors what they're doing.

MEEC Meetings, Events, Exhibitions, and Conventions. An acronym that describes an important sector of the hospitality industry that describes business events and activities.

Meetings A coming together of a group of people to discuss or exchange information. Meetings can include conferences, lectures, workshops, board meetings, training meetings, and corporate retreats. Meetings can be organized and held by corporations, associations, and government entities.

Missionary sales role The role typically taken on by the demand creator or a sales professional tasked with reminding the prospective or current customer of the products and services the MEEC organization has to offer. The missionary sales role is designed to develop the relationship between the organization and the customer.

Necessary budget Should be confirmed by the hospitality salesperson very early in establishing the dialogue.

Need Should be confirmed by the hospitality salesperson very early in establishing the dialogue.

Need discovery The objective of the sale dialogue is to uncover the needs of the prospect. These needs can then be converted into what is known as the buying objectives of the prospect. These buying objectives are the three-to-five objectives the prospect must achieve in order to complete the sale.

Need for approval emotion An emotion that subsides when much time is spent on prospecting and when sales professionals treat the tenth sales contact with a prospect the same as the first.

Need resistance When people resist buying because they want additional proof that they are making the right decision.

Need satisfaction theory This approach to sales relies on effective communication between the hospitality salesperson and the customer. The salesperson seeks to understand what buying motives or needs dominate the customer's buying process, then develops a sales strategy which addresses the buying motives in way that the customers realize value.

Negotiation Working to reach an agreement that is mutually satisfactory to both the buyer and the seller.

Networking Developing personal connections; can help the hospitality sales professional expand business opportunities.

Non-price consideration close Offers an incentive to act immediately.

Nonverbal communication Communication that is not verbal. The most common form is body language.

Now-or-never close   Creates a sense of urgency with the prospect, especially when the hospitality salesperson has a limited amount of space for a particular date or dates.

Objection   Specific reasons why the client believes that he or she is unable to purchase from the hospitality organization.

Objective fulfilment question   Seeks agreement on the part of the prospect that the product and services of the hospitality organization will satisfy his or her buying objectives.

Objective summary close   Emphasizes benefits important to the prospect. This technique is also called the summary close or the summary of benefits close. This method is very popular; it provides a review of the recognized benefits and proposes a course of action for the prospect that leads to commitment.

On-property service coordination   There are three different approaches to servicing the client and his or her event at the facility. In the first approach, responsibility for service before, during, and after the client's event is the responsibility of on-site event managers. The second, and most common, approach joins the hospitality salesperson with an on-property event manager who services the client's event. The final approach requires that the hospitality salesperson both sell and service the event.

On-property event manager   Joins with a hospitality salesperson to service the client's event.

On-site event managers   Responsible for service before, during, and after the client's event.

Open-ended questions   Allow prospects to answer as they wish and give the hospitality salesperson deeper meaning from the prospect's perspective. Open-ended questions allow the hospitality salesperson to probe deeper into understanding the needs of the prospect. Open-ended questions can help the hospitality salesperson "control" the sales dialogue.

Option questions   Used later in the sales dialogue, when the hospitality salesperson is working to uncover the prospect's tastes for various options.

Organizers   There's a place for everything and everything in its place. Organizers tend to be organized. With this type of person, there is an expectation that a project or activity will follow a process as well.

Outside influences   Impact the buying decision. This sales theory suggests that there are four interpersonal buying influences: economic, user, technical, and coach.

Packages   Combinations of products/services and pricing schemes.

Paternalism   An individual's autonomy is in conflict with the consumer's welfare.

People   Employees; impact the quality of service, and thus the marketing of the business.

Personal selling   A process where person-to-person communication takes place between a salesperson and a current or prospective customer.

Personal selling philosophy   Requires the hospitality salesperson to answer the questions that follow. When they start every day, what do they want to do as it relates to selling? What, as it relates to selling, directs their actions and decisions? After a day in the selling environment, what gives the hospitality salesperson satisfaction? Why are beliefs related to sales important? The ethics of hospitality sales must be a part of the personal selling philosophy. How does the ethical philosophy of the hospitality salesperson correspond with the individual's personal selling philosophy?

Persuaders   This is the kind of person who wants to draw attention to themselves. They want answers quickly, and are more likely to "solve the problem, then figure out how to do it."

Persuasive presentations   Seek to influence the prospect to act.

Persuasive sales dialogue   Meant to influence the prospect's opinions, point of view, and buying behaviors toward the hospitality salesperson and the organization he or she represents.

Place   Part of the four Ps of marketing; the location of the business, or what internet sites are used to sell the product or service.

Plan to close the sale   Hospitality salespeople must have a plan for closing the sale when the opportunity presents itself in the form of client cues. Prior to asking for commitment from the client, the hospitality salesperson should address objections, resolve concerns, then ask for the sale.

Planning The research and homework necessary to intelligently decide what to do.

Positioning Communicate a unique benefit to that target market.

Post-con Post-convention. The purpose of the post-convention meeting is to address the performance of the group, such as room nights (if applicable), banquet checks for review, and other miscellaneous charges that were incurred.

Post-event meeting Includes feedback and invoice review with the event planner and hospitality organization staff.

Post-event report (PER) Developed by the Events Industry Council; provides a documented record of the MEEC event for future reference by all stakeholders involved with the event.

Potential prospects The broad market of companies or individuals who have a need for the hospitality product or establishment.

Pre-con Pre-convention. Pre-convention meetings are meetings held with the event planner and appropriate vendors and operational managers 24 to 48 hours before the event.

Price One of the four Ps of marketing; what the customer is willing to pay.

Probing questions Used to collect more detail on a particular issue.

Process A series of steps or a course of action; the development of a marketing plan and careful examination of the effectiveness of the communication to the audience.

Procrastination Occurs when the delay or avoidance of an issue facing the hospitality salesperson arises due to the fear of making a mistake or calling an angry customer, or when other activities provide immediate gratification over activities that must be done in a timely fashion.

Product Part of the four Ps of marketing; an article or substance that is manufactured or refined for sale.

Production technicians Work with events that have trade show and/or theatrical/entertainment components. Position is front line, working with the client, third-party exhibit service companies, and entertainment production companies.

Profile Ranks each prospect for the potential of a successful or bountiful sales relationship.

Promotion One of the four Ps of marketing. Spreading positive information about an organization and its products and services.

Property demonstration Used later in the sales process; typically, the hospitality salesperson has met with the prospect at least once before, and the property demonstration is used as part of a persuasive sales dialogue. In this technique, the hospitality salesperson provides the prospect with a tour of the property, highlighting how features of the property will benefit the event planner and his or her attendees.

Props Materials that help support the solutions offered and the benefits stated in a sales presentation.

Prospect Potential customer.

Prospecting Developing plans to develop an inventory of prospects for hospitality products. These prospects can be current customers, former customers, or individuals who have never done business with the hospitality organization. Prospects can also be organizations or accounts.

Publicist A person who manages and generates publicity.

Qualification The evaluation of prospects. Qualifying a prospect involves considering 3 elements: 1) Does the prospect have a need for the hospitality product or service? 2) Does the prospect have the budget or financial ability to purchase the hospitality product or service? 3) Does the prospect have the authority or decision-making power to make the purchase decision?

Rapport Built when mutual trust, a business friendship, and like-mindedness are developed.

Reach The estimated number of potential customers who will see a specific type of promotional or advertising campaign.

Referral A sales lead that is collected from current customers.

Relational buyer Looking for the hospitality salesperson to be an expert that will consult and guide them to a purchase that will be the right choice for them.

Relationship buyers Can be seeking to develop a relationship such that one buying experience will lead to many more.

Reminder presentations Also known as check backs. These types of presentations work well with known or repeat clients, since there is an effort to continue the partnership or relationship and keep clients from switching to the competition. Many times, reminder presentations add service after a sale has been completed.

Reminder sales dialogues Typically come later in the sales process; prospects may have met with salespeople from multiple hospitality organizations. Then, the hospitality sales professional must remind the prospect of the benefits that will be derived from the products and services offered by the organization he or she represents.

Request for proposal (RFP) A document that an organization posts to elicit a response – a formal bid – from potential vendors for a desired solution. The RFP specifies what the customer is looking for and describes each evaluation criterion on which a vendor's proposal will be assessed.

Responsive A responsive person tends to be "out there" in their behavior, movements, and speech. They can be gregarious, using a great deal of body language and varying their speech.

Revenue management Selling the right product at the right price to the right market segment at the right time, through the right distribution channel in order to maximize revenue.

Sales blitz A popular form of cold calling used by hospitality sales professionals. The sales blitz technique is less intimidating, because the sales people drop off promotional materials when visiting office buildings targeted in advance.

Sales coordinators Provide the administrative support, customer service, and sales leads for the sales team.

Sales dialogue The hospitality salesperson establishes the customer's needs through a well-planned sales dialogue by engaging the client through different techniques to collect that information.

Sales process A step-by-step approach; each step of the process must be thoroughly addressed for the sale to be accomplished. The sales process includes looking for new accounts, making contact with these contacts, confirming that the prospect has a need for the MEEC product and services, presenting what the MEEC organization has to offer, overcoming objections, and closing the sale

Sales professionals Members of the hospitality management team who are responsible for selling to prospective customers.

Sales stop sign There are four sales stop signs that can derail a hospitality sale. 1) lack of need for the product or services represented by the hospitality salesperson; 2) concern about the hospitality product and service; 3) a destination, brand, or source concern; 4) it is the wrong time for the sale; 5) the price is not right.

Self-management skills Through practice and contemplation, and with experience, individuals can become successful hospitality salespeople.

Service organizations The purpose of such organizations can be educational, altruistic, communal, or a combination of all three.

Site visit After RFPs have been reviewed by the potential buyer, the buyer may wish to make a trip to review the locale in person.

Skin in the game When the hospitality salesperson who sells the services and event has more involvement in providing high quality service to the client.

Small talk A social interchange by which the hospitality salesperson establishes a rapport with the prospect. The most effective methods for developing rapport are: Seeking to uncover common interests or acquaintances, discussing current events or other observations pertinent to the prospect, and recognizing the prospect through compliments for achievements or other areas of realization.

SMERF One of the market segments in hospitality; stands for social, military, educational, religious, and fraternal.

Solution selling A selling methodology whereby the product and its characteristics are not at the center of the sales presentation. Instead, the hospitality salesperson focuses on the customer's problems and needs, then offers products and services that lead to problem resolution and satisfaction.

Specific benefits Meet the specific needs of the prospective buyer.

Strategic selling materials (SSMs) Tangible representations of the hospitality product and services. They help to establish a connection between the buying objectives of the prospect and the features of the hospitality organization.

Strategy What to do to accomplish a goal.

Summary confirmation questions Used by the hospitality salesperson to outline previous dialogues and understanding on various points in the sales process.

Supporting product Those products, services, or amenities that add value to the basic offering or core product. Supporting products, services, or amenities help to set the hospitality offering apart from its competition.

Synchronous presentations The face-to-face real-time presentation on the part of the hospitality sales professional.

Tactics How to go about enacting a strategy.

Third party A person or group besides the two primarily involved in a situation.

Third-party referrals One of the most powerful hospitality resistance busters; an authentic statement of support from a neutral third party can be the strongest means to negate a prospect's areas of concern. Gives the hospitality salesperson instant credibility.

Thirty-second commercial Also called an elevator speech. A clear-cut and succinct message or "commercial" about the person who is delivering the message. The central theme of the message is how the hospitality salesperson can help the other person.

Time management Not just about prioritizing activities, but also about using time wisely.

Trade shows Can be an excellent source of prospecting, because the prospects who are collected are pre-qualified based on their interests. In a typical trade show, prospects stop by vendor booths at random and may, or may not be, the person with purchasing authority.

Transactional buyer Tends to be focused on simple purchase decisions that emphasize efficiency.

Transactional buying process Buying process that is initiated by the prospect.

Trial close The hospitality salesperson is assessing interest on a particular feature, the proposal, or some other element of the hospitality organization's product and service.

Trial offers A form of resistance buster where the prospect tries the hospitality product or service without making a purchase commitment.

Unique selling proposition (USP) The hospitality salesperson explains the product or service that can be provided and how they are unique from other offerings. A description of how the listener will benefit must be included.

Upselling Offering additional products or services at an additional cost.

Value proposition The positioning statement that clarifies to the prospective customer what advantage they will gain by selecting the organization the hospitality salesperson represents over the competition.

INDEX

A

Above property sales, 233–234
Accountability, 60
Active listening, 166
Adaptive selling, 80
Advantages approach, 134
Affiliated industry desirability, 265–268
Affiliated suppliers, 265
After sale service. *See* Service after sale
AIDA principle, 180
Alternatives close, 205–206
AMCs. *See* Association management companies (AMCs)
Analyzers, 81
Artifacts, 86
Association management companies (AMCs), 102
Association market segment, 101–105
Assumptive close, 205
Asynchronous presentation format, 177
Augmented products, 126
Authentic reasons, 189

B

Balance sheet closing, 206–207
Beck-Farrar hospitality question model, 163–165
Benefits
    approach, 133, 173
    general, 134
    specific, 134
    statements, 173
Bleisure travel, 3
Booking coordinators, 221
Boyd, Bonnie, 230
Business discussion, 158
Business etiquette, 63–64
Business event, definition of, 4
Buyer resistance, 188
Buyer resolution theory, 93
Buyers
    hosted, 145
    relationship, 128
    transactional, 126

Buyer's remorse, 213
Buying motivations, 134
Buying objectives, 166, 91–92
Buying process, 90–91
Buying theories, customer, 93–95

C

Can-do attitude, 216
Canned presentations, 155
Capping, 202
Catering, 220–222
Check backs. *See* Reminder presentations
Closed-ended questions, 161
Close stage, 118
Closing process, 202
Code of ethics (international), sales and marketing, 60–61
Cold call, 260–261
Cold calling, 144
Communication etiquette, 65–66
Communication skills, 79–97, 239–240
    buying objectives, 91–93
    in buying process, 90–91
    interpersonal communication, 90
    introduction, 80
    styles, 80–88
    types of communication, 89
    verbal and nonverbal, 89
Communication style, 80
Compensation technique, 195
Competition
    analysis worksheet, 132
    direct, 130
    indirect, 130
Completed contract close, 206
Concern
    planning for addressing, 192–193
    reason for, 189
Confirmation questions, 162
Congress, 3
Controllers, 85–88
Conventions, 3, 220–222

Convention service managers (CSM), 52, 220
Convention & visitor bureaus (CVBs), 48, 145
Core products, 124
Corporate market segment, 106–107
Corporation, description of, 107
CSM. *See* Convention service managers (CSM)
C's of marketing, 16
Customer selling strategy, 100
Customer service representatives, 38
CVBs. *See* Convention & visitor bureaus (CVBs)

D

Delegation, 71
Delivery personnel, 37
Demand creator, 37
Demonstrations, 193
Destination management company (DMC), 6,
    256–262
Destination marketing organizations (DMOs),
    48, 145
Detailer, 180
Direct competition, 130
Direct denial technique, 193
Direct eye contact, 158
Direct marketing, 24–26
    advertising, 26
    email, 24
    mail, 24
    telephone, 25–26
Director of event services, 221
Director of marketing, 51
Director of sales, 51, 261–265
Direct request, 205
Discovery questions, 162
Distribution, 14
DMC. *See* Destination management company (DMC)
DMOs. *See* Destination marketing organizations
    (DMOs)

E

Effective listening, 165
EIC. *See* Event Industry Council (EIC)
Elevator speech, 73
Emotional intelligence, 60, 63
Ernest N. Morial Convention Center (ENMCC),
    238
    types of events in, 240

ESG. *See* Event specification guide (ESG)
Event coordinators, 221
Event Industry Council (EIC), 2, 4, 7, 226
Event services, 2, 220–222
    manager, 220
    supervisors, 221
Event specification guide (ESG), 7, 223
Executive meeting manager, 220
Exhibitions, 2
Exhibitor services assistants, 222
External marketing, 21

F

Facilitating products, 125
Feature-and-benefit methodology, 156
Feature approach, 133, 173
Feature spit, 175
Financial & Insurance Conference Professionals
    (FICP), 114
Force majeure, 210

G

Gatherer, 202
General benefits, 134
Global sales director, 236–237
Global sales manager, 235–236
Great hospitality salespeople, 62–63
Guerilla marketing, 27–28

H

Hospitality contracts, sales closing and, 208–212
Hospitality industry, description of, 2
Hospitality salesperson, 80
Hospitality sales process, 117–118, 122
    access, 117
    close *s*tage, 118
    defined, 117–118
    present *s*tage, 118
    proposal, 118
    qualification, 118
    service stage, 118
    upselling, 118
Hospitality sales professional, defined, 60
Hosted buyer, 145
HSF. *See* Hyatt Sales Force (HSF)
Hunter mentality, 202
Hyatt Sales Force (HSF), 233, 235

I

Incentive meetings, 107, 110
Indirect competition, 130
Indirect denial technique, 194
Indirect marketing, 26–28
  guerilla marketing, 27–28
  publicity, 28
  public relations, 28
  social media, 27
  viral marketing, 27
Informative presentations, 178
Internal marketing, 21
Interpersonal communication, 90

L

LaBadie, Jim, 230, 251
Lead generation, 258–259
Lead management, 260
LEARN, 225
Lukewarm call, 260–261

M

Management companies, 102
Market/marketing, 19, 26–28, 239–240
  vs. advertising, 21–22
  brand and, 21
  code of ethics, international, 60–61
  C's of, 16
  definition of, 14, 49
  description of, 9
  direct, 24–26
  function, 19–22
  indirect, 26–28
  learning through analogy, 16–18
  mnemonic devices, 15–16
  people and, 21
  principles, 14–16
  P's of, 15
  research, 18–19
  strategy and tactics, 22
  tactics, 23–28
    identification of target markets, 23
    targeting audience, 23–24
    types of marketing, 24–28
  types of, 24–28
Market segmentation, 19
Market segment behaviors, 99–119

  association and, 101–105
    selling to, 105–106
  corporate, 106–107
    meetings market, selling to, 108–111
  introduction, 100
  major in hospitality, 101
  others, 114–117
  sales process, hospitality, 117–118
  SMERF markets, 112–114
  target customers, 100–101
Matching and mirroring technique, 150
MEEC
  description of, 2
  hospitality sales and, nature of, 34–37
  planning, process of, 5–8
  professional development, 59–78
    appearance, 68
    business etiquette, 63–64
    communication etiquette, 65–66
    ethics, 74–76
    introduction to client or guest, 64
    management to self, 63
    networking, 71–72
    sales letter writing, 66–68
    shaking of hands, 64–65
    thirty-second commercial, 72–74
    time management, 69–71
  sales organization and, 49–50
  salesperson and, roles of, 37–38
    delivery personnel, 37
    demand creator, 37
    missionary sales role, 37
Meetings, 2
Missionary sales role, 37

N

Necessary budget, 189
Need, 189
"Need for approval" emotion, 141
Need resistance, 191
Need satisfaction theory, 93
Negotiation, 197
  techniques, 196–198
Networking, 71–72, 144
Non-price consideration close, 207
Nonverbal communication, 89
Now-or-never close, 207

O

Objections, 189
  forms of, 190
  techniques for overcoming, 193–195
Objective fulfillment question, 163
Objectives summary close, 206
Office configuration, types of, 257
On-property event manager, 219
On-property sales, 231–232
On-property service, 219–220
  coordination, 216
On-site service process, 222–224
Open-ended questions, 162
Option questions, 162
Organizers, 82
Outside influences, 94

P

Packages, 15
Paternalism, 74
People, 15
Personal selling, 34
  philosophy, 62
Persuaders, 82, 85
Persuasive presentations, 178
Persuasive sales dialogue, 157
Place, 15
Planning, 14
Positioning, 20, 133–136
Post-convention meetings (post-con), 55, 225
Post-event follow up, 225–226
Post-event meeting, 216
Post-event report (PER), 7, 226
Potential prospects, 141
Pre-convention meeting (pre-con), 53, 223
Presentation. *See* Sales presentation
Present *stage*, 118
Price, 15
Primary research, 18
Probing questions, 162
Process, 15
Procrastination, 70
Product, 15
Production technicians, 222
Product presentation. *See* Sales presentation
Professional development, MEEC and, 59–78
  appearance, 68

business etiquette, 63–64
  communication etiquette, 65–66
  ethics, 74–76
  introduction to client or guest, 64
  management to self, 63
  networking, 71–72
  sales letter writing, 66–68
  shaking of hands, 64–65
  thirty-second commercial, 72–74
  time management, 69–71
Professional services, buying of, 248–256
Profile, prospects and, 142
Promotion, 15
Property demonstration, 159
Proposal, 118, 243–244
Props, 172
Prospects, 139–151, 172
  of buying professional service, 248–256
  collection of information during, 147–149
  defined, 140
  description of, 140–143
  evaluation of, 142
  face-to-face meeting and, 149–150
  potential prospects, 141
  profile, 142
  qualification and, 142
  sources of, 144–146
P's of marketing, 15
Publicist, 28
Public relations (PR), 28

Q

Qualification, prospects and, 142
Questioning process, hospitality sales, 161–163

R

Rapport, 158
Reach, 24
Referral, 144
Relational buyer, 91
Relationship buyers, 128
Reminder presentations, 178
Reminder sales dialogues, 157
Rental, determination of, 242–243
Requests for proposals (RFPs), 6, 92, 177
Revenue management, 195–196
RFPs. *See* Requests for proposals (RFPs)
Rome, David E., 230, 256

S

Sales
  closing, 201–214
    hospitality contracts and, 208–212
    planning to, 203–204
    techniques, 204–208
  code of ethics, international, 60–61
  communication skills. *See* Communication
    skills
  coordinators, 52
  customer buying theories to, 93–95
  introduction, 34
  job descriptions, 40–48
  job opportunities, 38–40
  letter writing, 66–68
  managers, 40–41, 52
    organizational activities of, 56
  marketing and, 48–49
  MEEC and hospitality sales, nature of, 34–37
  meetings, 53–56
  organization, 50–52
    MEEC and, 49–50
  process, hospitality, 34, 117–118
  professionals, 34
  salesperson, MEEC, 37–38
    customer sales representatives, 38
    delivery personnel, 37
    demand creator, 37
    missionary sales role, 37
  strategy development. *See* Strategy development,
    sales
Sales blitz, 144
Sales communication, types of, 155–156
Sales contact plan, 156
Sales dialogue, 153–168
  Beck-Farrar hospitality question model,
    163–165
  buying objectives, establishment of, 166–167
  customer needs, determination of, 160–161
  introduction, 154–155
  listening and, 165–166
  objectives of, 156–157
  questioning process, hospitality sales, 161–163
  sales communication, types of, 155–156
  sales contact plan, 156
  techniques for, 158–160
Sales force and practical applications,
    management of, 229–268

Sales presentation, 171–185
  benefits, 173–174
  effective, 180–181
  features of, 173
    prevention of overload, 175
  formats, 177–178
  importance in hospitality industry, 172–173
  linking features, 174
  making of, 183–184
  planning of, 181
  practicing before, 184
  process, 175–177
  strategic selling materials, 182–182
    types of, 182–183
  techniques, 178–180
Sales stop sign, 190–192
Secondary research, 18
Self-management skills, 63
Service after sale, 215–227
  catering, 220–222
  convention, 220–222
  event services, 220–222
  introduction, 216
  issues, resolving of, 224–225
  on-property service, 219–220
  on-site service process, 222–224
  post-event follow up, 225–226
  relationship strengthening and, 216–219
  strategies, 216
Service stage, 118
SGMP. *See* Society of Government Meeting
    Professionals (SGMP)
Showmanship, 182
SITE. *See* Society for Incentive Travel Excellence
    (SITE)
Site visits, 92, 244–245
Small talk, 158
SMERF markets, 101, 112–114
Social media, 27
Society for Incentive Travel Excellence (SITE),
    115
Society of Government Meeting Professionals
    (SGMP), 114
Solution selling, 126–132
Special events, 111
Specific benefits, 134
Strategic selling materials (SSMs), 181–182
Strategy, 18

Strategy development, sales, 121–138
  levels of product, 124–126
    augmented products, 126
    core products, 124
    facilitating products, 125
    supporting product, 125
  positioning, 133–136
  solution selling, 126–132
Summary close, 206
Summary confirmation questions, 163
Supporting product, 125
Synchronous presentations, 178

T
Tactics, 18
Technology service coordinators, 221
Third-party referrals, 159, 194
Thirty-second commercial, 72–74
Time management, 63, 69–71
Tourism, defined, 2
Trade shows, 145

Transactional buyers, 91, 126, 167, 192
Transactional buying process, 177
Trial close, 204
Trial offers, 194

U
Unique Selling Proposition (USP), 73
Upselling, 118, 216
USP. *See* Unique Selling Proposition (USP)

V
Value proposition, 133
Verbal communication, 89
Viral marketing, 27
Vonderheide, Gus, 230, 237–239

W
Williams, Elaine, 230
Woodin, Terri, 230, 248
Written close, 206
Written proposals, 155–156